500 PSAT®

Practice Questions

The Staff of The Princeton Review

PrincetonReview.com

PENGUIN RANDOM HOUSE

The Princeton Review
24 Prime Parkway, Suite 201
Natick, MA 01760
E-mail: editorialsupport@review.com

Published in the United States by Random House, LLC, New York, and
simultaneously in Canada by Random House of Canada Limited, Toronto.

A Penguin Random House Company.

ISBN: 978-0-8041-2484-3
ISSN: 2333-9322

PSAT is a registered trademark of the College Board, which does not
sponsor or endorse this product.

The Princeton Review is not affiliated with Princeton University.

Editor: Aaron Riccio
Production Editor: Beth Hanson
Production Artist: Deborah A. Silvestrini

Printed in the United States of America on partially recycled paper.

10 9 8 7 6 5 4 3 2 1

Editorial

Rob Franek, Senior VP, Publisher
Casey Cornelius, VP Content Development
Mary Beth Garrick, Director of Production
Selena Coppock, Managing Editor
Calvin Cato, Editor
Meave Shelton, Editor
Alyssa Wolff, Editorial Assistant

Random House Publishing Team

Tom Russell, Publisher
Alison Stoltzfus, Publishing Manager
Dawn Ryan, Associate Managing Editor
Ellen Reed, Production Manager
Erika Pepe, Associate Production Manager
Kristin Lindner, Production Supervisor
Andrea Lau, Designer

Acknowledgments

This book could never have been created without the dedication and collective expertise of the staff and students of The Princeton Review.

Many thanks to Jonathan Chiu, the National Content Director for High School Programs.

Many thanks also to Chris Aylward, Brian Becker, Lisa Mayo, Amy Minster, Elizabeth Owens, and Stephen Shuck for their contributions in developing the content for this title.

Special thanks to Claudia Landgrover for masterfully managing the development and review processes for this title.

Special thanks also to Adam Robinson, who conceived of and perfected the Joe Bloggs approach to standardized tests as well as many other successful techniques used by The Princeton Review.

Contents

...So Much More Online!

More Practice...

- Free SAT online demonstration with a full-length practice SAT and interactive lessons

More Good Stuff...

- PSAT at-a-glance overview
- Articles on SAT techniques to get you ready for the next step

...then College!

- Detailed profiles for hundreds of colleges help you find the school that is right for you
- Dozens of Top 10 ranking lists including Quality of Professors, Worst Campus Food, Most Beautiful Campus, Party Schools, Diverse Student Population, and tons more
- Useful information about the admissions process
- Helpful information about financial aid and scholarships

princetonreview.com

Part I
Orientation

Chapter 1
Introduction

Who Writes the PSAT?

The PSAT is written and administered by Educational Testing Service (ETS), under contract by the College Board. You might think that the people at ETS are educators, professors of education, or teachers. They are not. The people who work for ETS are average people who just happen to make a living writing tests. In fact, they write hundreds of tests, for all kinds of organizations. They are a group of "testers-for-hire" who will write a test for anyone who asks.

The folks at ETS are not paid to educate; they are paid to write and administer tests. Furthermore, even though you will be paying ETS to take the PSAT, you are not their customer. The actual customers ETS caters to are the colleges, who get the information they want at no cost. This means that you should take everything that ETS says with a grain of salt and realize that its testing "advice" is not always the best advice. (Getting testing advice from ETS is a bit like getting baseball advice from the opposing team.)

Every test reflects the interests of the people who write it. If you know who writes the test, you will know a lot more about what kinds of answers will be considered "correct" answers on that test.

What Is The Princeton Review?

Shortcuts
The Princeton Review's techniques are the closest thing there is to a shortcut to the PSAT. However, there is no shortcut to learning these techniques.

The Princeton Review is the nation's leading test-preparation company. In just a few years, we became the nation's leader in SAT preparation, primarily because our techniques work. We offer courses and private tutoring for all of the major standardized tests, and we publish a series of books to help in your search for the right school. If you would like more information about how The Princeton Review can help you, go to PrincetonReview.com or call 800-2-Review.

How to Use this Book

This book is divided into three main parts. The first part of the book is a practice test that will give you an idea of your strengths and weaknesses, both of which can be sources of improvement. If you're already good at something, additional practice can make you great at it; if you're not so good at something, what you should do about it depends on how important it is.

The second part of the book contains the different sections of a full-length PSAT so that you can practice on timing or content or both! Focus on the problems that gave you trouble in the first test in this book. If you ultimately decide that you would like more practice, our *Cracking the PSAT* edition can give the additional work that you seek.

The third part of the book contains two additional full-length PSATs for you to use for evaluative purposes.

When You Take a Practice Test

Here are some guidelines for taking these tests:

- Time yourself strictly. Use a timer, watch, or stopwatch that will ring, and do not allow yourself to go over time for any section. If you try to do so at the real test, your scores will likely be canceled.
- Take a practice test in one sitting, allowing yourself breaks of no more than two minutes between sections. You need to build up your endurance for the real test, and you also need an accurate picture of how well you will do.
- Always take a practice test using an answer sheet with bubbles to fill in, just as you will for the real test. For the practice tests in the book, use the attached answer sheets. You need to be comfortable transferring answers to the separate sheet because you will be skipping around a bit.
- Each bubble you choose should be filled in thoroughly, and no other marks should be made in the answer area.
- As you fill in the bubble for a question, check to be sure you are on the correct number on the answer sheet. If you fill in the wrong bubble on the answer sheet, it will not matter if you worked out the problem correctly in the test booklet. All that matters to the machine scoring the test is the No. 2 pencil mark.

Chapter 2
All About National Merit Scholarships

The NMSQT part of the name PSAT/NMSQT stands for National Merit Scholarship Qualifying Test. That means that the PSAT serves as the test that will establish whether or not you are eligible for National Merit recognition. This chapter will help you figure out what that may mean for you.

How Do I Qualify for National Merit?

To qualify for any National Merit recognition, you must:

- Be a U.S. citizen or permanent resident who intends to become a U.S. citizen
- Be enrolled full-time in high school
- Take the PSAT in the third year of high school (for four-year programs; slightly different rules apply if you are in a three-year program or other course of study)
- Be fully endorsed and recommended for a Merit scholarship by your high school principal
- Have a record of strong academic performance throughout high school
- Complete the National Merit Scholarship Corporation (NMSC) Scholarship Application
- Obtain high scores on the SAT, which you will take later in the year

The Index

How does your PSAT score qualify you for National Merit? The National Merit Scholarship Corporation uses a selection index, which is the sum of your Math, Critical Reading, and Writing Skills scores. For instance, if your PSAT scores were 60 Math, 50 Critical Reading, and 60 Writing Skills, your index would be 170.

Math + Critical Reading + Writing Skills = National Merit Index

60 + 50 + 60 = 170

The Awards and the Process

In the fall of their senior year, about 50,000 students will receive one of two letters from NMSC: either a Letter of Commendation or a letter stating that they have qualified as semifinalists for National Merit.

Commended Students   Roughly two-thirds of these students (about 34,000 total students each year) will receive a Letter of Commendation by virtue of their high scores on the test. This looks great on your college application, so if you have a reasonable chance of receiving this recognition, it is definitely worth your time to prepare for the PSAT. Make no mistake, though, these letters are not easy to get. They are awarded to students who score between the 95th and the mid-99th percentiles—that means to the top three percent in the country.

If you receive this honorable mention from NMSC, you should be extremely proud of yourself. Even though you will not continue in the process for National Merit scholarships, this commendation does make you eligible for special scholarships sponsored by certain companies and organizations, which vary in their amounts and eligibility requirements.

Semifinalists   The other third of these students—those 16,000 students who score in the upper 99th percentile in their states—will be notified that they are National Merit semifinalists. If you qualify, you will receive a letter announcing your status as a semifinalist, along with information about the requirements for qualification as a finalist. These include maintaining high grades, performing well on your SAT, and getting an endorsement from your principal.

Becoming a National Merit semifinalist is quite impressive, and if you manage it, you should certainly mention it on your college applications.

What does "scoring in the upper 99th percentile in the state" mean? It means that you're essentially competing against the other people in your state for those semifinalist positions. Since some states have higher average scores than others, this means that if you're in states like New York, New Jersey, Maryland, Connecticut, or Massachusetts, you need a higher score to qualify than if you live in other states. However, the majority of the indices are in the range of 200–215. (This means approximate scores of 70 Critical Reading, 70 Math, 70 Writing Skills.)

Many students want to know exactly what score they need. Sadly, National Merit is notoriously tight-lipped about these numbers. It releases them only on rare occasions and generally does not like to announce them. However, it is not difficult to obtain some pretty reliable unofficial data on what it takes to be a semifinalist. Below you will find the most up-to-date qualifying scores for the class of 2013 National Merit semifinalists:

Alabama	209	Montana	203
Alaska	204	Nebraska	207
Arizona	212	Nevada	208
Arkansas	202	New Hampshire	211
California	220	New Jersey	221
Colorado	212	New Mexico	208
Connecticut	218	New York	215
D.C.	221	North Carolina	213
Delaware	215	North Dakota	200
Florida	211	Ohio	212
Georgia	214	Oklahoma	206
Hawaii	211	Oregon	213
Idaho	207	Pennsylvania	214
Illinois	213	Rhode Island	211
Indiana	211	South Carolina	208
Iowa	207	South Dakota	204
Kansas	212	Tennessee	210
Kentucky	208	Texas	216
Louisiana	209	Utah	205
Maine	210	Vermont	214
Maryland	219	Virginia	217
Massachusetts	221	Washington	216
Michigan	207	West Virginia	200
Minnesota	213	Wisconsin	207
Mississippi	204	Wyoming	200
Missouri	210		

Note, however, that while these numbers are probably roughly the same from year to year, they do change to a certain degree. These should be used only to give you a rough idea of the range of scores for National Merit recognition.

Finalists   The majority of semifinalists (more than 90 percent) go on to qualify as finalists. Students who meet all of the eligibility requirements will be notified in February of their senior year that they have qualified as finalists. This means that they are now eligible for scholarship money, though it does not necessarily mean that they will receive any. In fact, only about half of National Merit finalists actually win scholarships. What determines whether a student is awarded money or not? There is a final screening process, based on criteria that NMSC does not release to the public, to determine who actually receives these scholarships. This year, there will be 8,300 Merit Scholarship winners and 1,300 Special Scholarship recipients. Unlike the Merit Scholarships, which are given by the NMSC, the Special Scholarship recipients will receive awards from corporate sponsors and are selected from students who are outstanding, but not National Merit finalists.

Though the amounts of money are not huge, every little bit helps, and the award itself looks very impressive in your portfolio. So if you think you are in contention for National Merit recognition, study hard. If not, don't sweat it too much, but do prepare for the PSAT because it is good practice for the SAT.

What If I Miss the PSAT Administration My Junior Year?

If you are not concerned about National Merit scholarships, there is no reason to do anything in particular—except, perhaps, to obtain a few PSAT booklets to practice on, just to see what fun you missed.

However, if you want to be eligible for National Merit recognition, then swift action on your part is required. If an emergency arises that prevents you from taking the PSAT, you should write to the National Merit Scholarship Corporation *immediately* to request alternate testing dates. If your request is received soon enough, it should be able to accommodate you. (NMSC says that this kind of request must absolutely be received by March 1 following the missed PSAT administration.) You will also need a signature from a school official.

For More Information

If you have any questions or problems, the best person to consult is your school guidance counselor, who can help make sure you are on the right track. If you need further help, contact your local Princeton Review office at 800-2-REVIEW or **PrincetonReview.com**. Or, you can contact National Merit directly:

National Merit Scholarship Corporation
1560 Sherman Avenue, Suite 200
Evanston, IL 60201-4897
(847) 866-5100
NationalMerit.org

Part II
Practice Test

Chapter 3
Practice Test 1

PSAT

The Princeton Review

UR NAME: _____
(rint) Last   First   M.I.

NATURE: _____ DATE: ____ / ____ / ____

ME ADDRESS: _____
(rint)   Number and Street
                    E-MAIL: _____
City   State   Zip

ONE NO.: _____ SCHOOL: _____ CLASS OF: _____

IMPORTANT: Please fill in these boxes exactly as shown on the back cover of your text book.

SCANTRON F-17982-PRP   P3 2803 628 5 4 3 2 1
© The Princeton Review, Inc.

5. YOUR NAME

First 4 letters of last name				FIRST INIT	MID INIT
Ⓐ	Ⓐ	Ⓐ	Ⓐ	Ⓐ	Ⓐ
Ⓑ	Ⓑ	Ⓑ	Ⓑ	Ⓑ	Ⓑ
Ⓒ	Ⓒ	Ⓒ	Ⓒ	Ⓒ	Ⓒ
Ⓓ	Ⓓ	Ⓓ	Ⓓ	Ⓓ	Ⓓ
Ⓔ	Ⓔ	Ⓔ	Ⓔ	Ⓔ	Ⓔ
Ⓕ	Ⓕ	Ⓕ	Ⓕ	Ⓕ	Ⓕ
Ⓖ	Ⓖ	Ⓖ	Ⓖ	Ⓖ	Ⓖ
Ⓗ	Ⓗ	Ⓗ	Ⓗ	Ⓗ	Ⓗ
Ⓘ	Ⓘ	Ⓘ	Ⓘ	Ⓘ	Ⓘ
Ⓙ	Ⓙ	Ⓙ	Ⓙ	Ⓙ	Ⓙ
Ⓚ	Ⓚ	Ⓚ	Ⓚ	Ⓚ	Ⓚ
Ⓛ	Ⓛ	Ⓛ	Ⓛ	Ⓛ	Ⓛ
Ⓜ	Ⓜ	Ⓜ	Ⓜ	Ⓜ	Ⓜ
Ⓝ	Ⓝ	Ⓝ	Ⓝ	Ⓝ	Ⓝ
Ⓞ	Ⓞ	Ⓞ	Ⓞ	Ⓞ	Ⓞ
Ⓟ	Ⓟ	Ⓟ	Ⓟ	Ⓟ	Ⓟ
Ⓠ	Ⓠ	Ⓠ	Ⓠ	Ⓠ	Ⓠ
Ⓡ	Ⓡ	Ⓡ	Ⓡ	Ⓡ	Ⓡ
Ⓢ	Ⓢ	Ⓢ	Ⓢ	Ⓢ	Ⓢ
Ⓣ	Ⓣ	Ⓣ	Ⓣ	Ⓣ	Ⓣ
Ⓤ	Ⓤ	Ⓤ	Ⓤ	Ⓤ	Ⓤ
Ⓥ	Ⓥ	Ⓥ	Ⓥ	Ⓥ	Ⓥ
Ⓦ	Ⓦ	Ⓦ	Ⓦ	Ⓦ	Ⓦ
Ⓧ	Ⓧ	Ⓧ	Ⓧ	Ⓧ	Ⓧ
Ⓨ	Ⓨ	Ⓨ	Ⓨ	Ⓨ	Ⓨ
Ⓩ	Ⓩ	Ⓩ	Ⓩ	Ⓩ	Ⓩ

TEST FORM
_____

DATE OF BIRTH

MONTH		DAY		YEAR	
○ JAN					
○ FEB					
○ MAR	⓪	⓪	⓪	⓪	
○ APR	①	①	①	①	
○ MAY	②	②	②	②	
○ JUN	③	③	③	③	
○ JUL		④	④	④	
○ AUG		⑤	⑤	⑤	
○ SEP		⑥	⑥	⑥	
○ OCT		⑦	⑦	⑦	
○ NOV		⑧	⑧	⑧	
○ DEC		⑨	⑨	⑨	

3. TEST CODE   4. PHONE NUMBER

(columns of bubbles ⓪ ① ② ③ ④ ⑤ ⑥ ⑦ ⑧ ⑨)

7. SEX
○ MALE
○ FEMALE

8. OTHER
1 Ⓐ Ⓑ Ⓒ Ⓓ Ⓔ
2 Ⓐ Ⓑ Ⓒ Ⓓ Ⓔ
3 Ⓐ Ⓑ Ⓒ Ⓓ Ⓔ

1 READING

1 Ⓐ Ⓑ Ⓒ Ⓓ Ⓔ
2 Ⓐ Ⓑ Ⓒ Ⓓ Ⓔ
3 Ⓐ Ⓑ Ⓒ Ⓓ Ⓔ
4 Ⓐ Ⓑ Ⓒ Ⓓ Ⓔ
5 Ⓐ Ⓑ Ⓒ Ⓓ Ⓔ
6 Ⓐ Ⓑ Ⓒ Ⓓ Ⓔ
7 Ⓐ Ⓑ Ⓒ Ⓓ Ⓔ
8 Ⓐ Ⓑ Ⓒ Ⓓ Ⓔ
9 Ⓐ Ⓑ Ⓒ Ⓓ Ⓔ
10 Ⓐ Ⓑ Ⓒ Ⓓ Ⓔ
11 Ⓐ Ⓑ Ⓒ Ⓓ Ⓔ
12 Ⓐ Ⓑ Ⓒ Ⓓ Ⓔ
13 Ⓐ Ⓑ Ⓒ Ⓓ Ⓔ
14 Ⓐ Ⓑ Ⓒ Ⓓ Ⓔ
15 Ⓐ Ⓑ Ⓒ Ⓓ Ⓔ
16 Ⓐ Ⓑ Ⓒ Ⓓ Ⓔ
17 Ⓐ Ⓑ Ⓒ Ⓓ Ⓔ
18 Ⓐ Ⓑ Ⓒ Ⓓ Ⓔ
19 Ⓐ Ⓑ Ⓒ Ⓓ Ⓔ
20 Ⓐ Ⓑ Ⓒ Ⓓ Ⓔ
21 Ⓐ Ⓑ Ⓒ Ⓓ Ⓔ
22 Ⓐ Ⓑ Ⓒ Ⓓ Ⓔ
23 Ⓐ Ⓑ Ⓒ Ⓓ Ⓔ
24 Ⓐ Ⓑ Ⓒ Ⓓ Ⓔ

2 MATHEMATICS

1 Ⓐ Ⓑ Ⓒ Ⓓ Ⓔ
2 Ⓐ Ⓑ Ⓒ Ⓓ Ⓔ
3 Ⓐ Ⓑ Ⓒ Ⓓ Ⓔ
4 Ⓐ Ⓑ Ⓒ Ⓓ Ⓔ
5 Ⓐ Ⓑ Ⓒ Ⓓ Ⓔ
6 Ⓐ Ⓑ Ⓒ Ⓓ Ⓔ
7 Ⓐ Ⓑ Ⓒ Ⓓ Ⓔ
8 Ⓐ Ⓑ Ⓒ Ⓓ Ⓔ
9 Ⓐ Ⓑ Ⓒ Ⓓ Ⓔ
10 Ⓐ Ⓑ Ⓒ Ⓓ Ⓔ
11 Ⓐ Ⓑ Ⓒ Ⓓ Ⓔ
12 Ⓐ Ⓑ Ⓒ Ⓓ Ⓔ
13 Ⓐ Ⓑ Ⓒ Ⓓ Ⓔ
14 Ⓐ Ⓑ Ⓒ Ⓓ Ⓔ
15 Ⓐ Ⓑ Ⓒ Ⓓ Ⓔ
16 Ⓐ Ⓑ Ⓒ Ⓓ Ⓔ
17 Ⓐ Ⓑ Ⓒ Ⓓ Ⓔ
18 Ⓐ Ⓑ Ⓒ Ⓓ Ⓔ
19 Ⓐ Ⓑ Ⓒ Ⓓ Ⓔ
20 Ⓐ Ⓑ Ⓒ Ⓓ Ⓔ

3 READING

25 Ⓐ Ⓑ Ⓒ Ⓓ Ⓔ
26 Ⓐ Ⓑ Ⓒ Ⓓ Ⓔ
27 Ⓐ Ⓑ Ⓒ Ⓓ Ⓔ
28 Ⓐ Ⓑ Ⓒ Ⓓ Ⓔ
29 Ⓐ Ⓑ Ⓒ Ⓓ Ⓔ
30 Ⓐ Ⓑ Ⓒ Ⓓ Ⓔ
31 Ⓐ Ⓑ Ⓒ Ⓓ Ⓔ
32 Ⓐ Ⓑ Ⓒ Ⓓ Ⓔ
33 Ⓐ Ⓑ Ⓒ Ⓓ Ⓔ
34 Ⓐ Ⓑ Ⓒ Ⓓ Ⓔ
35 Ⓐ Ⓑ Ⓒ Ⓓ Ⓔ
36 Ⓐ Ⓑ Ⓒ Ⓓ Ⓔ
37 Ⓐ Ⓑ Ⓒ Ⓓ Ⓔ
38 Ⓐ Ⓑ Ⓒ Ⓓ Ⓔ
39 Ⓐ Ⓑ Ⓒ Ⓓ Ⓔ
40 Ⓐ Ⓑ Ⓒ Ⓓ Ⓔ
41 Ⓐ Ⓑ Ⓒ Ⓓ Ⓔ
42 Ⓐ Ⓑ Ⓒ Ⓓ Ⓔ
43 Ⓐ Ⓑ Ⓒ Ⓓ Ⓔ
44 Ⓐ Ⓑ Ⓒ Ⓓ Ⓔ
45 Ⓐ Ⓑ Ⓒ Ⓓ Ⓔ
46 Ⓐ Ⓑ Ⓒ Ⓓ Ⓔ
47 Ⓐ Ⓑ Ⓒ Ⓓ Ⓔ
48 Ⓐ Ⓑ Ⓒ Ⓓ Ⓔ

The Princeton Review
PSAT

MATHEMATICS

21 Ⓐ Ⓑ Ⓒ Ⓓ Ⓔ
22 Ⓐ Ⓑ Ⓒ Ⓓ Ⓔ
23 Ⓐ Ⓑ Ⓒ Ⓓ Ⓔ
24 Ⓐ Ⓑ Ⓒ Ⓓ Ⓔ

25 Ⓐ Ⓑ Ⓒ Ⓓ Ⓔ
26 Ⓐ Ⓑ Ⓒ Ⓓ Ⓔ
27 Ⓐ Ⓑ Ⓒ Ⓓ Ⓔ
28 Ⓐ Ⓑ Ⓒ Ⓓ Ⓔ

ONLY ANSWERS ENTERED IN THE OVALS IN EACH GRID AREA WILL BE SCORED.
YOU WILL NOT RECEIVE CREDIT FOR ANYTHING WRITTEN IN THE BOXES ABOVE THE OVALS.

29 · 0 1 2 3 4 5 6 7 8 9
30 · 0 1 2 3 4 5 6 7 8 9
31 · 0 1 2 3 4 5 6 7 8 9
32 · 0 1 2 3 4 5 6 7 8 9
33 · 0 1 2 3 4 5 6 7 8 9

34 · 0 1 2 3 4 5 6 7 8 9
35 · 0 1 2 3 4 5 6 7 8 9
36 · 0 1 2 3 4 5 6 7 8 9
37 · 0 1 2 3 4 5 6 7 8 9
38 · 0 1 2 3 4 5 6 7 8 9

WRITING SKILLS

1 Ⓐ Ⓑ Ⓒ Ⓓ Ⓔ
2 Ⓐ Ⓑ Ⓒ Ⓓ Ⓔ
3 Ⓐ Ⓑ Ⓒ Ⓓ Ⓔ
4 Ⓐ Ⓑ Ⓒ Ⓓ Ⓔ
5 Ⓐ Ⓑ Ⓒ Ⓓ Ⓔ
6 Ⓐ Ⓑ Ⓒ Ⓓ Ⓔ
7 Ⓐ Ⓑ Ⓒ Ⓓ Ⓔ
8 Ⓐ Ⓑ Ⓒ Ⓓ Ⓔ
9 Ⓐ Ⓑ Ⓒ Ⓓ Ⓔ
10 Ⓐ Ⓑ Ⓒ Ⓓ Ⓔ
11 Ⓐ Ⓑ Ⓒ Ⓓ Ⓔ
12 Ⓐ Ⓑ Ⓒ Ⓓ Ⓔ
13 Ⓐ Ⓑ Ⓒ Ⓓ Ⓔ

14 Ⓐ Ⓑ Ⓒ Ⓓ Ⓔ
15 Ⓐ Ⓑ Ⓒ Ⓓ Ⓔ
16 Ⓐ Ⓑ Ⓒ Ⓓ Ⓔ
17 Ⓐ Ⓑ Ⓒ Ⓓ Ⓔ
18 Ⓐ Ⓑ Ⓒ Ⓓ Ⓔ
19 Ⓐ Ⓑ Ⓒ Ⓓ Ⓔ
20 Ⓐ Ⓑ Ⓒ Ⓓ Ⓔ
21 Ⓐ Ⓑ Ⓒ Ⓓ Ⓔ
22 Ⓐ Ⓑ Ⓒ Ⓓ Ⓔ
23 Ⓐ Ⓑ Ⓒ Ⓓ Ⓔ
24 Ⓐ Ⓑ Ⓒ Ⓓ Ⓔ
25 Ⓐ Ⓑ Ⓒ Ⓓ Ⓔ
26 Ⓐ Ⓑ Ⓒ Ⓓ Ⓔ

27 Ⓐ Ⓑ Ⓒ Ⓓ Ⓔ
28 Ⓐ Ⓑ Ⓒ Ⓓ Ⓔ
29 Ⓐ Ⓑ Ⓒ Ⓓ Ⓔ
30 Ⓐ Ⓑ Ⓒ Ⓓ Ⓔ
31 Ⓐ Ⓑ Ⓒ Ⓓ Ⓔ
32 Ⓐ Ⓑ Ⓒ Ⓓ Ⓔ
33 Ⓐ Ⓑ Ⓒ Ⓓ Ⓔ
34 Ⓐ Ⓑ Ⓒ Ⓓ Ⓔ
35 Ⓐ Ⓑ Ⓒ Ⓓ Ⓔ
36 Ⓐ Ⓑ Ⓒ Ⓓ Ⓔ
37 Ⓐ Ⓑ Ⓒ Ⓓ Ⓔ
38 Ⓐ Ⓑ Ⓒ Ⓓ Ⓔ
39 Ⓐ Ⓑ Ⓒ Ⓓ Ⓔ

SECTION 1
Time — 25 minutes
24 Questions
(1–24)

Directions: For each question in this section, select the best answer from among the choices given and fill in the corresponding circle on the answer sheet.

Each sentence below has one or two blanks, each blank indicating that something has been omitted. Beneath the sentence are five words or sets of words labeled A through E. Choose the word or set of words that, when inserted in the sentence, best fits the meaning of the sentence as a whole.

Example:

Desiring to ------- his taunting friends, Mitch gave them taffy in hopes it would keep their mouths shut.

(A) eliminate   (B) satisfy   (C) overcome
    (D) ridicule   (E) silence

---

1. Excited about ------- new cooking techniques, Raquel pored over cookbooks and bought a few important kitchen utensils.

    (A) resisting   (B) mitigating   (C) entertaining
        (D) neglecting   (E) investigating

2. By successfully publishing poems, short stories, and novels throughout his career, the author proved himself to have a ------- writing ability.

    (A) finite   (B) radical   (C) diversified
        (D) middling   (E) visionary

3. Although the armadillo has armor-like scales that form a shield over its shoulders, back, and hips, its ------- underside is covered only with skin and fur.

    (A) guarded   (B) vulnerable   (C) complex
        (D) youthful   (E) sallow

4. The return home for failed Olympic hopeful Cecily Carter was -------: she was happy to see everyone but ------- to explain why she hadn't made the team.

    (A) exhilarating . . depressed
    (B) distressing . . hesitant
    (C) ambivalent . . amused
    (D) inconvenient . . challenged
    (E) bittersweet . . loath

5. Many large-pot lottery winners, lacking the financial savvy to appropriately deal with such a(n) -------, eventually wind up -------.

    (A) deficiency . . thriving
    (B) insight . . ingenious
    (C) paucity . . bankrupt
    (D) windfall . . insolvent
    (E) abundance . . illustrious

6. Rarely -------, Juan tended to demand his way with those he worked with, never bothering to consult or ask anyone else's opinion.

    (A) synergistic   (B) imperious   (C) overbearing
        (D) extroverted   (E) disjointed

7. Many in the film industry considered the producer the ------- of -------; he was the quintessential professional.

    (A) paragon . . malevolence
    (B) connoisseur . . immaturity
    (C) extension . . accomplishment
    (D) epitome . . proficiency
    (E) personification . . philanthropy

8. Knitters apprehensive about attempting more intricate patterns will be motivated by Lee Hartwell's ------- instructional videos, which ------- even the trickiest stitches.

    (A) abstruse . . obscure
    (B) munificent . . critique
    (C) straightforward . . muddle
    (D) vocational . . explicate
    (E) pellucid . . demystify

GO ON TO THE NEXT PAGE

The passages below are followed by questions based on their content; questions following a pair of related passages may also be based on the relationship between the paired passages. Answer the questions on the basis of what is <u>stated</u> or <u>implied</u> in the passage and in any introductory material that may be provided.

Questions 9-12 are based on the following passages.

Passage 1

Line
Without fail, the same thing happens in every romantic comedy I ever see. Boy and girl meet, fall in love, and live happily ever after. There are witty best friends and complicated misunderstandings. Then everything works out
5 perfectly. I have always been frustrated by this formula. I have never seen a romantic comedy that I truly enjoyed. For quite a while, I thought I was just overly cynical; now, I'm not so sure the problem is with me. Romance and humor are wonderful things to have in life, but the romantic comedy
10 sets us up to fail. Our experiences will never be like those we see on the big screen. Therefore, instead of making us happy, the romantic comedy makes us feel like there is always something better for us that we're missing out on.

Passage 2

For as long as I can remember, I have been enthralled by
15 romantic comedies—mostly because of their unapologetically optimistic outcomes, though some may argue the films are unrealistic or cheesy. Although the structure of most of them is similar at the most basic level (main characters meet, deal with complications, work everything out), the individual
20 movies are vastly different. A multitude of characters, back stories, locations, time periods, and other factors come together to create myriad distinct stories. Romantic comedies, detractors complain, are not believable—real life never works out the way it does in the movies. That's exactly why I love
25 them. Watching happily ever after happen on the big screen is a wonderful reminder that even when things don't seem to be going your way, you might just run out of an elevator and into the person of your dreams.

9. Both authors do which of the following in these passages?

    (A) Incorporate critics' reviews.
    (B) Write in the first person.
    (C) Mention specific films.
    (D) Refer to the reader's romantic experiences.
    (E) Refute the arguments of others.

10. In line 17 the word "cheesy" most nearly means

    (A) genuine
    (B) shoddy
    (C) melted
    (D) inauthentic
    (E) charming

11. The author of Passage 1 would most likely respond to the "detractors" (Passage 2, line 23) with

    (A) total approval
    (B) mild frustration
    (C) sarcasm
    (D) hesitancy
    (E) resentment

12. Which best captures the attitude of each author toward romantic comedies?

    (A) The author of Passage 1 feels romantic comedies are less realistic than they used to be, whereas the author of Passage 2 thinks they are a good bargain.
    (B) The author of Passage 1 is slightly bored by the improbability of the films, whereas the author of Passage 2 is completely fed up with it.
    (C) The author of Passage 1 disdains the phoniness of romantic comedies, whereas the author of Passage 2 supposes them to be accurate representations of real life.
    (D) The author of Passage 1 is frustrated by the unrealistic standards set in romantic comedies, whereas the author of Passage 2 enjoys the optimistic consistency of the films.
    (E) The author of Passage 1 is annoyed by the recent increase in movie ticket prices, whereas the author of Passage 2 believes the films help people feel optimistic about their lives.

GO ON TO THE NEXT PAGE >

Questions 13-24 are based on the following passage.

This passage is adapted from a book published in 2012.

Google, Yahoo!, Bing, and other search engines are all over the internet, seeming to promise us all the information we could ever need. With such a profusion of information at our fingertips, we wonder how previous generations of
5 scholars slaved away at libraries, pulling dusty books from the shelves and hoping that those books could reveal all the world's secrets.

Because the internet search has become such an essential part of our daily routines—because we can do it on our
10 phones and TVs as well as our computers—we can finally begin to assess how this information saturation has affected our minds. Now that we have all this information at our behest, are we smarter? Or, as one writer in the *Atlantic Monthly* asked, "Is Google Making Us Stoopid?"
15 In many ways, our informational field has reflected our understanding of the universe: where we once thought of the "heavens" as the things that we could see in the sky, we now theorize the universe as infinite, containing literally countless numbers of worlds like our own in literally countless
20 figurations. Just as the universe is too large to conceptualize, there's now too much information available for anyone ever to know. In the days of traditional library research, the search for the appropriate sources was itself part of the process. Researchers did the selecting themselves and assimilated a
25 good deal of peripheral knowledge into the bargain. A scholar likes James Frazer, author of *The Golden Bough* (1890), could be fairly certain that he was assembling all of the world's myths and folklore in a single book.

Now, we know that Frazer's project was a very limited
30 one. A single Google search for the word "myth" will show us how many billions of things he missed. In fact, projects like Frazer's must necessarily have changed. Because we know how much information is out there, we can't possibly dream of trying to assemble it all into anything as manageable as
35 a single book. We instead generate theories to support our impossible positions, as if to say that because there is too much information, nothing can be knowable in any real depth.

Indeed, this shift from the finite to the infinite is another version of the globalization that we experience every day:
40 cars from Japan, electronics from Korea, and furniture from Sweden are parts of our daily lives, which we no longer experience as foreign. Ours is truly a world community, where the lines between nations have become blurred and where people have more in common than ever before.

45 In an earlier age, this kind of global consumption would have only been available to the exorbitantly wealthy—not only to buy the goods, but to travel the globe…It's now available to anyone who can drive to the store or order something online. We can have global experiences at mall
50 food courts. No matter whether one lives in an urban or rural area, whether one has a fast or slow internet connection, the entire world is there for our consumption and perusal at any time of the day or night. Just as our ancestors' ways of life seem incomprehensibly difficult to us, so too must ours seem
55 impossibly large to them, some bit of witchcraft that allows us to be everywhere at once.

Because the whole world and all its information are at our fingertips, how can we possibly begin to understand this new world that has grown up around us? How do we evaluate
60 something that we can hardly understand? The researcher of a century ago spent many hours poring over a single text, and often had to learn entirely new languages to do so. The computer-savvy researcher of today, by contrast, can have that information instantaneously and can even search within it for
65 whatever bits of information seem relevant.

To ask the question in the most simpleminded of ways, are we smarter? All this information is now at our fingertips, but can we really be said to *have* it? Those older scholars and thinkers may have known what they knew more intimately.
70 They may have worked harder to acquire it. But there was simply less for them to know, and it's no mistake that scholars from our own era are constantly improving upon and refining what those older scholars have done. They may have known everything there was to know, but that was a very limited
75 everything indeed. Still, our own omniscience is not without its limitations. Rather than delving more deeply into this or that topic, we are much more likely to throw up our hands, to say that if we can't know everything, then it's not worth it to try to know anything at all. How can we take seriously any
80 attempt at knowing when the remainder of all that we don't know is there as a constant reminder? It is at the very least my hope—and the hope, I suspect, of many others—that there must be some way between the two extremes. We don't want to return to the era of the very small world, nor can we
85 allow ourselves to drift off into the infinite immensity of the informational world that is available now.

GO ON TO THE NEXT PAGE

13. The first paragraph (lines 1-7) most directly focuses on the

   (A) predicted downfall of internet search engines
   (B) death of true research in contemporary scholarship
   (C) distinction between topics of old scholarship and new
   (D) reduction of intelligence in the modern age
   (E) contemporary availability of large amounts of information

14. In context, the reference to "previous generations of scholars" (lines 4-5) is significant in that it

   (A) demonstrates the contrast between old and new methods of research
   (B) states that people from earlier eras had more time to spend reading
   (C) emphasizes the contemporary scholar's contempt for libraries
   (D) indicates the accuracy provided by basic internet searches
   (E) shows that new research methods can reveal universal knowledge

15. In line 11, the phrase "information saturation" describes the

   (A) mode of thinking that has crippled contemporary research methods
   (B) contrast between effective and ineffective methods of acquiring information
   (C) moment at which an intelligent human being can no longer learn new information
   (D) change in contemporary thinking about the usefulness of scholarly research
   (E) emerging situation in which information becomes too much for one person to know

16. In lines 12-13, "at … behest" most nearly means

   (A) under our control
   (B) beyond our understanding
   (C) in our books
   (D) available to us
   (E) within our grasp

17. In lines 15-16, "our understanding" represents a shift away from

   (A) online databases
   (B) universal knowledge
   (C) inadequate explanations
   (D) faith-based interpretations
   (E) a knowable world

18. The author mentions "researchers" (line 24) and "a scholar" (line 25) primarily to

   (A) underline the importance of traditional modes of study
   (B) warn against the dangers of traditional research
   (C) wonder at the importance of printed books
   (D) compare the researchers of previous ages unfavorably to those of today
   (E) demonstrate instances of one type of study

19. In context, the book cited in line 26 supports the notion that

   (A) the scope of contemporary research has changed
   (B) scholars no longer have ambitious research goals
   (C) the study of mythology has disappeared from contemporary scholarship
   (D) one particular book answers more questions than the internet can
   (E) researchers are more accurate when they work with limited information

20. The author suggests that "Now" (line 29) scholars have become

   (A) hopeless
   (B) collaborative
   (C) inundated
   (D) smarter
   (E) aggressive

GO ON TO THE NEXT PAGE

21. In lines 38-42 ("Indeed ... foreign"), the author notes a parallel between

(A) contemporary research and the makeup of mall food courts

(B) a desire for complete knowledge and cultural and ethnic diversity

(C) the amount of information and the excesses of consumerism

(D) trends in research and preferences for foreign goods

(E) the range of available information and economic globalization

22. The word "witchcraft" (line 55) refers to

(A) one of the new forms of information available to contemporary scholars

(B) a recently developed power made possible by internet searching

(C) lives lived in an era without modern conveniences

(D) the ability to experience many parts of the world in a single place

(E) the overwhelming amount of information that is available at all times

23. The example of the "computer-savvy researcher" (line 63) is primarily used to illustrate

(A) rampant procrastination

(B) technological sophistication

(C) deep knowledge

(D) mental handicaps

(E) informational availability

24. The primary purpose of the last paragraph (lines 66-86) is to

(A) doubt that the new modes of acquiring information will ever generate important discoveries

(B) suggest that some compromise is possible between old and new ways of acquiring information

(C) long for an earlier mode of research that relied on the deep study of long printed books

(D) defend the rights of computer-literate people to use whatever bits of information they find relevant

(E) outline the differences between those who use computers to access information and those who do not

STOP
If you finish before time is called, you may check your work on this section only.
Do not turn to any other section in the test.

SECTION 2
Time — 25 minutes
20 Questions
(1–20)

Directions: For this section, solve each problem and decide which is the best of the choices given. Fill in the corresponding circle on the answer sheet. You may use any available space for scratchwork.

Notes

1. The use of a calculator is permitted.

2. All numbers used are real numbers.

3. Figures that accompany problems in this test are intended to provide information useful in solving the problems. They are drawn as accurately as possible EXCEPT when it is stated in a specific problem that the figure is not drawn to scale. All figures lie in a plane unless other wise indicated.

4. Unless otherwise specified, the domain of any function f is assumed to be the set of all real numbers x for which $f(x)$ is a real number.

Reference Information

  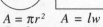   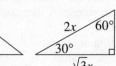

$A = \pi r^2$
$C = 2\pi r$
$A = lw$
$A = \frac{1}{2}bh$
$V = lwh$
$V = \pi r^2 h$
$c^2 = a^2 + b^2$

Special Right Triangles

The number of degrees of arc in a circle is 360.

The sum of the measures in degrees of the angles of a triangle is 180.

1. If $y + 3 = 7$, what is the value of $2y + 3$?

    (A) −5
    (B) 8
    (C) 11
    (D) 14
    (E) 23

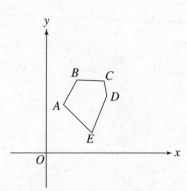

2. In the figure above, which side of 5-sided polygon *ABCDE* has the greatest negative slope?

    (A) *EA*
    (B) *AB*
    (C) *BC*
    (D) *CD*
    (E) *DE*

GO ON TO THE NEXT PAGE

3. Rhys has a bucket of candy containing 15 lollipops, 25 gumballs, 35 licorice sticks, and no other types of candy. If Rhys selects one type of candy at random, what is the probability that the chosen candy will be a licorice stick?

(A) $\dfrac{1}{5}$

(B) $\dfrac{1}{3}$

(C) $\dfrac{3}{10}$

(D) $\dfrac{7}{15}$

(E) $\dfrac{8}{15}$

4. If $(b + 2)(3b - 6) = z$, then $(b + 2)(b - 2) =$

(A) $\dfrac{1}{6}z$

(B) $\dfrac{1}{3}z$

(C) $\dfrac{1}{2}z$

(D) $3z$

(E) $6z$

5. If three lines intersect to form six equal angles, what is the measure of one of these angles?

(A) 15°
(B) 30°
(C) 45°
(D) 50°
(E) 60°

NUMBER OF QUESTIONS ANSWERED
VERSUS HOMEWORK TIME

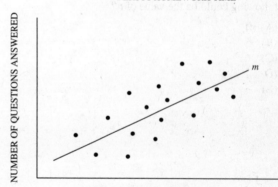

6. Brian surveyed the 18 students in his algebra class to determine the amount of time they spent doing homework and the number of questions answered on the last test. The scatterplot above shows the homework time and the number of test questions answered for each of the 18 students. Line m is the best fit line. For how many students was the number of test questions answered fewer than what the best fit line predicted for the corresponding homework time?

(A) 8
(B) 9
(C) 10
(D) 11
(E) 13

GO ON TO THE NEXT PAGE

7. The expression $3p + 6$ could be represented by which of the following operations?

   (A) 3 times 6 more than a number p
   (B) 3 times 6 less than a number p
   (C) 3 more than 6 times a number p
   (D) 6 less than 3 times a number p
   (E) 6 more than 3 times a number p

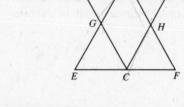

9. In the figure above, $AD = DB = EC = CF$. If $\triangle ABC$ and $\triangle DEF$ are equilateral, and $AB = 10$, what is the perimeter of quadrilateral $CGDH$?

   (A) 10
   (B) 15
   (C) 20
   (D) 25
   (E) 35

8. If the quantity $(2t - 5)$ is divisible by t, which of the following could be the value of t ?

   (A) 4
   (B) 5
   (C) 6
   (D) 7
   (E) 8

10. Helene lists her zip code on an application form. She notices that the first and last digits are both prime, the middle digit is a divisor of 45, and the least common multiple of remaining two digits is 6. Which of the following numbers could be her zip code?

   (A) 22935
   (B) 23924
   (C) 32437
   (D) 35563
   (E) 52732

GO ON TO THE NEXT PAGE

11. What number is 4 less than $\frac{1}{2}$ of itself?

(A) −11
(B) −10
(C) −9
(D) −8
(E) −6

13. The side of square S is twice the diameter of circle C. What is the greatest possible number of points of intersection of the perimeter of square S and the circumference of circle C ?

(A) Two
(B) Three
(C) Four
(D) Six
(E) Eight

12. Ringo is a dog that is not brown. From which of the following statements can it be determined whether or not Ringo is a Labrador?

(A) Any dog that is not brown is not a Labrador.
(B) Some dogs that are brown are not Labradors.
(C) All dogs that are brown are Labradors.
(D) No dogs are both brown and Labradors.
(E) Any dog that is brown is not a Labrador.

$$y = -x$$
$$y = x + n$$

14. If the ordered pair $(t, 2)$, where $x = t$ and $y = 2$, is the intersection of the two lines above, then what is the value of n ?

(A) −2
(B) 0
(C) 2
(D) 4
(E) 6

GO ON TO THE NEXT PAGE

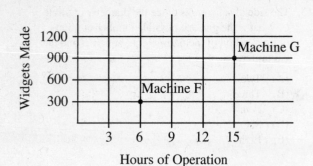

15. The graph above shows the number of widgets made by two machines, F and G, plotted against the number of hours in operation. On average, for each hour of operation, how many more widgets did machine G make than machine F?

(A)   9
(B)   10
(C)   22
(D)   50
(E)   60

16. If w is an integer and 8 is a factor of $2w$, which of the following must be true?

   I. w is an even integer
   II. w is divisible by 4
   III. w is divisible by 8

(A) I only
(B) II only
(C) I and II only
(D) II and III only
(E) I, II, and III

17. If q and s are greater than 0 and $\dfrac{q^{12}}{q^2} = s^5$, then $\dfrac{s^{12}}{s^2} =$

(A) q^5
(B) q^6
(C) q^{10}
(D) q^{12}
(E) q^{20}

18. Line l, defined by the equation $x + 2y = 4$, is graphed in the xy-plane. Line m is the reflection of line l across the x-axis. Which is the following is an equation of line m ?

(A) $x - 2y = -4$
(B) $x + 2y = -4$
(C) $x - 2y = 4$
(D) $x + 2y = 4$
(E) $2x - y = -2$

GO ON TO THE NEXT PAGE

19. A lock requires a 3-digit code such that each digit is a positive even number less than 9. How many such codes are possible?

    (A) 4
    (B) 8
    (C) 16
    (D) 24
    (E) 64

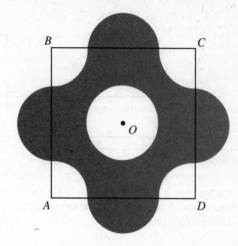

20. The figure above shows a square with side of length 4. The center of the square, point O, is also the center of circle O, with radius 1. Four semicircles with radius 1 are centered on each side of the square. If the arcs shown have centers at A, B, C, and D, what is the area of the shaded region?

    (A) 4π
    (B) 16
    (C) $8\pi - 8$
    (D) $8 + 4\pi$
    (E) $16 - 2\pi$

STOP
If you finish before time is called, you may check your work on this section only.
Do not turn to any other section in the test.

SECTION 3
Time — 25 minutes
24 Questions
(25–48)

Directions: For each question in this section, select the best answer from among the choices given and fill in the corresponding circle on the answer sheet.

Each sentence below has one or two blanks, each blank indicating that something has been omitted. Beneath the sentence are five words or sets of words labeled A through E. Choose the word or set of words that, when inserted in the sentence, best fits the meaning of the sentence as a whole.

Example:

Hoping to ------- the dispute, negotiators proposed a compromise that they felt would be ------- to both labor and management.

(A) enforce . . useful
(B) end . . divisive
(C) overcome . . unattractive
(D) extend . . satisfactory
(E) resolve . . acceptable

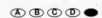

25. Though the training methods were rigorous and exhausting, the results were so -------- that the athletes kept up with the program.

(A) calming   (B) astonishing   (C) disastrous
 (D) subtle   (E) brutal

26. Among the hundreds of siblings in professional football are brothers Peyton and Eli Manning, both quarterbacks but with -------- throwing styles: while Eli has a much stronger arm, Peyton is the more accurate passer.

(A) uniform   (B) vigorous   (C) complicated
 (D) trendy   (E) distinct

27. The novice jungle explorers were concerned about getting lost in the rainforest, but the maps they brought were so ------- that their fears of never returning from the expedition were much -------.

(A) meticulous . . alleviated
(B) vibrant . . justified
(C) systematic . . exacerbated
(D) inaccurate . . lightened
(E) antiquated . . panicked

28. Although the pufferfish is the second-most ------- vertebrate on the planet, producing toxins that can kill a human within 24 hours, its big eyes and comically rotund appearance ------- its lethality.

(A) virulent . . communicate
(B) distended . . belie
(C) poisonous . . witness
(D) toxiferous . . disaffirm
(E) trafficable . . ridicule

29. The article described the appearance of goose bumps under stress as a ------- reflex because for our ancestors, having their hair stand on end made them look more intimidating to would-be predators, but for modern humans, there is really no purpose for the reaction.

(A) genealogical   (B) defunct   (C) primitive
 (D) pedantic   (E) vestigial

GO ON TO THE NEXT PAGE

The passages below are followed by questions based on their content; questions following a pair of related passages may also be based on the relationship between the paired passages. Answer the questions on the basis of what is <u>stated</u> or <u>implied</u> in the passage and in any introductory material that may be provided.

Questions 30-31 are based on the following passage.

Biographers' perspectives on Thomas Jefferson* differ greatly. Some view the influential politician as an opponent of the slave trade who introduced a 1778 law prohibiting the importation of slaves and penned the famous "all men are created equal" statement, while others portray him as a wealthy land and slave owner who formally freed only two of his many slaves during his lifetime, failing to match his actions to his strong rhetoric. A third view holds that he was simply a product of his time: in order to maintain the land and wealth necessary to be significant politically, owning slaves was a necessary evil. The biographers all agree on one thing, however: Thomas Jefferson was one of the most prominent leaders in our nation's history.

*U.S. President 1801-1809

30. The author indicates that the "others" (line 5) view Jefferson as a man who

(A) practiced what he preached
(B) had strong political aspirations
(C) believed all men are created equal
(D) had a significant amount of land
(E) said one thing but did another

31. The primary purpose of this passage is to

(A) summarize Thomas Jefferson's political career
(B) concede Thomas Jefferson's role in the slave trade
(C) present varying perspectives on Thomas Jefferson
(D) challenge Thomas Jefferson's status as an eminent politician
(E) connect Thomas Jefferson's political success to his financial success

Questions 32-33 are based on the following passage.

Online shoppers do not intentionally make their personal information available to identity thieves, but they can leave an unintentionally traceable trail if they don't take precautions. As shoppers browse and purchase merchandise on websites, it's easy for those who aren't paying attention to ingenuously leave a trail of email addresses, passwords, and credit card numbers—all bits of data that wily identity thieves can scoop up and use as they like. The FTC estimates that nearly 9 million Americans are victims of identity theft every year, falling prey to convincing but phony websites, quick-talking phone scammers, or phishing emails. A stolen identity can be a quick buck for a criminal but a lifetime of hassle for the victim.

32. The author uses "ingenuously" (line 5) to mean that online shoppers

(A) accidentally use the wrong credit card
(B) don't understand how the Internet works
(C) deliberately use wrong information to throw off thieves
(D) don't realize their information is insecure
(E) are savvy about how they make online purchases

33. The author cites the figure of "9 million" (lines 8-9) in order to suggest that

(A) using a credit card is safer than using a debit card
(B) large retailers are less secure than smaller retailers
(C) some victims of identity theft have had information stolen multiple times
(D) the FTC keeps meticulous data about online hackers
(E) online shopping is less secure than many shoppers might think

GO ON TO THE NEXT PAGE ⟩

Questions 34-39 are based on the following passage.

Each passage below discusses rabies. Passage 1 was published in July 2012; Passage 2 was published in October 2012.

Passage 1

For as long as the disease has existed, rabies has been considered incurable. Even when the human diploid cell rabies vaccine was first given in 1967, it had to be
Line administered within six days of the patient's contraction
5 of the virus, before symptoms started to appear. After this six-day period, the fatality rate was 100%, and even now, the disease kills about 55,000 people each year.

But a doctor at the Children's Hospital of Wisconsin, Dr. Rodney Willoughby, may have finally found a way to
10 conquer this seemingly unconquerable disease. In 2004, American teenager Jeanna Giese contracted the disease and was not vaccinated before the onset of symptoms. Willoughby hypothesized that the detrimental effects of rabies on the brain could be halted by a more general halting of brain
15 functions. Willoughby's team induced a coma and gave Jeanna heavy doses of ketamine, midazolam, ribavirin, and amantadine. After 31 days of isolation and 76 days of hospitalization, Jeanna was essentially cured of the virus and maintained all of her higher brain functions. Willoughby's
20 result gives researchers hope that the chemical effects of rabies can be altered to prevent the disease's deteriorating effects. Jeanna was the first patient to survive the disease unvaccinated, and she gives the medical community hope that her recovery was not merely an outlier.

Passage 2

25 Rabies researchers would like to be able to change the odds. Recent findings have given these researchers hope, but the findings may not hold the promise they initially seemed to—the disease remains fatal in an overwhelming number of cases, and even the furthest advances of medical science may
30 not yet have found the cure.

Dr. Rodney Willoughby gave researchers hope in 2004 when his experimental treatment cured an unvaccinated case of rabies in an American teenager. Since 2004, there have been more cures with what is now called the "Milwaukee
35 protocol," but the results have not been quite as miraculous as researchers initially believed. Under the initial protocol, only two of the 25 treated patients survived. Some critics of Willoughby's method have even begun to suggest that the protocol is only effective on particularly mild cases of

40 the infection. Furthermore, those cured have typically been young people with exceptionally strong immune systems, and the bites from which they contracted the disease may have occurred far enough away from the brain that their effects were diluted. Willoughby's method remains the subject of
45 heated debate within the scientific community, a large portion of which continues to believe that rabies is an incurable disease. "Medical miracles happen," says rabies researcher Jun Hong, "but we can't start believing that these are general or reproducible cases."

34. In their discussion of rabies, the authors of Passage 1 and Passage 2 each make use of

    (A) recent findings and theories from medical researchers
    (B) emotionally charged addresses to the reader
    (C) complex metaphors and figurative language
    (D) citations from amateur rabies researchers
    (E) descriptions of the brain's chemical makeup

35. The mention of the "human diploid cell rabies vaccine" (Passage 1, lines 2-3) and "the initial protocol" (Passage 2, line 36) would best support the idea that

    (A) rabies can be cured with an induced coma and a combination of medicines
    (B) rabies is predominantly incurable after a certain stage
    (C) the effects of rabies on the brain cannot be reversed
    (D) rabies was curable for a short period but is no longer curable
    (E) other diseases similar to rabies are not so damaging to the brain

36. The primary purpose of Passage 2 is to

    (A) underline the importance of debate within the scientific community
    (B) offer a warning that recent scientific findings are not fully conclusive
    (C) detail the ways in which the brain's chemistry is resistant to induced coma
    (D) warn against the deteriorating effects of the Milwaukee protocol
    (E) praise the recent discoveries of Dr. Willoughby and others in the field

GO ON TO THE NEXT PAGE ➤

37. The author of Passage 2 would most likely respond to the findings discussed in Passage 1 with

 (A) agreement, given his general appreciation for advances in medical science
 (B) dismissal, because he disagrees so strongly with the Milwaukee protocol
 (C) skepticism, since the research presented have not been adequately proven
 (D) shock, because the statistics are so precisely aligned with his own argument
 (E) grudging approval, since the findings in the first passage are so conclusive

38. If the sample of "25 treated patients" (Passage 2, line 37) had a greater survival rate, the greater rate would most likely have had what effect on the author's argument in Passage 1?

 (A) Strengthen the argument by providing additional statistical support
 (B) Weaken the argument by showing a fault in the argument's logic
 (C) Provide an insoluble contradiction to the argument with empirical data
 (D) Reduce the coherence of the argument by introducing new data
 (E) No effect, because the findings have already been dismissed by the author of Passage 1

39. The evidence provided about rabies cures in Passage 1 and Passage 2, respectively, is best described as

 (A) encouraging vs. disputed
 (B) fantastic vs. grounded
 (C) scientific vs. anecdotal
 (D) amateurish vs. medical
 (E) mature vs. irrelevant

GO ON TO THE NEXT PAGE

Questions 40-48 are based on the following passage.

This passage is adapted from a 2009 novel set in Egypt and the United Kingdom.

Naim loved squash as he did, he thought, because he was never *quite* as good as he wanted to be. Certainly, a large part of it was the competition—no matter how many
Line players you could beat, there were always new ones who
5 could beat you—but if that had been the only hurdle, things might have been easier: after a loss or an unsatisfying win, he spent extra hours at the court, practicing with an almost machine-like consistency, drilling until he couldn't breathe anymore, and hitting hundreds, thousands of shots, trying
10 to store that perfect stroke in his muscle memory. On top of that, his biggest challenge came from his coach, Mr. Shabana, who wanted Naim to play the English style—consistency, endurance, humility—that had never felt right; Naim's own take on the game, more characterized by quick, deceptive
15 movements, odd changes in pace, fancy trick shots, felt much more like the game he was meant to play, much more an expression of himself than the characterless devotion to some sport that existed long before he came along to play it.

But if it wouldn't win his matches or tournaments, or
20 allow him to go pro (his lifelong dream, but one that seemed too hard with a unique, personalized style of play), then why keep playing what Mr. Shabana called this "dead-end" style of squash? Naim couldn't say. He loved to watch the greats from squash history, both the English and the Egyptian
25 champions, and their methodical, uncannily consistent styles of play. Naim himself wanted to be part of this great legion of players. His hope to change the way the game was played and for his name to be known made him think he might be better suited to the bigger stage of tennis: where styles were not so
30 regimented, and the best players were like movie stars.

Naim would not switch to tennis because as he watched a new player on the pro tour, he found the inspiration he had been missing. The player's name was Mohamed El Shorbagy—a young man, not much older than Naim, and
35 also from Naim's home town of Alexandria—but Naim was much more captivated by his style of play. On the same court and against many of the same players that Naim had been watching all these years, El Shorbagy played the traditional game, but he did it with such flair, such incredible
40 confidence and style, that he seemed totally self-taught; he was almost, it seemed, expressing his very soul as he played, the same way one might do in a poem. If Naim watched him carefully—and he did watch him, over and over again—he would occasionally wonder if El Shorbagy's feet were even
45 on the ground. While El Shorbagy would often win, and by wide, convincing margins, he was not a traditional player: to be sure, Mr. Shabana likely would've called his play "savage." But his results spoke for themselves, and he was such a pleasure to watch that the crowds at his matches were always
50 notably large.

Naim himself had been the first to use the word "inspiration" when talking about El Shorbagy's play (and many years after El Shorbagy retired, as Naim told his own students about El Shorbagy's early performances, he would
55 explain his professional career and his subsequent coaching life as impossible without El Shorbagy's influence). Naim took the word from his teachers. If inspiration was the feeling that the sky was the limit, that one could do anything, that one's world had changed in a way that could never be
60 undone—then Naim had experienced that very thing.

40. The first two paragraphs (line 1-30) primarily suggest that Naim was

  (A) more interested in becoming a celebrity than in improving his skills
  (B) working to change his game to be more consistent with what his coach suggested
  (C) exasperated by his attempts to become a great squash player
  (D) wishing that he had become a tennis player
  (E) contemptuous of his squash coach

41. In line 11, the word "that" refers to which of the following from lines 1-10?

  (A) Naim's difficult training regimen
  (B) Naim's wavering devotion to the sport of squash
  (C) Naim's inability to become a great player
  (D) The overreaction to a loss in tournament play
  (E) The talented players against whom Naim played

42. The parenthetical remarks in lines 20-21 anticipate which of the following in the passage?

  (A) Naim's search for true inspiration
  (B) Naim's ultimate wish to give up squash for tennis
  (C) Naim's belief in the teachings of Mr. Shabana
  (D) Naim's choice to become a squash professional
  (E) Naim's admiration for Mohamed El Shorbagy

GO ON TO THE NEXT PAGE ➡

43. The sentence in lines 26-27 ("Naim ... players") indicates that Naim wanted to

(A) be listed among the great squash players of all time
(B) perfect the English style of playing squash
(C) appear on televised sporting events
(D) improve upon what Mr. Shabana advised
(E) show that his style of play could be learned by other players

44. Lines 29-30 ("where ... stars") suggest which of the following about Naim?

(A) His appreciation of the English style of squash
(B) His egotism in believing that his style of squash is superior
(C) His level of admiration for well-known squash players
(D) The disappointment he would face if he were to switch to tennis
(E) His wish to be a unique and well-respected athlete

45. In line 30, "regimented" most nearly means

(A) military
(B) uncreative
(C) little-known
(D) difficult
(E) disciplined

46. The third paragraph (lines 31-50) primarily serves to

(A) show a renewal of interest
(B) highlight a willingness to mature
(C) defend a difficult choice
(D) cheer a series of victories
(E) concede an earlier point

47. What Naim found most appealing in El Shorbagy's play was its

(A) expressive creativity
(B) disciplined form
(C) Egyptian squash style
(D) popular appeal
(E) technical perfection

48. The final paragraph most directly elaborates on which point made earlier by the narrator?

(A) "his biggest challenge came from his coach" (line 11)
(B) "Naim couldn't say" (line 23)
(C) "the best players were like movie stars" (line 30)
(D) "he found the inspiration he had been missing" (lines 32-33)
(E) "El Shorbagy played the traditional game" (lines 38-39)

STOP

If you finish before time is called, you may check your work on this section only.
Do not turn to any other section in the test.

SECTION 4
Time — 25 minutes
18 Questions
(21–38)

Directions: For this section, solve each problem and decide which is the best of the choices given. Fill in the corresponding circle on the answer sheet. You may use any available space for scratchwork.

Notes

1. The use of a calculator is permitted.

2. All numbers used are real numbers.

3. Figures that accompany problems in this test are intended to provide information useful in solving the problems. They are drawn as accurately as possible EXCEPT when it is stated in a specific problem that the figure is not drawn to scale. All figures lie in a plane unless other wise indicated.

4. Unless otherwise specified, the domain of any function f is assumed to be the set of all real numbers x for which $f(x)$ is a real number.

Reference Information

 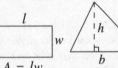

$A = \pi r^2$
$C = 2\pi r$

$A = lw$

$A = \frac{1}{2}bh$

$V = lwh$

$V = \pi r^2 h$

$c^2 = a^2 + b^2$

Special Right Triangles

The number of degrees of arc in a circle is 360.

The sum of the measures in degrees of the angles of a triangle is 180.

21. If r is an integer and 7.3×10^r is a number between 8,000 and 80,000, what is the value of r ?

(A) 1
(B) 2
(C) 3
(D) 4
(E) 5

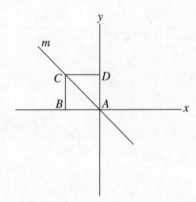

22. In the xy-plane above, $ABCD$ is a square with a side length of 8. If line m passes through points A and C, which of the following points lies on line m ?

(A) $(-5, 0)$
(B) $(0, -5)$
(C) $(-5, 5)$
(D) $(0, 5)$
(E) $(5, 5)$

GO ON TO THE NEXT PAGE

STUDENTS ATTENDING COLLEGE Q, BY GPA

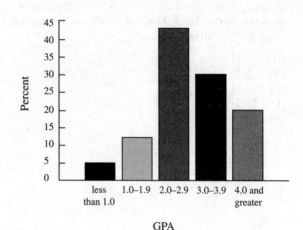

23. A total of 30,000 students attend College Q. How many of the students have a GPA that is less than 4.0 ?

(A)   3,000
(B)   6,000
(C)   12,000
(D)   20,000
(E)   24,000

3, 15, 35, 63, ...

24. The sequence above is formed by multiplying each odd integer by the next odd integer, starting with 1. What is the difference between the 7th and 8th term of the sequence?

(A)   1
(B)   28
(C)   60
(D)   128
(E)   256

25. When Gilbert rents a car from the Cars4U dealership, he is charged a constant rate per mile the car is driven plus a fixed cost for a carwash. On Monday he was charged a total of $13 after driving the rental car for 20 miles. On Friday he was charged $11.50 for driving the rental car 14 miles. Which of the following equations expresses the total charge T, in dollars, when Gilbert drives the rental car for m miles?

(A) $T = m - 7$
(B) $T = 0.25m$
(C) $T = 0.25m + 8$
(D) $T = 0.5m + 4$
(E) $T = 8m + 0.50$

26. The function g is defined by $g(x) = 33 - 4x$. If $g(b) = 5$, what is the value of b ?

(A) $-\dfrac{19}{2}$

(B) -7

(C) 7

(D) $\dfrac{19}{2}$

(E) 13

GO ON TO THE NEXT PAGE

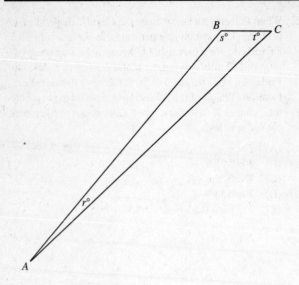

27. In the figure above, $AB = 200$ and $BC = 5$. Which of the following must be true?

(A) r is less than s and t
(B) s is greater than r and t
(C) t is greater than r and s
(D) s is equal to t
(E) r is greater than s and t

28. At a certain department store, the only sizes of shirts sold are small, medium, and large. At that store, the ratio of small shirts to medium shirts is 5:2, and the ratio of medium shirts to large shirts is 6:5. What is the ratio of small shirts to all <u>other</u> shirts?

(A)   5:11
(B)   5:16
(C)   7:11
(D)   11:5
(E)   15:11

GO ON TO THE NEXT PAGE

Directions for Student-Produced Response Questions

Each of the remaining 10 questions requires you to solve the problem and enter your answer by marking the ovals in the special grid, as shown in the examples below. You may use any available space for scratch work.

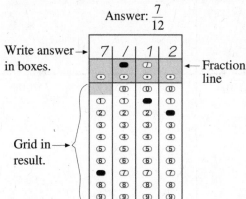

Answer: $\frac{7}{12}$

Write answer in boxes.

← Fraction line

Grid in result.

Answer: 2.5

← Decimal point

Note: You may start your answers in any column, space permitting. Columns not needed should be left blank.

- Mark no more than one circle in any column.
- Because the answer sheet will be machine-scored, **you will receive credit only if the circles are filled in correctly.**
- Although not required, it is suggested that you write your answer in the boxes at the top of the columns to help you fill in the circles accurately.
- Some problems may have more than one correct answer. In such cases, grid only one answer.
- No question has a negative answer.
- **Mixed numbers** such as $3\frac{1}{2}$ must be gridded as 3.5 or 7/2. (If | 3 | 1 | / | 2 | is gridded, it will be interpreted as $\frac{31}{2}$, not $3\frac{1}{2}$.)

- **Decimal Answers:** If you obtain a decimal answer with more digits than the grid can accommodate, it may be either rounded or truncated, but it must fill the entire grid. For example, if you obtain an answer such as 0.6666..., you should record your result as .666 or .667. **A less accurate value such as .66 or .67 will be scored as incorrect.**

Acceptable ways to grid $\frac{2}{3}$ are:

29. Each of the 8 salesmen at a used car dealership met his sales quota of 5 cars last month. In addition, 3 of the salesmen each sold exactly 3 additional cars, and 2 of the salesmen each sold 1 additional car. What is the total number of cars sold by these 8 salesmen?

30. In 1976 the world record distance for throwing a discus was 230 feet, and by 1983 the record distance had increased to 235 feet and 3 inches. If the record distance continues to increase at the same rate, in what year will the record distance for throwing a discus reach $261\frac{1}{2}$ feet?

GO ON TO THE NEXT PAGE →

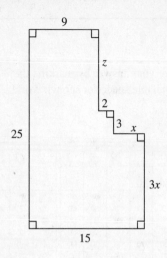

31. In the figure above, what is the value of z ?

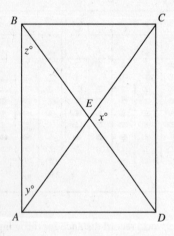

32. In the figure above, AC and BD are the diagonals of rectangle $ABCD$. If $x = 123$, what is the value of z ?

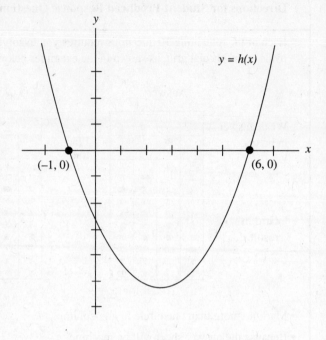

33. In the graph above, $h(x)$ is a quadratic function. For what x value does $h(x)$ reach its least value?

34. On her first four quizzes, Jan score 12, 8, 1, and 15 points. After Jan took her fifth quiz, she found that the average (arithmetic mean) of the five quiz scores was equal to the median of the five quiz scores. What is one possible value for the number of points Jan scored on her fifth quiz?

GO ON TO THE NEXT PAGE

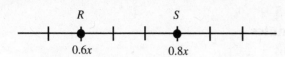

35. On the number line above, the distance between point R and point S is 3. What is the value of x ?

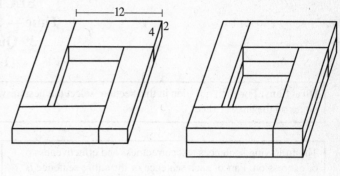

37. Four boards each measuring 2 inches by 4 inches by 12 inches are laid on a flat floor to form a square, as shown in the figure on the left. Another four boards of the same dimensions are laid on top of the first four in the same way, as shown in the figure on the right. This process is repeated until the boards are stacked a total of 10 boards high. The box created by these boards is then filled with sand until the sand is perfectly level with the highest point of the box. What is the volume, in cubic inches, of the sand in the box?

36. Sara created a list of 500 consecutive multiples of 4. What is the result if Sara subtracts the smallest number in her list from the largest number her the list?

38. If $5 < \dfrac{80}{x+2} < 6$, then what is one possible value of $\dfrac{40}{x+2}$?

STOP

If you finish before time is called, you may check your work on this section only.
Do not turn to any other section in the test.

SECTION 5
Time — 30 minutes
39 Questions
(1–39)

Directions: For each question in this section, select the best answer from among the choices given and fill in the corresponding circle on the answer sheet.

The following sentences test correctness and effectiveness of expression. Part of each sentence or the entire sentence is underlined; beneath each sentence are five ways of phrasing the underlined material. Choice A repeats the original phrasing; the other four choices are different. If you think the original phrasing produces a better sentence than any of the alternatives, select choice A; if not, select one of the other choices.

In making your selection, follow the requirements of standard written English; that is, pay attention to grammar, choice of words, sentence construction, and punctuation. Your selection should result in the most effective sentence—clear and precise, without awkwardness or ambiguity.

EXAMPLE:

Bobby Flay baked his first cake <u>and he was thirteen years old then</u>.
(A) and he was thirteen years old then
(B) when he was thirteen
(C) at age thirteen years old
(D) upon the reaching of thirteen years
(E) at the time when he was thirteen

1. One remarkable aspect of the platypus' ankles is <u>how it produces</u> venom.

   (A) how it produces
   (B) the production of
   (C) it produces
   (D) when they produce
   (E) by producing

2. <u>Wuthering Heights is a dark, tragic novel, while it</u> causes many of its readers to shed tears.

   (A) *Wuthering Heights* is a dark, tragic novel, while it
   (B) Because *Wuthering Heights* is darkly tragic, and as such, it
   (C) Being that it is a dark, tragic novel, *Wuthering Heights*
   (D) *Wuthering Heights*, although a dark, tragic novel, it
   (E) *Wuthering Heights* is a dark, tragic novel that

3. <u>Having swum from Cuba to the United States, Diana Nyad</u> became the first individual to complete the journey without a shark cage, even though she received multiple jellyfish stings.

   (A) Having swum from Cuba to the United States, Diana Nyad
   (B) Swimming from Cuba to the United States, Diana Nyad she
   (C) When Diana Nyad swam from Cuba to the United States, so she
   (D) Diana Nyad having swum from Cuba to the United States, and she
   (E) To swim from Cuba to the United States, Diana Nyad

4. Jessica decided to take the bus rather than the train for the simple reason <u>that it was much less expensive in cost than the train that she could take</u>.

   (A) that it was much less expensive in cost than the train that she could take.
   (B) because the train was much more expensive.
   (C) that it was much less expensive than the train.
   (D) being that the train was much more expensive.
   (E) of it being much less expensive than the train.

GO ON TO THE NEXT PAGE

5. In 1958 Chinua Achebe attempted to print his novel *Things Fall Apart*, sending the manuscript to several publishers, <u>some of them</u> rejected it immediately.

    (A) some of them
    (B) that, out of some
    (C) some of whom
    (D) and some which
    (E) some of those people

6. Of the many works of art from the Renaissance period, Leonardo da Vinci's <u>oddly compelling *Mona Lisa* is more</u> famous.

    (A) oddly compelling *Mona Lisa* is more
    (B) odd, compelling *Mona Lisa* is more
    (C) *Mona Lisa* is oddly compelling, plus most
    (D) *Mona Lisa*, which is oddly compelling, is the more
    (E) oddly compelling *Mona Lisa* is the most

7. It was more probably disease and a lack of supplies than cold weather that hindered <u>Napoleon's troops from successfully conquering Russia</u>.

    (A) Napoleon's troops from successfully conquering Russia
    (B) Russia being successfully conquered by Napoleon's troops
    (C) Napoleon's troops to successfully conquer Russia
    (D) Napoleon's troops having successfully conquered Russia
    (E) the successful conquering of Russia by Napoleon's troops

8. In 1783, while only thirteen years old, <u>three piano sonatas composed by Ludwig van Beethoven established</u> his reputation as a musical prodigy.

    (A) three piano sonatas composed by Ludwig van Beethoven established
    (B) three piano sonatas that Ludwig van Beethoven composed established
    (C) three piano sonatas were composed by Ludwig van Beethoven, establishing
    (D) Ludwig van Beethoven composed three piano sonatas, they established
    (E) Ludwig van Beethoven composed three piano sonatas that established

9. If Xavier <u>had regularly completed his physics assignments</u>, he will be more likely to succeed in the class.

    (A) had regularly completed his physics assignments
    (B) regularly completes his physics assignments
    (C) could regularly complete what he is assigned in physics
    (D) can regularly complete what he is assigned in physics
    (E) could have regularly completed his physics assignments

10. After digging for several years, <u>the discovery of King Tutankhamun's tomb by Howard Carter and George Herbert sparked renewed interest in ancient Egypt</u>.

    (A) the discovery of King Tutankhamun's tomb by Howard Carter and George Herbert sparked renewed interest in ancient Egypt
    (B) the discovering of King Tutankhamun's tomb by Howard Carter and George Herbert sparked renewed interest in ancient Egypt
    (C) Howard Carter and George Herbert discovering King Tutankhamun's tomb, this sparked renewed interest in ancient Egypt
    (D) Howard Carter and George Herbert discovering King Tutankhamun's tomb, they were sparking renewed interest in ancient Egypt
    (E) Howard Carter and George Herbert discovered King Tutankhamun's tomb and sparked renewed interest in ancient Egypt

GO ON TO THE NEXT PAGE

11. The professions of both psychiatrists and psychologists involve research and diagnosis, but being unlike psychiatrists, psychologists' professions do not involve prescribing medications.

   (A) being unlike psychiatrists, psychologists' professions
   (B) psychiatrists' professions are unlike psychologists' professions,
   (C) psychiatrists' professions, and unlike those of psychologists,
   (D) psychiatrists' professions, unlike those of psychologists,
   (E) by being unlike psychiatrists, psychologists' professions

12. The Foreign Legion is technically a branch of the French army, but French citizens making up only twenty five percent of their recruits in 2007.

   (A) French citizens making up only twenty-four percent of their recruits in 2007
   (B) French citizens made up only twenty-four percent of its recruits in 2007
   (C) French citizens making up only twenty-four percent of the total number of recruits in 2007
   (D) only twenty-four percent of their recruits being made up by French citizens
   (E) only twenty-four percent of the recruits were French citizens in 2007

13. In 1945 the International Court of Justice established its headquarters in The Hague, Netherlands, this is a place where more than 150 international organizations now have offices.

   (A) this is a place
   (B) being
   (C) it being a place
   (D) a place
   (E) it is a place

14. Although they rarely attack humans, sharks, powerful predators that are capable of both severely injuring and killing if provoked.

   (A) sharks, powerful predators that are capable of both
   (B) sharks, which are powerful predators and capable of both
   (C) sharks are powerful predators, both being capable of
   (D) sharks are powerful predators and both capable of
   (E) sharks are powerful predators that are capable of

15. Some trout that have been bait for striper fish once by fishermen are now no longer used as such because they can spread damaging organisms.

   (A) trout that have been bait for striper fish once by fishermen
   (B) trout once used by fishermen as bait for striper fish
   (C) trout, which has been used for baiting striper fish by fishermen
   (D) trout, while by fishermen baiting striper fish
   (E) trout, by which striper fish have been baited by fishermen

16. Citizens in large cities tend to live in smaller homes than the countryside.

   (A) tend to live in smaller homes than
   (B) tend to live in smaller homes than with the citizens in
   (C) tend to live in smaller homes than do citizens in
   (D) have tended to live in smaller homes than did
   (E) tend to live in smaller homes than the homes of

GO ON TO THE NEXT PAGE

17. <u>No one will boost the chess team's excitement like Abigail's victory tonight</u>.

  (A) No one will boost the chess team's excitement like Abigail's victory tonight.
  (B) Nothing will boost the chess team's excitement as much as Abigail's success tonight will.
  (C) The excitement of the chess team will be boosted by Abigail's success more than any.
  (D) Abigail's success tonight will boost the chess team's excitement like none other.
  (E) No one will boost the excitement of the chess team like Abigail's success will.

18. Every band that performed at the rock concert on Friday <u>had a theft of their guitars</u> after the show.

  (A) had a theft of their guitars
  (B) had their guitars stolen
  (C) that stole the guitars
  (D) that had its guitars stolen
  (E) had its guitars stolen

19. Many college students rarely visit the grocery store and prefer to order takeout or eat at restaurants <u>rather than cook</u> meals at home.

  (A) rather than cook
  (B) instead of
  (C) rather than cooked
  (D) instead of to cook
  (E) rather than

20. <u>He was a much less famous supporter</u>, the janitor did more to bolster the charity's cause than did the well-known actress.

  (A) He was a much less famous supporter
  (B) Despite him being a much less famous supporter
  (C) As a supporter he was much less famous
  (D) While a much less famous supporter
  (E) As opposed to being much less famous as a supporter

GO ON TO THE NEXT PAGE

The following sentences test your ability to recognize grammar and usage errors. Each sentence contains either a single error or no error at all. No sentence contains more than one error. The error, if there is one, is underlined and lettered. If the sentence contains an error, select the one underlined part that must be changed to make the sentence correct. If the sentence is correct, select choice E. In choosing answers, follow the requirements of standard written English.

EXAMPLE:

The other players and her significantly improved
    A   B   C

the game plan created by the coaches. No error
             D   E

21. Before he became the host of a children's television show
               A

in 1968, Fred Rogers is attending Rollins College in
                  B

Florida, where he majored in music composition.
        C   D

No error
  E

22. The remarkable skills of Meriwether Lewis and William

Clark as a frontiersman contributed much to Thomas
       A   B

Jefferson's decision to have them lead an expedition
          C

of such importance. No error
     D   E

23. Many in the field of medicine indicating that one of the
        A   B

key factors to maintaining good health, nearly as vital

as eating a healthy diet, is exercising daily. No error
  C   D   E

24. When orchestra conductors, who are responsible for
   A   B C

setting the tempo of a musical performance,

directs musicians, they communicate through Gestures
          D

and nuances of expression. No error
             E

25. Either the regular staff and the temporary employees
    A

worked enough hours during the week to qualify for
   B   C   D

overtime pay. No error
        E

26. Because the staff there frequently overbooks the rooms,
         A   B

everyone should confirm his or her reservation before
             C

driving to the hotel. No error
   D   E

27. Unfortunately, in many schools, such as my last high
          A   B

school, cheating on tests have become so common that
             C

some students do not even worry about getting caught

anymore and even brag about it to their friends. No error
       D   E

28. Like the situation with Bill, who decided to major in
         A   B

engineering in college only after first considering five
               C

other majors, I struggled to choose a definite field of
    D

study. No error
   E

GO ON TO THE NEXT PAGE →

29. The new employees at the firm, eager to make a good

    impression on their boss, have been working overtime
    _____A_____B_____
    and arrive early to work each day. No error
    ___C___D_____E

30. Riding in an airplane for the first time, there were too
    _____A_____

    many pockets of turbulence during the flight for Liam

    to feel comfortable enough to fall asleep easily. No error
    ___B___C_____D_____E

31. While traveling by train is convenient, bus tickets
    ___A_____

    can usually be purchased more inexpensive
    _____B_____C_____

    than can train tickets. No error
    ___D_____E

32. Even though I left home an hour earlier than I
    ___A_____

    was suppose to leave, the traffic on the expressway was
    _____B_____C_____

    so dreadful that I was still twenty minutes late for work.
    ___D___

    No error
    E

33. On the table in the hallway lie the library books that I
    _____A_____B_____

    borrowed last month but have not yet returned. No error
    ___C_____D_____E

34. Despite the fact that there appears to be several
    ___A_____B_____

    openings in my schedule tomorrow, I know that in reality
    ___C_____

    I will be extremely busy. No error
    ___D_____E

GO ON TO THE NEXT PAGE ⟹

Directions: The following passage is an early draft of an essay. Some parts of the passage need to be rewritten.

Read the passage and select the best answers for the questions that follow. Some questions are about particular sentences or parts of sentences and ask you to improve sentence structure or word choice. Other questions ask you to consider organization and development. In choosing answers, follow the requirements of standard written English.

Questions 35-39 are based on the following passage.

(1) The Broadway play *Les Miserables,* based on a novel written by Victor Hugo in 1862, has been very successful because of its musical numbers and its captivating story. (2) The songs are very well written. (3) The play follows the adventures of the hero Jean Valjean after he breaks parole from prison and starts a new life. (4) The play is equally popular though because it combines action scenes, which they all enjoy, and emotional scenes, which give the characters depth.

(5) In this play, Valjean progresses from being an escaped convict to becoming mayor of the city of Vigo. (6) His search for redemption plays a large part in the story. (7) For example, at one point police inspector Javert falsely accuses another man of being Jean Valjean, and wants to put the man in prison. (8) Many men might have been content to let an innocent person take the blame. (9) Instead of that Valjean sought to redeem himself by stepping forward and identifying himself as the guilty party.

(10) As a man, Valjean changes from an uncouth convict into an educated man and finally into a caring father. (11) At first, Valjean stole and assaulted others because he needed to eat, not because he was an evil person. (12) He simply did what he needed to in order to survive. (13) However, as he experiences kindness from others, he transforms into a gentle, thoughtful, and civilized man.

35. Sentence 2 (shown below) would be more effective if it began with which of the following?

    The songs are very well written.

    (A) The play has much popular music
    (B) The play containing much popular music
    (C) In other words, audiences enjoy the play because
    (D) It is worth noting that the play, containing a lot of popular music
    (E) The musical numbers contribute to the play's success because

36. In context, sentence 4 (shown below) requires which of the following changes?

    The play is equally popular though because it combines action scenes, which they all enjoy, and emotional scenes, which give the characters depth.

    (A) Delete "though."
    (B) Change "because" to "in that."
    (C) Change "emotional" to "moving."
    (D) Delete "which give the characters depth."
    (E) Change "they all" to "audiences always."

37. In the context of the passage, which of the following effectively revises and combines sentences 8 and 9 (shown below)?

    Many men might have been content to let an innocent person take the blame. Instead of that Valjean sought to redeem himself by stepping forward and identifying himself as the guilty party.

    (A) Many would have been content to let an innocent person take the blame, but Valjean instead redeems himself by stepping forward to identify himself as the guilty party.
    (B) Many are content to let an innocent person take the blame; however Valjean redeems himself by stepping forward to identify himself as the guilty party.
    (C) Seeking to redeem himself by stepping forward and identifying himself as the guilty party, Valjean does what many might not have done.
    (D) Redeeming himself by stepping forward to identify himself as the guilty party was what he sought, many people would have let an innocent person take the blame.
    (E) A redeemed man was what Valjean wanted to become instead; many others let an innocent person take the blame.

GO ON TO THE NEXT PAGE

38. If the author of the passage wants to more thoroughly develop the final paragraph, then the author should do which of the following?

  (A) Refer to an authority regarding the differences between Valjean and typical convicts of his time.

  (B) Provide further details regarding the ways in which Valjean changed.

  (C) Discuss the way that convicts were treated during the 1860s.

  (D) Explain what Valjean did when he became mayor of Vigo.

  (E) Give examples of other successful Broadway musicals.

39. Where could the author most logically add the following sentence?

Many plays and novels written in the 1860s feature downtrodden characters who change their lives and achieve moral redemption.

  (A) After sentence 1

  (B) After sentence 3

  (C) At the beginning of the second paragraph

  (D) Before sentence 11

  (E) At the very end of the passage

STOP

If you finish before time is called, you may check your work on this section only.
Do not turn to any other section in the test.

PRACTICE TEST 1 ANSWERS

Section 1	Section 2	Section 3	Section 4	Section 5	
1. E	1. C	25. B	21. D	1. B	31. C
2. C	2. D	26. E	22. C	2. E	32. B
3. B	3. D	27. A	23. E	3. A	33. E
4. E	4. B	28. D	24. C	4. C	34. B
5. D	5. E	29. C	25. C	5. C	35. E
6. A	6. A	30. E	26. C	6. E	36. E
7. D	7. E	31. C	27. A	7. A	37. A
8. E	8. B	32. D	28. E	8. E	38. B
9. B	9. C	33. E	29. 51	9. B	39. C
10. D	10. A	34. A	30. 2,018	10. E	
11. A	11. D	35. B	31. 10	11. D	
12. D	12. A	36. B	32. 28.5	12. B	
13. E	13. C	37. C	33. 2.5	13. D	
14. A	14. D	38. A	or	14. E	
15. E	15. B	39. A	$\frac{5}{2}$	15. B	
16. D	16. C	40. C		16. C	
17. E	17. E	41. E	34. 4, 9,	17. B	
18. E	18. C	42. E	24	18. E	
19. A	19. E	43. A	35. 15	19. A	
20. C	20. B	44. E	36. 1,996	20. D	
21. E		45. E	37. 1,280	21. B	
22. D		46. A		22. A	
23. E		47. A	38. 2.5	23. B	
24. B		48. D	$< \dfrac{40}{x+2}$	24. D	
			< 3	25. A	
				26. E	
				27. C	
				28. A	
				29. C	
				30. A	

You will find a detailed explanation for each question beginning on page 55.

SCORING YOUR PRACTICE PSAT

Critical Reading

After you have checked your answers against the answer key, you can calculate your score. For the two Critical Reading sections (Sections 1 and 3), add up the number of correct answers and the number of incorrect answers. Enter these numbers on the worksheet on the next page. Multiply the number of incorrect answers by .25 and subtract this result from the number of correct answers. Then round this to the nearest whole number. This is your Critical Reading "raw score." Next, use the conversion table to convert your raw score to a scaled score.

Math

Calculating your Math score is a bit trickier, because some of the questions have five answer choices (for these, the incorrect answer deduction is .25), and some are Grid-Ins (which have no deduction for wrong answers).

First, check your answers to all of the problem-solving questions on Sections 2 and 4. For Section 2 and questions 21–28 of Section 4, enter the number of correct answers and the number of incorrect answers into the worksheet on the next page. Multiply the number of incorrect answers by .25 and subtract this result from the number of correct answers. For questions 29–38 of Section 4, the Grid-In questions, simply enter the number of correct answers. Now, add up the totals for both types of math questions to give you your total Math raw score. Then you can use the conversion table to find your scaled score.

Writing Skills

The Writing Skills section should be scored just like the Critical Reading sections. Add up the number of correct answers and the number of incorrect answers from Section 5, and enter these numbers on the worksheet on the next page. Multiply the number of incorrect answers by .25 and subtract this result from the number of correct answers. Then round this to the nearest whole number. This is your Writing Skills raw score. Next, use the conversion table to convert your raw scores to scaled scores.

WORKSHEET FOR CALCULATING YOUR SCORE

Critical Reading

	Correct	**Incorrect**

A. Sections 1 and 3   _____ – (.25 × _____) =

A

B. Total rounded Critical Reading raw score

B

Math

	Correct	**Incorrect**

C. Sections 2 and 4—Problem Solving _____ – (.25 × _____) =

C

D. Section 4—Grid-Ins _____ =

D

E. Total unrounded Math raw score (C + D)

E

F. Total rounded Math raw score

F

Writing Skills

	Correct	**Incorrect**

Section 5   _____ – (.25 × _____) =

Total rounded Writing Skills raw score

SCORE CONVERSION TABLE

Math Raw Score	Math Scaled Score	Critical Reading Raw Score	Critical Reading Scaled Score	Writing Skills Raw Score	Writing Skills Scaled Score
38	80	48	80	39	80
37	77	47	80	38	80
36	74	46	78	37	78
35	72	45	76	36	77
34	70	44	74	35	76
33	68	43	72	34	74
32	66	42	71	33	73
31	65	41	69	32	71
30	64	40	68	31	69
29	62	39	67	30	68
28	61	38	66	29	66
27	60	37	64	28	65
26	59	36	63	27	63
25	58	35	62	26	62
24	57	34	62	25	60
23	55	33	61	24	59
22	54	32	60	23	57
21	53	31	59	22	56
20	52	30	58	21	55
19	51	29	57	20	54
18	50	28	56	19	52
17	48	27	55	18	51
16	47	26	54	17	50
15	46	25	54	16	49
14	45	24	53	15	48
13	44	23	52	14	46
12	43	22	51	13	45
11	42	21	50	12	44
10	41	20	49	11	43
9	40	19	48	10	41
8	39	18	47	9	40
7	38	17	46	8	39
6	36	16	45	7	37
5	35	15	44	6	36
4	34	14	43	5	35
3	32	13	42	4	33
2	30	12	41	3	32
1	29	11	40	2	31
0	26	10	39	1	30
		9	38	0	29
		8	37		
		7	36		
		6	34		
		5	33		
		4	32		
		3	30		
		2	29		
		1	27		
		0	25		

Chapter 4
Practice Test 1:
Answers and
Explanations

Section 1

1. **E**   You know that Raquel is *excited* and that she *pored over cookbooks* and *bought utensils.* She's learning something new, and she's excited about it, so your missing word is going to be positive. Eliminate choices (A) and (D). "Learning" would be a good word to put in the blank, which makes choice (E) the correct answer.

2. **C**   The author wrote many different things, including *poems, short stories, and novels,* so you know he has a "varied" writing ability. Choice (C) is closest to that meaning, making it the correct answer.

3. **B**   The sentence tells you that the armadillo has *armor-like scales that form a shield,* meaning the animal is well-protected. The trigger *although* sets up a contrast between the clue and the blank, so you need to look for a word that is the opposite of *protected. Vulnerable* means exactly that, making choice (B) the correct answer.

4. **E**   Start with the second blank. The second part of the sentence tells you Cecily was *happy to see everyone,* however the trigger *but* indicates a change in direction. The second blank will be something negative, so you can eliminate choice (C). With a contrast set up in the second part of the sentence, and a colon (same direction trigger) connecting the two parts of the sentence, you know that the first blank will mean something like "mixed." The first blank in Choice (A) is only positive, and choice (B) is only negative, so both of those can be eliminated. There is no context to support her return home being *inconvenient,* so you can eliminate (D). Both *bittersweet* and *loath* fit the context of the sentence, making choice (E) the correct answer.

5. **D**   Start with the first blank. Because we know the winners are *large-pot winners,* the missing word must mean "large amount of money." Eliminate choices (A), (B), and (C). For the second blank, you know they *lack the financial savvy,* so they aren't good at dealing with money. Therefore, in a few years, they are likely to be "broke." Choice (D) is the correct answer.

6. **A**   You know that Juan *demands his way* and never *asks anyone else's opinion.* The *rarely* time trigger lets you know that you will be looking for a word that's the opposite of those characteristics. *Synergistic* means "cooperative and working together for a greater good," which makes choice (A) the correct answer.

7. **D**   The second part of the sentence defines both of the missing words. Recycle the words that come after the semicolon to fill in the blanks, placing *quintessential* into the first blank and *professional* into the second. Choice (D) is the correct answer.

8. **E**   Start with the first blank. Because you know the knitters are *apprehensive* about the *intricate patterns,* but the videos will *motivate* them, the videos must be *clear* or *easy to follow.* Eliminate choices (A), (B), and (D). For the second blank, if the videos are clear, they must "clearly explain" the tricky stitches. That makes choice (E) the correct answer.

9. **B**   Both authors use the "I" format.

10. **D**   The author mentions that *some may argue the films are unrealistic or cheesy*. Using *unrealistic* synonymously with *cheesy* gives you a solid context. You can eliminate all answers except choice (D), inauthentic, which is also synonymous with *unrealistic*.

11. **A**   The *detractors* mentioned in Passage 2 argue that the films are not believable. The author of Passage 1 also feels this way. This should lead you to look for an answer choice that contains a positive response. Choices (B) and (E) are clearly negative, so you can eliminate them. Choices (C) and (D) may describe the author's tone in Passage 1, but the question is asking about the author's response to the detractors, not the author's general tone. Choice (A) is the correct answer.

12. **D**   Use POE with one passage at a time. Starting with Passage 1, you can eliminate choice (A) because there's no comparison in Passage 1 between older and newer romantic comedies. You can also eliminate choice (E) because there's no discussion of ticket prices. Now look at Passage 2 and the second half of the answers. Choice (B) can be eliminated because the author of Passage 2 actually quite likes the romantic comedies, and isn't at all fed up. Choice (C) also doesn't work, because the author of Passage 2 never claims to believe the films are realistic. That leaves choice (D), which fits with both Passage 1 and Passage 2 and is the correct answer.

13. **E**   Each sentence in the first paragraph refers to something about the new wealth of information available. The first sentence mentions *all the information we could ever need*. The second mentions the *profusion of information*. Although the author does go on to say that our approach to this information has changed, he does not speak of it disparagingly, as choices (A), (B), and (D) suggest.

14. **A**   The previous generations of scholars are described as *slav[ing] away at libraries, pulling dusty books from the shelves and hoping that those books could reveal all the world's secrets*. This information is given in contrast to the first sentence of the first paragraph, which shows that now that information is all more readily available. The author does not indicate a preference in these lines for either method, which eliminates choices (D) and (E). And while choice (B) may be true, the author does not state it, and it is not his main point.

15. **E**   The term *information saturation* refers back to *all the information we could ever need* and the *profusion of information* mentioned in the previous paragraph. The term does not refer to scholars specifically, which eliminates choices (A) and (D). Nor does the author suggest that contemporary human beings are unable to learn any new information, eliminating choice (C), only that there is too much available information for any single human being to know, as in choice (E).

16. **D**   The author continually refers to the new wealth of information as available (as in choice (D)), but he does not indicate that we have a complete grasp or understanding of that information, which eliminates choices (A) and (E). Because we can still access and use some of this information, it cannot be described as "beyond our understanding," as in choice (B).

17.　E　Pay close attention to the question. It does not ask about "our understanding," which might lead one to pick (A), (B), or (C). Instead, it asks from what this understanding is a *shift away*. Note the next line: *where we once thought of the 'heavens' as the things that we could see in the sky*. In other words, the universe used to be knowable because it was something we could see, as in choice (E).

18.　E　The researchers and scholar mentioned in this part of the passage are given as examples of the older mode of study. While they might be contrasted with newer scholars, they are not being contrasted with newer researchers in these lines, eliminating choice (D). Choice (B) can be eliminated because the author is not warning against this mode of study; he is merely describing it. Only choice (E) can work because, while it is less specific than the others, it does not contain any errors.

19.　A　Note the contrast between choices (A) and (B). These two answers have some similarities, but choice (B) is more extreme and should therefore be eliminated. Choice (A) is supported in the transition between the third and fourth paragraphs: *A scholar like James Frazer, author of* The Golden Bough *(1890), could be fairly certain that he was assembling all of the world's myths and folklore in a single book. Now, we know that Frazer's project was a very limited one.*

20.　C　Read the fourth paragraph carefully: *Because we know how much information is out there, we can't possibly dream of trying to assemble it all into anything as manageable as a single book. We instead generate theories to support our impossible positions.* The author's use of hyperbole here is used to underline the extent to which contemporary researchers are overwhelmed or "inundated," as in choice (C), by the wealth of information available.

21.　E　In this part of the passage, the author discusses goods from different countries and then goes on to say that we *can have global experiences at mall food courts* and that *the entire world is there for our perusal at any time of the day or night.* As with all the information that is constantly at our fingertips, so too is the world constantly at our fingertips. This agrees with choice (E). Choice (A) focuses too narrowly on food courts. Choice (C) refers to consumerism as "excess," a value judgment that the author does not place on consumerism. Choice (D) refers to a preference for foreign goods, where the author refers only to their availability.

22.　D　The word "witchcraft" appears in the following sentence: *Just as our ancestors' ways of life seem incomprehensibly difficult to us, so too must ours seem impossibly large to them, some bit of witchcraft that allows us to be everywhere at once.* Note the last part of the sentence: the witchcraft *allows us to be everywhere at once.* The author is not discussing information in this part of the essay, which eliminates choices (A) and (E). Choice (C) refers to the older, less international mode of consumerism. Only choice (D) agrees with the passage.

23.　E　The mention of the "computer-savvy researcher" appears in the following line: *The computer-savvy researcher of today, by contrast, can have that information instantaneously and can even search within it for whatever bits of information seem relevant.* In other words, this researcher has an abundance of information available to him at all times, as choice (E) suggests.

24. **B** The crucial line appears at the end of the final paragraph: *It is at the very least my hope—and the hope, I suspect, of many others—that there must be some way between the two extremes.* This "way" agrees with the "compromise" mentioned in choice (B). The author is dismissive of neither the new nor the old modes of research, which eliminates choices (A) and (C). Nor is the author completely in support of the new type of research, which eliminates choices (D) and (E).

Section 2

1. **C** The first step is to solve the first equation for y. To do that, subtract 3 from each side, yielding $y = 4$. Now plug that value into the second equation. This results in $2(4) + 3 = 8 + 3 = 11$, so (C) is the credited response.

2. **D** The question asks for the greatest negative slope, so the sides with positive slopes, AB and DE, can be eliminated. Side BC is practically a horizontal line; it has no slope and can also be eliminated. Of the two remaining sides, CD has the steepest slope, making (D) the credited response.

3. **D** Probability is defined as the number of things that fit the requirements divided by the total number of things. In this case, the number of licorice sticks would be divided by the total number of pieces of candy. This yields $\frac{35}{75}$, which reduces to $\frac{7}{15}$. Therefore, (D) is the credited response.

4. *B* With variables in the answer choices, the best option is to Plug In. Choose an easy number for b such as 4. This makes the first equation $(4 + 2)(3(4) - 6)$, which equals $(6)(6)$. Therefore $z = 36$. The second equation is $(4 + 2)(4 - 2)$, which equals $(6)(2)$ or 12. This is the target answer. Now, plug 36 in for z in the answer choices, trying to find the one that equals 12. (A) is $\frac{1}{6}(36)$, which is 6, so (A) can be eliminated. (B) is $\frac{1}{3}(36)$, which is 12, but the rest of the answers need to be checked. (C) is (36), which equals 18, (D) is 3(36), which equals 108, and (E) is 6(36), which equals 216. Therefore, (C), (D), and (E) can be eliminated, leaving (B) as the credited response.

5. **E** There are 360° in a plane. If three lines meet a plane to form 6 equal angles, the lines will divide the total 360° by 6, leaving 60° per angle. Therefore, (E) is the credited response.

6. **A** Each dot on the scatterplot represents one student. To find the number of students who answered fewer questions than expected, count the number of dots below the best fit line. There are 8, so (A) is the credited response.

7. **E** Use process of elimination. The answer must include "3 times" something, so (C) can be eliminated. The expression in the question adds 6, so eliminate (B) and (D), since they indicate "less than." Finally, by adding 6 *after* multiplying p by 3, (A) can be eliminated, leaving (E) as the credited response.

8. B   When a question asks for a specific amount and the answer choices are numbers, Plug in the Answers (PITA). This question asks which number "could be" the value of t, so start at the top instead of with the middle answer. Label the answer choices "t," then plug in 4 for t. The quantity $2t - 5$ becomes $2(4) - 5$, which is 3. This is not divisible by 4, so (A) can be eliminated. Choice (B) is $2(5) - 5$, which equals 5. This is divisible by 5, so (B) is the credited response. With PITA, only one answer choice will work, so there is no need to try the others.

9. C   Start by marking all the information given in the problem on the figure. If $\triangle ABC$ and $\triangle DEF$ are equilateral, then all the long sides are 10, and $AD = DB = EC = CF = 5$. Because C and D are midpoints of AB and EF, those lines are parallel. This means that all the small triangles are also equilateral triangles, with side lengths of 5. If each side of quadrilateral $CGDH$ is 5, the perimeter is 20, making (C) the credited response.

10. A   Use process of elimination on the answer choices. The first digits are all prime numbers, so no answers can be eliminated from that. Since the last digit of (B) is 4, which is not prime, (B) can be eliminated. The middle digit must be a divisor of 45, such as 5 or 9. Choice (C) has 4 in the middle and (E) has 7, so both of those can be eliminated. Finally, the second and fourth digits need to have 6 as their least common multiple. Choice (D) has a 5 as the second digit, which does not have 6 as a multiple, so the credited response is (A).

11. D   When the question asks for a specific number, use PITA. The first step is taking half of the number, which won't come out evenly with odd numbers. Therefore, (A) and (C) can be eliminated. Choice (B) is –10, half of which is –5. Four less than that would be –9, which isn't the original number, so (B) is can be eliminated. Choice (D) is –8, half of which is –4. Four less than that is –8, the original number, so (D) is the credited response.

12. A   This is a logic question, so check each answer to determine if it helps provide more necessary information about Ringo. (A) states that dogs that aren't brown aren't Labradors. Since Ringo is not brown, this means she is not a Labrador. Check the other answers choices to be certain (A) is the best one. (B), (C), and (E) reveal information about some or all brown dogs. Since Ringo is not brown, this is not useful, and (B), (C) and (E) can be eliminated. (D) indicates that no dogs are brown Labradors, which still does not apply to Ringo, who is not brown, so (D) can be eliminated. (A) is the credited response.

13. C   To determine the possible number of points of intersection between two shapes, draw them a few different ways. Move the shapes around and try to overlap them as much as possible. If the circle is completely within the square, there will be no points of intersection. If the circle overlaps one side of the square, there will be two points of intersection. If the circle overlaps the corner of the square, there are four points of intersection.

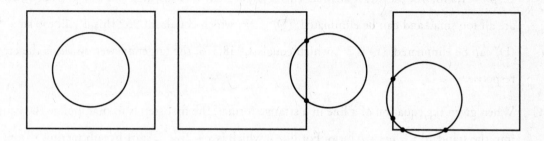

There is no other way to draw the two shapes that will result in more points of intersection. Therefore, (C) is the credited response.

14. D   This question has a lot of variables, so start by plugging in the given information. The language about the ordered pair is confusing, but it clearly states "$x = t$ and $y = 2$." Plug those values in to the two equations, which yields

$2 = -t$

$2 = t + n$

When dealing with simultaneous equations, the best approach is to stack them and add them together in an attempt to make one variable disappear. When these equations are added together, the result is $4 = n$, so (D) is the credited response.

15. B   To answer this question, the number of widgets each machine makes in one hour must be calculated. According to the chart, Machine F makes 300 widgets in 6 hours of operation. Divide 300 by 6 to get 50 widgets per hour for machine F. Machine G makes 900 widgets in 15 hours of operation. Divide 900 by 15 to get 60 widgets per hour for machine G. To find the difference in number of widgets made for each hour of operation, subtract 50 from 60, which equals 10. Therefore, (B) is the credited response.

16. C   When a question contains a variable, Plug In. Since $2w$ must be divisible by 8, pick a number for w that will make $2w$ a multiple of 8. If $2w = 8$, then $w = 4$, which is both even and divisible by 4. It is not divisible by 8, however, so case III is false. Answers that contain case III can be eliminated, so (D) and (E) are not the credited response. To determine what "must be true," Plug In a few more times, using some different numbers. If $2w = 80$, then $w = 40$, and cases I and II are still true. If $2w = -24$, then $w = -12$, which is also even and divisible by 4. Therefore, (C) is the credited response.

17. E   With variables in the problem, Plugging In is the way to go. However, these exponents are large, so simplify first. $\dfrac{q^{12}}{q^2}$ equals q^{10}, since division of bases means to subtract the exponents. Now plug in something small for q, such as 2. $2^{10} = 1{,}024 = s^5$. To solve this for s, take the fifth root of each side, which means that $s = 4$. This can be plugged in to the second equation, once it is simplified to

s^{10}. 4^{10} = 1,048,576, the target answer. This is larger than 1,024, which was q^{10}, so (A), (B), and (C) are all too small and can be eliminated. (D) is 2^{12}, which equals 4,096. This is still too small, and (D) can be eliminated. (E) is 2^{20}, which equals 1,048,576, the target answer, so (E) is the credited response.

18. C When given the equation of a line in a strange format, the first step is to manipulate the equation into the standard $y = mx + b$ form. For line l, which is $x + 2y = 4$, start by subtracting x from each side, which yields $2y = -x + 4$. Divide both sides by 2, giving the equation for line l as $y = -\frac{1}{2}x + 2$. Draw a sketch of this line, with the y-intercept at 2 and a slight negative slope. Then, sketch in line m as the reflection of line l across the x-axis. It will look something like the following:

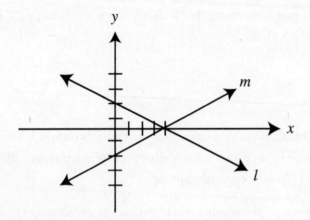

From the sketch, it is clear that the slope of line m will be positive and the y-intercept will be negative. This is enough to use POE on the answer choices. Get each one into $y = mx + b$ form and eliminate any choices with negative slopes or positive y-intercepts. (A) is $y = \frac{1}{2}x + 2$, which has a positive y-intercept and can be eliminated. (B) is $y = -\frac{1}{2}x - 2$, which has a negative slope and can be eliminated. (C) is $y = \frac{1}{2}x - 2$, which has the correct sign on the slope and the y-intercept. (D) is $y = -\frac{1}{2}x + 2$, which is the same as line l in the question, so it can be eliminated. (E) is $y = 2x + 2$, which has a positive y-intercept and can be eliminated. (C) is the only remaining choice and is the credited response.

19. E For a question that asks "how many" different possibilities exist, draw a dash for each of the positions to be filled. There are 3 digits in the code, so draw three dashes. Now fill in each dash with the number of options possible for that position. There are 4 even numbers less than 9: 2, 4, 6, and 8. Therefore, the number on the first dash will be 4. The question does not state that the numbers must be distinct, or different, from one another. As a result, there are also 4 options for each of

the other two dashes. Now multiply all three numbers together to get the total number of possible codes. $4 \times 4 \times 4 = 64$, so (E) is the credited response.

20. **B** This is a very odd-looking figure, and there is no formula for the area of such a shape. The figure could be broken down into pieces, the area of each piece found, and the whole thing added together. That process would be time-consuming, so try to find a shortcut. The circle cut from the middle of the square has the same radius as the semicircles on the sides. If the semicircles on the left and right sides were cut off and placed in the center of the square, they would exactly fill that hole, as shown below.

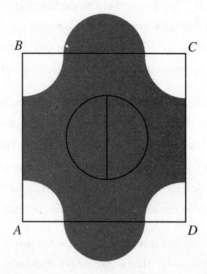

The two remaining semicircles are centered on the sides of the square. If each has a radius of 1, each has a diameter of 2, leaving 1 unit on each side for the radius of the arcs. This is also the same radius as the semicircles. Each of the two remaining semicircles could then be cut in half, creating 4 arc pieces that would exactly fill the remaining holes, as shown below.

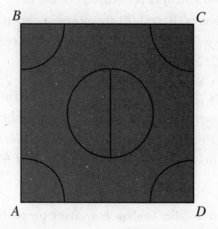

The whole square has been filled in and no extra pieces are left. Therefore, the area of the shaded region is equal to the area of the square. With a side length of 4, the area of the square is 16, so (B) is the credited response.

Section 3

25. **B** The training methods are *rigorous and exhausting*, yet the athletes are *keeping up with the program*. They must be getting something out of it, so the results must be "impressive." Choice (B) is the correct answer.

26. **E** The styles are "different." The colon is a same direction trigger, so you are looking for a word that means "different." Choice (E) is the correct answer.

27. **A** Start with the second blank. You know that the explorers are *concerned about getting lost*. The second blank deals with their *fears of never returning*. Because you have a change direction trigger, *but*, the fears aren't going to come true. Eliminate choices (B), (C), and (E). Now look at the first blank. If their fears are lessened, the maps are going to be "really good." Choice (A) is the correct answer.

28. **D** Start with the first blank. The sentence tells you that the pufferfish *produces toxins that can kill a human within 24 hours,* so the missing word must mean "poisonous." Eliminate choices (B) and (E). In the second part of the sentence, you have a contrast. You know the fish is really dangerous, but there's a description of *big eyes and comically rotund appearance,* so the missing word must mean something like "don't accurately represent." Choice (A) and (C) are the opposite of what you're looking for, but both words in choice (D) fit the given context. Choice (D) is the correct answer.

29. **C** The authors states that our *ancestors* had *goose bumps* because they *made them look more intimidating to would-be predators* but today that is no longer necessary. So replace the blank with "something from the past." *Primitive* works well with this definition, so choice (C) is the correct answer.

30. **E** The author says of the others that they believed Jefferson failed to *match his actions to his strong rhetoric.* This most closely aligns with choice (E), the correct answer.

31. **C** The passage does mention Jefferson's political career, but that's not the main point of the passage. Eliminate choice (A). Choices (B) and (E) are mentioned briefly in the passage, but again, are not the purpose of the passage. The author is addressing different perspectives on the man, and choice (C) states that. Choice (C) is the correct answer.

32. **D** The author states that the shoppers *aren't paying attention.* There's nothing deliberate about their actions, so you can eliminate choices (C) and (E). They know how the Internet works, because they are using it, so you can eliminate choice (B). There's no indication that they've used the wrong credit card, so you can eliminate choice (A). Choice (D) best fits the context of the passage and is the correct answer.

33. **E** The statistic is mentioned in order to show how many people have fallen victim to identify theft. Choices (A) and (B) are not mentioned at all. Choice (C) could be true, but there's no specific evidence about who those 9 million are. Choice (D) may also be true, but specific details of the 9 million are not given. That leaves choice (E), which fits the context of the passage and is the correct answer.

34. **A** Both passages discuss the recent findings of Dr. Rodney Willoughby, so each draws upon recent findings and theories from a medical researcher. While both passages mention that rabies attacks the brain's chemical makeup, neither "describes" the brain's chemical makeup, eliminating choice (E).

35. **B** Although Passage 1 is more approving of Dr. Willoughby's findings, those findings are not part of Passage 1's discussion of the "human diploid cell rabies vaccine," which, according to the passage *had to be administered within six days of the patient's contraction of the virus, before symptoms started to appear.* In Passage 2, the author states that, *Under the initial protocol, only two of the 25 treated patients survived.* Both lines suggest that rabies remains predominantly incurable, as in choice (B).

36. **B** Passage 2 does address debate within the scientific community, but the importance of that debate is not its primary focus, eliminating choice (A). Passage 2 is critical of the Milwaukee protocol, but not so critical as to call its effects "deteriorating." Only choice (B) can work, as Passage 2 is primarily concerned with warning against a full acceptance of the Milwaukee protocol, which remains the subject of heated debate within the medical community.

37. **C** While the authors of Passage 1 and Passage 2 discuss the same findings, the author of Passage 1 does so approvingly, and the author of Passage 2 does so with some doubt. Passage 2 warns against the full acceptance of the Milwaukee protocol, so he would not fully "agree" or "approve" of the argument in Passage 1 (eliminating choices (A) and (E)), nor would he "dismiss" the argument, eliminating choice (B). His attitude is more cautious, or "skeptical," as suggested by choice (C).

38. **A** The author of Passage 1 is approving of the Milwaukee protocol, so any further evidence of the protocol's success would strengthen his argument. A higher survival rate in the "25 treated patients" would certainly provide this kind of support.

39. **A** The author of Passage 1 offers a hopeful message about the Milwaukee protocol, suggesting that Jeanna's cure *gives the medical community hope that her recovery was not merely an outlier.* The author of Passage 2 offers a more qualified message, suggesting that *Willoughby's method remains the subject of heated debate within the scientific community, a large portion of which continues to believe that rabies is an incurable disease.* Only choice (A) fully captures this contrast. Passage 1 is not fantastic or amateurish, eliminating choices (B) and (D). Passage 2 is not anecdotal or irrelevant, eliminating choices (C) and (E).

40. **C** Before Naim learns about El Shorbagy (in the third paragraph), he is frustrated with his game as described by words and phrases like *never* quite *as good as he wanted to be, his biggest challenge came from his coach, characterless devotion,* and *why keep playing.* Choice (C) best paraphrases these terms. The other choices use words from the passage but are not supported by evidence from the passage, and choice (E) is only one small part of the first two paragraphs, in addition to the fact that it is too extreme.

41. **E**   The word *that* appears in the previous sentence: *if that had been the only hurdle.* This "that" and the one in the question refer to the same thing, *the competition,* or the players that Naim has to face, as choice (E) suggests. Choices (A), (C), and (D) are all minor aspects of his difficult competition, but the word *that* refers directly to the competition itself.

42. **E**   The parentheses appear after the words *to go pro,* and the words in the parentheses are as follows: *his lifelong dream, but one that seemed too hard with a unique, personalized style of play.* These lines anticipate the later discussion of Mohamed El Shorbagy, who managed to become a pro (and inspired Naim to do so), even with his unique style of play. Choice (E) captures this idea most effectively. Choice (A) does contain the word *inspiration*, but there is no indication in the passage that Naim is specifically searching for that inspiration. Choice (E) is more precise and refers to a specific moment in the passage.

43. **A**   This sentence appears in the following context: *He loved to watch the greats from squash history, both the English and the Egyptian champions, and their methodical, uncannily consistent styles of play. Naim himself wanted to be part of this great legion of players.* There is a good deal of emphasis in these lines on *greatness* and *champions,* thus expressing Naim's wish to be one among these great champions, as choice (A) suggests. Choice (B) refers only to the English style and cannot account for the mention of *Egyptian champions.* Choice (C) might be an indirect effect of becoming a great squash player, but it is not directly mentioned in the passage.

44. **E**   Don't be distracted by the word *suggest.* Any *suggestion* on this test must have direct support in the passage, so pay attention to the lines in question—*His hope to change the way the game was played and for his name to be known made him think he might be better suited to the bigger stage of tennis: where styles were not so regimented, and the best players were like movie stars*—which essentially state that Naim looked to tennis as a sport that was both more creative and better known, thus implying his wish to be unique and well-known, as in choice (E).

45. **E**   In this sentence, *styles* are being described as *regimented.* In other parts of the passage, the traditional squash style is described as *methodical* and *consistent.* The word *regimented* must mean something similar, and choice (E) provides a reasonable substitute. The other choices share roots or alternate meanings with the word *regimented*, but they do not work in this context.

46. **A**   Just as Naim is considering switching to a different sport, he discovers *a new player on the pro tour* who is to become *the inspiration he had been missing.* The third paragraph describes this change of heart and *renewal of interest,* as choice (A) suggests. Choice (B) cannot work because there is no indication that Naim has *matured,* only that he has changed.

47. **A**   For Naim, *El Shorbagy played the traditional game, but he did it with such flair, such incredible confidence and style, that he seemed totally self-taught; he was almost, it seemed, expressing his very soul as he played, the same way one might do in a poem.* Naim is therefore moved by the creativity and personality of El Shorbagy's game, as choice (A) states. El Shorbagy also has *popular appeal,* but this is not what Naim is so drawn to, thus eliminating choice (D).

48. **D** The final paragraph discusses the ways that El Shorbagy would be a lasting influence in Naim's life, expanding on his initial *inspiration*, thus making choice (D) the best of these answer choices. El Shorbagy does not appear until the third paragraph, thus eliminating choices (A), (B), and (C). Finally, even though El Shorbagy does play a *traditional game*, Naim is more drawn to the *non-traditional* aspects of his play, thus eliminating choice (E).

Section 4

21. **D** "Find the value" with numbers in the answer choices: PITA! Start with choice (C). Plug in 3 for r (use the calculator to be safe) and get 7,300. Too small, so eliminate choices (C), (B), and (A) and go bigger. Plug in 4 for r and get 73,000, which is between 8,000 and 80,000. The credited response is (D).

22. **C** The figure can be trusted, so point A has coordinates of (0, 0). Since the square has a side of 8, point C has coordinates of (–8, 8). Use the slope formula, $\dfrac{y_2 - y_1}{x_2 - x_1}$, to find the slope of line m: $\dfrac{0 - 8}{0 - (-8)} = -1$. Plug the answer choices into the slope formula to get the same slope. Plug in choice (C) to get: $\dfrac{0 - 5}{0 - (-5)} = -1$. Alternatively, plot the answer choices to visually see which answer makes sense. The credited response is (C).

23. **E** Read The Full Question (RTFQ). The question asks for the number of students whose GPA is <u>less</u> than 4.0. Since 20% of the students scored 4.0 and greater, 80% of the students scored less than 4.0. Take 80% of the 30,000 students, (30,0000 × 0.80), to get 24,000 students. The credited response is (E).

24. **C** Don't get fancy. Just write out the pattern. 1st is 1 × 3 = 3. 2nd is 3 × 5 = 15. 3rd is 5 × 7 = 35. 4th is 7 × 9 = 63. 5th is 9 × 11 = 99. 6th is 11 × 13 = 143. 7th is 13 × 15 = 195. 8th is 15 × 17 = 255. The question asked for the difference between the 7th and 8th term, so subtract: 255 – 195 = 60. The credited response is (C).

25. **C** Variables in the answer choices: Plug In! In this case the problem provides the numbers to plug in. The correct expression will work for both situations. Using choice (C), plug in the number of miles Gilbert drove the car for m and check the result against his total charge. First plug in the numbers for Monday. He drove 20 miles, so (.25)(20) + 8 = 13, which matches Gilbert's charge of $13. Now plug in the numbers for Friday. He drove 14 miles, so (.25)(14) + 8 = 11.50, which matches Gilbert's charge of $11.50. Since both situations check out, the credited response is (C).

26. **C** "Find the value" with numbers in the answer choices: PITA! The question asks for the value of b, which is the x value in the function. Start with choice (C). So $g(7) = 33 – 4(7) = 5$, which matches the target of 5. The credited response is (C).

27. **A** Be careful: the figure is not drawn to scale and will need to be redrawn. Two properties of triangles are needed to answer this question. First, the largest side is opposite the largest angle and the smallest side is opposite the smallest angle. Second, the third side of a triangle must be less than the sum of the other two sides and greater than the difference of the other two sides. Since $AB = 200$ and $BC = 5$, $(200 - 5) < AC < (200 + 5)$. Therefore $195 < AC < 205$. If the triangle is drawn so that $AC = 196$, then AB is the largest side, BC is the smallest side, and AC is in between. Therefore $r < s < t$, which eliminates choices (B), (D), and (E). But if the triangle is drawn so that $AC = 204$, then AC is the largest side, BC is the smallest side, and AB is in the middle. Therefore $r < t < s$, which eliminates choice (C). The credited response is (A).

28. **E** There are two ratios given, both of which contain "medium shirts." Use the ratio box to find the overall ratio of small to medium to large.

	Small	Medium	Large	Total
Ratio	5	2		
Multiplier				
Actual	?	6	5	

Use the medium column to find that the multiplier is 3. Fill in the multiplier and find the value for small.

	Small	Medium	Large	Total
Ratio	5	2		
Multiplier	3	3	3	
Actual	15	6	5	

The question asks for is the ratio of small shirts to all <u>other</u> shirts, so that's 15:(6 + 5) which is 15:11. The credited response is (E).

29. **51** Take it in bite-sized pieces. The 8 salesmen each sold 5 cars, so $8 \times 5 = 40$ cars. Then 3 of the salesmen each sold 3 more cars, so $3 \times 3 = 9$ more cars. Then 2 salesmen each sold 1 more car, so $2 \times 1 = 2$ more cars. Add them all together to get a total of $40 + 9 + 2 = 51$ total cars sold.

30. **2,018** First, it might be easier to convert the feet to inches. There are 12 inches in a foot, so 230 feet is 2,760 inches and 235 feet is 2,820 inches. Therefore the distance in 1976 is 2,760 inches and in 1983 is 2,823 inches. Then find the rate. The difference between 1983 and 1976 is 7 years and the difference between 2,823 inches and 2,760 inches is 63 inches. At this rate, the distance will increase 63 inches every 7 years. The simplest way to continue is to add the rate until you reach 261.5 feet, which is 3,138 inches. For example, starting from 1983, add 7 years to get 1990 and add 63 inches to get 2,886 inches. Continue that pattern. In 1997 the distance is 2,949 inches. In 2004 the distance is 3,012 inches. In 2011, the distance is 3,075 inches. In 2018, the distance is 3,138 inches.

31. **10** Since all of the angles are right angles, the figure can be cut up into a bunch of rectangles. The horizontal base is 15, so the sum of the other horizontal pieces must also equal 15. Solve $9 + 2 + x = 15$ to find that $x = 4$. Now, the vertical side labeled $3x$ must equal 12. The vertical height on the left is 25, so the sum of the vertical heights on the right must also equal 25. Solve $12 + 3 + z = 25$ to find that $z = 10$.

32. **28.5** Vertical angles are equal and $x = 123$, so $\angle AEB = 123$. *ABCD* is a rectangle, so the diagonals are the same length and intersect at each other's midpoint, making $AE = BE$. Therefore *ABE* is an isosceles triangle and $y = z$. The sum of all the angles in a triangle is 180°, so $y + z + 123 = 180$. Solve the equation to find that $y + z = 57$. Since $y = z$, substitute to find that $z + z = 57$. Solve to find that $2z = 57$, so $z = 28.5$.

33. **2.5 or $\dfrac{5}{2}$**

A quadratic equation is symmetrical. Draw a vertical line down the center of the curve, which should pass through its lowest point. The points to the left and the right will be the same distance from the vertical line, so the line will be halfway between two points with the same y value. The two points given have the same y value, so the vertical line will be halfway between –1 and 6. To find the halfway point, take the average of –1 and 6: $\dfrac{-1 + 6}{2} = \dfrac{5}{2} = 2.5$. Therefore, the vertical line is $x = 2.5$, which is the x-coordinate of the lowest point (least value) of the function.

34. **4, 9, 24**

Put the numbers in order: 1, 8, 12, 15. But where to place the unknown fifth number? It could go <u>above</u> the median, <u>below</u> the median, or it could <u>be</u> the median. Do one of the following.

If the fifth test score is placed above the median then the list is now 1, 8, 12, 15, x, which makes the median of the list 12. The median is equal to the mean, so the mean is also 12. Use the average pie to solve for x. The number of things is 5 and the average is 12. Multiply to find that the sum of the test equals 60. Therefore $1 + 8 + 12 + 15 + x = 60$ and $x = 24$.

If the fifth test score is placed below the median then the list is now x, 1, 8, 12, 15, which makes the median of the list 8. The median is equal to the mean, so the mean is also 8. Use the average pie to solve for x. The number of things is 5 and the average is 8. Multiply to find that the sum of the test equals 40. Therefore $1 + 8 + 12 + 15 + x = 40$ and $x = 4$.

If the fifth test score <u>is</u> the median then the list is now 1, 8, x, 12, 15, which makes the median of the list x. The median is equal to the mean, so the mean is also x. Use the average pie to solve for x. The number of things is 5 and the average is x. Multiply to find that the sum of the test equals $5x$. Therefore $1 + 8 + 12 + 15 + x = 5x$ so $4x = 36$ and $x = 9$.

35. **15** Don't worry about the markings on the number line. The two points are given and the distance between them is known. Set those equal to each other. The difference between the two points equals the distance, so $0.8x - 0.6x = 3$, then $0.2x = 3$, and $x = 15$.

36. **1,996** 500 numbers are too many to write out, so pick an easy number to start with and then extrapolate. The easiest number to start with is the first multiple of 4, so the first number in the list is $4 \times 1 = 4$. The second number in the list is $4 \times 2 = 8$. Using this pattern, the five hundredth number in the list is $4 \times 500 = 2,000$. Subtracting the smallest from the largest results in $2,000 - 4 = 1,996$.

37. **1,280** Write down the volume formula: $v = l \times w \times h$. The key to this question is to find the dimensions <u>inside</u> the box. The board on the top right is labeled with a length of 12 inches, but it is overlapped by the board on the right. The overlap is 4 inches, so the length inside the box is 8 inches. The inside width is also 8 inches for the same reason. The height of each board is 2 inches. The boards are stacked 10 high, so the total height is $2 \times 10 = 20$ inches. Use the volume formula to solve. $8 \times 8 \times 20 = 1,280$.

38. $$2.5 < \frac{40}{x + 2} < 3$$

The question looks more complicated than it is. It is not necessary to solve for x to answer this question. RTFQ and look for similarities. The question contains $\frac{80}{x + 2}$ and the goal is $\frac{40}{x + 2}$. What is the relationship between them? Notice that $\frac{40}{x + 2}$ is half of $\frac{80}{x + 2}$. Therefore, divide all sides of the inequality by 2 to find that $2.5 < \frac{40}{x + 2} < 3$. Choose any number in that range, for example 2.8.

Section 5

1. **B** The pronoun *it* is singular, but refers to *ankles*, which are plural. Therefore, this sentence contains a pronoun agreement error. Eliminate choices (A) and (C), which both use *it*. Introducing either the word *when* or the word *by* turns the sentence into a fragment, so choices (D) and (E) are also incorrect. Choice (B) fixes the pronoun agreement error and makes the sentence complete, so choice (B) is the correct answer.

2. **E** The word *while* suggests that this sentence contains a contrast. However, since the sentence does not introduce another contrasting thought at the end of the phrase, this sentence is currently a fragment. Therefore, you can eliminate choice (A). Choice (D) repeats this error by using *although*, which is also a contrast word, so you can eliminate choice (D). Choice (B) uses *because*, which similarly makes the sentence incomplete. Choice (C) uses the word *being*. In general, avoid choosing an answer that uses the word *being* whenever possible. Therefore, choice (E) is the correct answer.

3. **A** *Having swum* may sound odd, but the phrase contains the correct verb tense. Therefore, keep choice (A) for now. Choice (B) uses *she* immediately after *Diana Nyad,* and therefore contains a redundancy error. Choice (C) incorrectly uses *so,* and is therefore incorrect. Use a comma and select conjunctions—For And Nor But Or Yet So (FANBOYS)—to join two complete thoughts. Since the phrase *Diana Nyad having swum from Cuba to the United States* is not a complete thought, you cannot use a comma and a conjunction to join this phrase to the rest of the sentence. Therefore, choice (D) is not the credited answer. Choice (E) changes the intended meaning of the sentence, and is incorrect. Since choice (A) does not contain any grammatical errors, it is the correct answer.

4. **C** The phrase *much less expensive in cost* is redundant, since *less expensive* already refers to *cost.* Therefore, you can eliminate choice (A). Using *reason* with *because* is also redundant, so you can eliminate choice (B). Choice (C) does not contain any redundancies or introduce any new errors, and is the correct answer. Both choices (D) and (E) incorrectly use the word *being.* If possible, avoid choosing answers that contain *being.*

5. **C** The clause *In 1958 Chinua Achebe attempted to print his novel* Things Fall Apart, *sending the manuscript to several publishers* is a complete thought. The clause *some of them rejected it immediately* is also a complete thought. Therefore, this sentence contains a comma splice. Choice (E) repeats this error, so eliminate choices (A) and (E). Choice (B) unnecessarily uses *that* and is therefore not as concise as choice (C). Choice (D) uses *which,* rather than *whom.* Since the pronoun refers to *publishers,* who are people rather than things, you want to use *whom.* The correct answer is therefore choice (C).

6. **E** Use *more* to compare two things, but use *most* to compare more than two things. Since this sentence compares *many works of art* and the *Mona Lisa,* you need *most* rather than *more.* Eliminate choices (A), (B), and (D). Choice (C) incorrectly uses *plus* and is therefore not the credited answer. Choice (E) fixes the original error and does not introduce any new errors, so it is the correct answer.

7. **A** Choice (B) incorrectly uses *being* and is therefore incorrect. Choice (C) uses *hindered…to.* Since the correct idiom is *hindered from,* this choice is incorrect. Choice (D) repeats the idiom error because it does not contain a preposition at all. Choice (E) changes the verb from active voice to passive voice, and is therefore incorrect. Choice (A) does not contain any grammatical errors and is therefore correct.

8. **E** The phrase *In 1783, while only thirteen years old* is a modifying phrase and must describe whatever comes after the comma. Since Beethoven, and not the piano sonatas, was thirteen years old, then Beethoven must come immediately after the comma. Choices (A), (B), and (C) repeat the original error and are therefore incorrect. Choice (D) contains two complete thoughts joined by a comma, and is therefore a comma splice. Choice (E) fixes the error in the original sentence, and does not contain a comma splice. Therefore, the correct answer is choice (E).

9. **B** The verb *had...completed* is in the past perfect tense. To correctly use the past perfect tense, you must be referring to a past event that occurred before some other past event. Since you do not have two separate past events in this sentence, the verb *had completed* is incorrect. Eliminate choice (A). The verb *could complete* does not agree with *will be*, which is in the future tense. Therefore, eliminate choices (C) and (E). The verb *can complete* also does not agree with the future tense verb *will be*, so choice (D) is also incorrect. Choice (B) fixes the original error in the sentence, and does not introduce any new verbs, so it is the correct answer.

10. **E** The phrase *After digging for several years* is a modifying phrase that must describe whatever appears right after the comma. Since *Howard Carter and George Herbert*, not *the discovery*, dug for several years, you need *Howard Carter and George Herbert* to come immediately after the comma. Eliminate choices (A) and (B). Choices (C) and (D) incorrectly use *discovering* rather than *discovered*. The correct answer is therefore choice (E).

11. **D** This sentence incorrectly compares *psychiatrists* to *psychologists' professions*. Since you want to compare professions to other professions, rather than people to professions, eliminate choice (A). Choice (E) repeats the original comparison error and is therefore incorrect. Choice (B) uses the verb *are*, which makes the phrase *do not involve prescribing medications* into a fragment. Choice (C) correctly compares *psychiatrists' professions* and *those of psychologists*, but uses the same direction conjunction *and* to link the two. However, since the sentence is discussing a contrast, rather than a similarity, *and* is not the correct conjunction to use here. Eliminate choice (C). Choice (D) fixes the original error by using *those of* to refer to the professions of psychiatrists and is therefore the correct answer.

12. **B** This sentence contains a parallelism error, since *The Foreign Legion is* is not parallel with *French citizens making*. Therefore, you can eliminate choices (A) and (C), both of which use *making*. Choice (D) uses *being*, and is also incorrect. Choice (E) changes the meaning slightly by suggesting that the people who were recruits were simply not French citizens in 2007, but might be French citizens now. It also incorrectly uses the definite article *the*, when there are no specific recruits involved. Choice (B) fixes the parallelism error and retains the original meaning of the sentence, and is therefore the correct answer.

13. **D** The clause *In 1945 the International Court of Justice established its headquarters in The Hague, Netherlands* is a complete thought. The clause *this is a place where more than 150 international organizations now have offices* is also a complete thought. Since only a comma divides these two thoughts, this sentence contains a comma splice. Choices (A) and (E) repeat the original error, and are incorrect. Choices (B) and (C) use *being*. If possible, avoid choosing grammar answers that use the word *being*. Therefore, you can eliminate choices (B) and (C). Choice (D) fixes the original error and does not introduce any new errors, so it is the correct answer.

14.   E   The phrase *Although they rarely attack humans* is an incomplete thought. Since the phrase *sharks, powerful predators that are capable of both severely injuring and killing if provoked* is also an incomplete thought, this sentence is a fragment. Choices (A) and (B) repeat the original error. Choice (C) uses *being*, and if possible, you want to avoid choosing grammar answers that use *being*. The phrase *are capable of severely injuring and killing if provoked* describes sharks, and is not a new, separate thought, so you want to use *that* rather than *and*. Therefore, choice (E) is the correct answer.

15.   B   This sentence is missing a verb, since you cannot describe trout as bait, but rather must say that they have been used as bait. Therefore, choice (A) is incorrect. Choice (B) fixes the error by introducing the verb *used*. In order to maintain the original meaning of the sentence, *by fisherman* should come before, rather than after *striper fish*. Therefore you can eliminate choices (C) and (E). Note that choice (C) also uses the singular verb *has* to refer to *trout*, while the non-underlined portion uses the plural verb *are*. Choice (D) turns the sentence into a fragment and is therefore incorrect. The correct answer is choice (B).

16.   C   This sentence compares *citizens in large cities* to *the countryside*. Since you want to compare citizens to other citizens, not to areas, this sentence contains a comparison error. Choices (A), (D), and (E) repeat this error. Since the sentence needs to compare the homes in which one group lives to the homes in which another group lives, the sentence needs to include verbs in both parts of the comparison. Choice (B) incorrectly uses *with*, rather than *do*, and is therefore not the credited answer. Choice (C) fixes the comparison error by phrasing the sentence so that it compares the homes in which citizens in large cities live to homes in which citizens in the countryside live. Choice (C) is the correct answer.

17.   B   As the sentence is currently written, it compares *No one*, or a person, to *Abigail's victory*, or a thing. Since you must compare people to people and things to things, this sentence contains a comparison error. Choices (A) and (E) repeat the original error. Choice (C) uses the passive phrase *will be boosted* and also contains the phrase *more than any,* which does not directly refer to anything else in the sentence. Choice (D) changes the intended meaning of the sentence by suggesting that no other success will boost the chess team's excitement as much as Abigail's success will, while the original sentence suggests that nothing else at all will boost the chess team's excitement as much as Abigail's success will. Choice (B) is therefore the correct answer.

18.   E   This sentence uses the plural pronoun *their* to refer to the noun *band*, which is singular, so this sentence contains a pronoun agreement error. Choices (A) and (B) repeat the original error. Choice (C) changes the intended meaning of the sentence by suggesting that the band stole the guitars, rather than that the band's guitars were stolen. Choice (D) uses *that*, which turns the sentence into an incomplete thought. Therefore, the correct answer is choice (E).

19. **A** This sentence correctly contrasts two things that college students do: they prefer to order take out rather than to cook. Since the sentence contrasts two actions, it does not contain a comparison error. However, choices (B) and (E) contrast an action (preferring to order take out) and a noun (meals at home). Therefore, these two choices are incorrect. Choice (C) incorrectly changes the verb to past tense, and is therefore not the credited answer. Choice (D) incorrectly changes the comparison word to *instead*, and unnecessarily adds the word *to*. Since the original sentence is correct as written and is more concise, choice (A) is the correct answer.

20. **D** The clause *He was a much less famous supporter* is a complete thought. Since the clause *the janitor did more to bolster the charity's cause than did the well-known actress* is also a complete thought, this sentence contains a comma splice. Choices (A) and (C) repeat the original error. Choices (B) and (E) both use the word *being*, and if possible you want to avoid choosing answers that use *being*. Choice (D) fixes the error in the original sentence and does not introduce any new errors, so it is the correct answer.

21. **B** The verb in the non-underlined portion of the sentence is *majored*, which is in the past tense. Therefore, *is attending*, which refers to an action occurring in the present, is not in the correct tense. The verb should be *attended*.

22. **A** This sentence incorrectly refers to the two men *Meriwether Lewis and William Clark* as *a frontiersman*. Since *a frontiersman* is singular, it cannot refer to two individuals. This sentence contains a noun agreement error.

23. **B** In this sentence the word *indicating* is in the wrong verb form because it creates a fragment. In order to be complete, the sentence should use the verb *indicate*.

24. **D** Choice (D) uses the singular verb *directs*. However, the subject of the sentence is *conductors*, which is plural. Therefore, this sentence contains a subject-verb agreement error, and choice (D) is the credited answer.

25. **A** If you use the word *either* in a sentence, you must also include the word *or* later in the sentence. Since this sentence uses *and* instead, the use of the word *either* is incorrect. Use *both* if you are referring to one thing *and* another.

26. **E** The pronoun *there* must refer to a place, and in this case it correctly refers to *the hotel*. Therefore, choice (A) does not contain an error. Choice (B) contains the singular verb *overbooks*. Since the subject of the verb is *staff*, which is also singular, this choice does not contain a subject verb agreement error. Nothing in the sentence indicates that the verb should be in a different tense, so there are no tense errors, and the verb is not in a list, so there are no parallelism errors. Choice (B) is therefore error-free. Choice (C) correctly uses the singular pronouns *his* and *her* to refer to *everyone*, which is also singular, so choice (C) does not contain an error. Choice (D) contains a verb in the correct tense, and does not contain any subject-verb agreement errors. Additionally, *driving to* is the correct idiom, so choice (D) does not contain any errors. The correct answer is therefore choice (E).

27. **C** Choice (C) contains the plural verb *have become*. Since the subject of that verb is *cheating*, which is singular, choice (C) contains an error. Use the singular verb *has*, rather than the plural verb *have*, with singular subjects.

28. **A** This sentence compares *the situation with Bill* and the pronoun *I*. You can compare situations to situations and people to people, but you cannot compare situations to people. Therefore, choice (A) contains a comparison error.

29. **C** This sentence lists two things that the new employees have been doing: they *have been working overtime* and they *arrive early to work each day*. However, remember that items in a list should be parallel. Thus, the verbs *have been working* and *arrive* should be in the same form. Since *working* is not underlined, *arrive* must be the verb that is in the incorrect tense. Therefore, choice (C) contains an error and is the correct answer.

30. **A** The phrase *Riding in an airplane for the first time* is a modifying phrase that should describe whatever appears immediately after the comma. *Liam* is the person who is riding the in the airplane, but his name does not appear immediately after the comma. Since the part of the sentence that comes right after the comma is not underlined, you cannot change that part of the sentence. Therefore, the error must be in the modifying phrase itself. Changing the phrase to *When he rode in an airplane* would fix the problem by using the pronoun *he* to ensure that the phrase refers to *Liam* instead of *there were too many pockets of turbulence*.

31. **C** Here, the adjective *inexpensive* modifies the verb *can be purchased*. However, you must use adverbs, rather than adjectives, to modify verbs. Thus, *inexpensive* should be changed to *inexpensively*, and the correct answer is choice (C).

32. **B** The word *suppose* means *to think*. However, *supposed* means *required*. Since this sentence refers to something the author was required to do, rather than something that he or she thought, choice (B), which uses *suppose*, contains a diction error.

33. **E** Choice (A) contains the phrase *in the hallway*. The word *in* is the correct preposition to describe something inside the hallway. The article *the* refers to the singular specific noun *hallway*, and is therefore correct. The noun *hallway* is singular, and does not have any agreement problems with verbs or other nouns in the sentence. Therefore, choice (A) does not contain an error. The verb *lie* is in the present tense, and since the books are currently on the table, the verb is in the correct tense. The subject of the plural verb *lie* is the plural noun *books*, so this subject and verb agree. The verb *lie* is not in a list of things, so there are no parallelism errors. Therefore, choice (B) does not contain an error. The verb *borrowed* is in the past tense, and since the act of borrowing occurred *last month*, the past tense is appropriate. The subject *I* agrees with the verb *borrowed*, so there are no subject verb agreement errors in choice (C). Finally, the verb *borrowed* is not in a list of things, so there are no parallelism errors in this choice. Therefore, choice (C) is correct as written. The adverb *yet* in choice (D) modifies the verb *returned*, so the adverb is correctly used. Finally, the verb *have not…*

returned is in the correct tense, and agrees with the subject *I*. Therefore, choice (D) does not contain an error. This sentence is correct as written, so the correct answer is choice (E).

34. **B** The singular verb *appears* does not agree with the plural *openings*. Therefore, choice (B) contains a subject-verb agreement error.

35. **E** The previous sentence describes two reasons for the play's success: *it has been very successful because of its musical numbers and its captivating story*. Therefore, in order to transition from the reasons for its success into a discussion of the music, the next sentence should relate the play's songs to the play's success. Choice (A) contains a complete thought, and since the original sentence also contains a complete thought, joining the two would create a run-on. Choice (B) uses the incorrect verb form *containing*. Choice (C) is grammatically acceptable, but the phrase *In other words* suggests that what follows should simply restate the previous sentence. However, since that is not the case, choice (C) is incorrect. Choice (D) contains two fragments, which, if joined with the original sentence, would not create a complete thought. Choice (E) relates the previous sentence, which discusses the fact that the play's music is one reason for its success, to sentence 2, which discusses the fact that the music is well written. Therefore, choice (E) is the correct answer.

36. **E** The word *though* correctly refers to a contrast between the thoughts presented in sentence 3, which discusses the play's music, and the thoughts presented in sentence 4, which discusses the nature of the play's scenes. Therefore, you can eliminate choice (A). The phrase *in that* is not a conjunction, so you would not want to use it to replace the conjunction *because*, which is correctly used in the sentence. Therefore, you can eliminate choice (B). Changing *emotional to moving* does not significantly alter the meaning or the grammar of the sentence, so the sentence does not require this change. Therefore, you can eliminate choice (C). If you deleted the phrase *which give the characters depth*, the sentence would still be grammatically correct. However, the sentence does not require this change, since the phrase is correctly used. Therefore, you can eliminate choice (D). The pronoun *they* does not clearly refer to anyone in the sentence, and is therefore ambiguous. Replacing *they all* with *audiences always* would fix this error. Therefore, choice (E) is the correct answer.

37. **A** Choice (A) correctly links the two sentences and does not introduce any new errors. Choice (B), however, changes the verb *would have been* to *are*. Since the sentence discusses a hypothetical situation and not one that is actually occurring, *are* is incorrect. Choice (E) similarly uses the present tense verb *let*, which would also refer to a real rather than a hypothetical situation. Therefore you can eliminate choice (E). Choice (C) combines the two sentences, but uses many *–ing* verbs. If you have a choice between an answer that uses many *–ing* verbs and one that does not, you should choose the answer that does not contain as many *–ing* verbs. Therefore, choice (A) is more effective than choice (C). Finally, choice (D) contains two complete thoughts joined by a comma, and is therefore a comma splice. It is also in the passive voice. The correct answer is choice (A).

38.   **B**   The final paragraph focuses on the ways in which Valjean changes, so the correct answer should refer to this topic. Since the passage never discusses ways in which Valjean differs from other convicts of his time, the author does not need to refer to an authority on this matter. Choice (A) is therefore incorrect. Choice (B) refers to the ways in which Valjean changes throughout the story, and is therefore the correct answer. The final paragraph does discuss the fact that Valjean was a convict, but the way that he was treated during that time is not the focus of the paragraph, so you can eliminate choice (C). Paragraph two, not paragraph three, refers to Valjean's time as a mayor, so this topic would be out of place in paragraph three. Choice (D) is thus incorrect. Broadway musicals are mentioned in the first paragraph, not the third paragraph. Therefore, this topic would be out of place in paragraph three. The correct answer is choice (B).

39.   **C**   Sentence 1 does discuss the fact that *Les Miserables* is a play based on a novel that was written in the 1860s. However, nothing in sentence 1 or the sentence that follows discusses downtrodden characters who change their lives and seek to achieve moral redemption. The next sentence discusses the play's music, so placing the new sentence after sentence 1 would not create a smooth transition between the two. Sentence 3 discusses the play's topic, and sentence 4 refers to the fact that the play is popular because of the types of scenes it portrays. Since neither of these thoughts is related to plays and novels of the 1860s in general or to downtrodden characters who change their lives, choice (B) is incorrect. Paragraph one discusses the fact that *Les Miserables* is a play written in the 1860s, and paragraph two focuses on the ways in which Valjean changes and searches for redemption, so placing the new sentence at the beginning of paragraph two would serve to link the two paragraphs. Sentence 10 discusses the fact that Valjean changes throughout the story, but sentence 11 contains information about the reasons that Valjean acted as he did. Information regarding plays and novels of the 1860s would be irrelevant to either of these sentences, so this choice is incorrect. The final paragraph focuses on the ways that Valjean changes throughout the story, but does not discuss plays and novels of the 1860s in general. The new sentence contains information unrelated to the rest of the paragraph, so choice (E) is not the credited answer. The correct answer is choice (C).

Part III
Drills

Chapter 5
Drills

SECTION 1
Time — 25 minutes
24 Questions
(1–24)

Directions: For each question in this section, select the best answer from among the choices given and fill in the corresponding circle on the answer sheet.

Each sentence below has one or two blanks, each blank indicating that something has been omitted. Beneath the sentence are five words or sets of words labeled A through E. Choose the word or set of words that, when inserted in the sentence, <u>best</u> fits the meaning of the sentence as a whole.

Example:

Desiring to ------- his taunting friends, Mitch gave them taffy in hopes it would keep their mouths shut.

(A) eliminate   (B) satisfy   (C) overcome
(D) ridicule   (E) silence

1. Those who were leaving for the holiday were excited to ------- the campus, since the semester had been both challenging and stressful.

   (A) reenter   (B) vacate   (C) weaken
       (D) initiate   (E) resume

2. The fact that Henry had earned a position as a starter on the varsity basketball team made him the ------- of his less ------- second-string teammates who were jealous of his success.

   (A) pleasure . . motivated
   (B) rival . . studious
   (C) symbol . . coordinated
   (D) mystery . . motivated
   (E) envy . . athletic

3. Already one of the most famous scientists in the world, Albert Einstein continued to ------- scientific ------- when he won the Nobel Prize for Physics in 1921.

   (A) earn . . apathy
   (B) ignore . . derision
   (C) establish . . accolades
   (D) disdain . . notoriety
   (E) garner . . acclaim

4. The black mamba snake's lethality, evident in its high toxin levels, quick strikes, and aggressive unpredictability, presents a fearsome example of -------.

   (A) vagrancy   (B) agility   (C) virulence
       (D) agitation   (E) destruction

5. The reviewer denounced the actress's ------- style: her flat performance reduced the well-written script to a tedious recitation.

   (A) brusque   (B) sanctioned   (C) arbitrary
       (D) dramatic   (E) monotonous

6. The Senate majority voted to change the chamber's rules on -------, on speaking at inordinate length to obstruct a legislative assembly.

   (A) filibustering   (B) vetoing   (C) oppression
       (D) falsification   (E) initiating

7. The chance that a wide-reaching enterprise will ------- consumers increases when the enterprise has a monopoly on a market; thus ------- is highly beneficial.

   (A) exploit . . competition
   (B) manipulate . . vitality
   (C) capitalize . . allocation
   (D) assist . . opposition
   (E) sustain . . coercion

8. Since a vast majority of the bacteria on the human body are advantageous to their host, a tricky question is how to distinguish the few pathogens that are ------- from the preponderance that are -------.

   (A) allies . . beneficial
   (B) invaders . . contaminated
   (C) menaces . . propitious
   (D) parasites . . noxious
   (E) portents . . hardy

The passages below are followed by questions based on their content; questions following a pair of related passages may also be based on the relationship between the paired passages. Answer the questions on the basis of what is <u>stated</u> or <u>implied</u> in the passage and in any introductory material that may be provided.

Questions 9-12 are based on the following passages.

Passage 1

Seventeenth-century philosopher John Locke formulated an influential idea about the development of human traits and ideas. Specifically, he claimed that humans are not born with ideas or behavioral traits (characteristics that distinguish one person from another), but instead must gain them from personal experience. "Let us suppose the mind to be," he said, "white paper, void of all characters." His "tabula rasa," or "blank slate," view concludes that humans develop only from external environmental influences, not from any innate characteristics. Our experiences must "write" who we are on our minds. This view forms one side of a centuries-old nature versus nurture debate that questions whether humans become who they are because of external influences (nurture) or hereditary traits (nature). Can we be completely formed based on factors outside ourselves?

Passage 2

"Which contributes more to the area of a rectangle," asks twentieth-century psychologist Donald Hebb, "its length or its width?" He wasn't talking about geometry, but rather answering a journalist's question about whether nature or nurture has a stronger impact on an individual's development. He agrees that an environment and experiences are important to a person's development, but no more so than that same person's genetic makeup and hereditary traits. As far as the nature versus nurture question is concerned, according to Hebb and most other modern psychologists and anthropologists, there is no question. Current research and modes of thought hold that both genetic and environmental factors influence a person's development. The two criteria are so tightly knitted, it's impossible to say which determines an individual's characteristics.

9. Both Locke and Hebb suggest that environmental factors are

(A) crucial for tabula rasa
(B) interwoven with genetic traits
(C) subject to government regulations
(D) secondary to hereditary factors
(E) influential to human development

10. Hebb uses the geometry analogy (lines 16-18) in order to suggest that "nature" is

(A) easily understood through a formula
(B) less understood by psychologists
(C) a combination of hereditary and environmental factors
(D) inseparable from "nurture"
(E) of little benefit to anyone other than anthropologists

11. Passage 1 suggests that Locke would most likely respond to what Hebb says (lines 24-26, Passage 2) by

(A) pointing out that twins with similar genetic material have different characteristics
(B) criticizing Hebb for not defining "nature" and "nurture"
(C) restating his belief that humans do not have innate rules for processing information
(D) arguing that Hebb's analogy is too broad for the topic
(E) denying that the question is relevant for modern scientists

12. Which best describes the relationship between Passage 1 and Passage 2?

(A) Passage 2 offers a scientific perspective on a theory outlined in Passage 1.
(B) Passage 2 contradicts a modern assumption made in Passage 1.
(C) Passage 2 presents a contemporary analysis of a theory stated in Passage 1.
(D) Passage 2 synthesizes two disparate views presented in Passage 1.
(E) Passage 2 explores a solution to a problem described in Passage 1.

Questions 13-24 are based on the following passage.

In this passage, a literary critic discusses some of the issues he encountered while researching the life of Jean Toomer (1894-1967), an author from the early to mid-twentieth century. Most famous as the author of the seminal book Cane *(1923), Toomer was also a deeply private individual, whose views of race were often in conflict with those of others from his time.*

Though lauded as one of the central figures in the Harlem Renaissance, Jean Toomer the man has remained a mystery to literary historians. In an article published in *The Crisis*

Line in 1924, race leader W.E.B. DuBois pointed to some of the
5 mystery surrounding Toomer: "All of his essays and stories, even when I do not understand them, have their strange flashes of power, their numerous messages and numberless reasons for being." Essayist William Stanley Braithwaite is unreserved in his praise for Toomer's major book, *Cane*
10 (1921): "*Cane* is a book of gold and bronze, of dusk and flame, of ecstasy and pain, and Jean Toomer is a bright morning star of a new day of the race in literature." Toomer gained huge accolades from the white literary world as well, and well-known authors such as Sherwood Anderson and Waldo
15 Frank considered him one of their own. But Toomer's full connection to the white world remains a mystery, and critics have begun to wonder whether Toomer is the paragon of racial representation that he was initially represented, by Braithwaite especially, to be.
20 For many black artists in the 1930s and 1940s, Jean Toomer was an inspiration. He helped to broaden the definition of what "race literature" could be. He was not constrained, as many other black authors of the time were, to writing only about race oppression and race conflict. He
25 could incorporate influences from white as well as black artists, and he melded them into a new, innovative style that mixed poetry, prose, jazz, folklore, and spiritualism. He showed that an African American author didn't have to be defined by his race but could enjoy, and even surpass, the
30 artistic freedom enjoyed by white artists. Furthermore, he was able to cross over the color line to reach white audiences, who, in the 1920s especially, remained widely uninformed about cultural production by African Americans.

Still, his relationship to civil rights and the African
35 American community has been difficult to determine. After the success of *Cane*, Toomer contributed only a few more essays before withdrawing from the literary world altogether. In the 1930s, he had nearly disappeared from the literary scene, and his two marriages, in 1931 and 1934, were
40 interracial, both to white women. Although intermarriage between blacks and whites was still socially vilified at the time, Toomer's attitude toward this social restriction is vague. Toomer himself may not have thought of these marriages as interracial: particularly by the 1940s, Toomer insisted that his
45 race was "American" and by the end of his life, he may have even identified as a white man. These scraps are all historians have.

By the 1960s, race activism reached its apex with such figures as Martin Luther King, Jr., and Malcolm X. Black
50 and white artists alike joined together in the fight that became known as the Civil Rights movement. By that time, however, Jean Toomer was nestled in a deeply private life in Doylestown, Penn., and was not one of the voices in the fight for black equality. By then, and until his death in 1967,
55 Toomer was much more taken with local issues, and his main concern was with his church, the Friend's Society of Quakers, and the high school students whom he taught there.

If Toomer's early literary output can be more thoroughly understood than his later personal life, or his later racial
60 identification, it can only be because Toomer himself wanted it to be so. His own sense of race and personality was so complex that he likely did not want to become embroiled in debates that were literally so black and white. In a 1931 essay, Toomer announced that "the old divisions into white, black,
65 brown, red, are outworn in this country. They have had their day. Now is the time of the birth of a new order, a new vision, a new ideal of man." Whether we consider Toomer's view naïve or not, there can be no question that he thought himself a part of this "new order."
70 Because Toomer was such a truly great artist, literary historians will always long for more information about his life. Unfortunately, there's little hope that more of that information will emerge, and Jean Toomer the man must remain an inscrutable piece in our understanding of Jean
75 Toomer the artist. Perhaps such inscrutability is good for us, too. We should be wary of the rigid categories that Toomer fought against all his life, and if anything, perhaps Toomer's refusal to fit into these categories can help us to modify our own.

13. The author suggests that Toomer's relationship with the black community "has remained a mystery to literary historians" (lines 2-3) because

(A) details of Toomer's later life are insufficient to explain his personal attitudes

(B) Toomer's literary reputation was dismissed by many of his contemporaries

(C) Toomer's fame in literary circles was not acknowledged by white authors

(D) Toomer's essays provide inconsistent representations of his views

(E) evidence shows that Toomer worked against the Civil Rights movement

14. In lines 1-33, the author's discussion of Toomer's contemporaries and later artists is used to

(A) show how one particular era viewed the role of race in art
(B) state that Toomer lived in an era of radical social change
(C) give evidence of their views of Toomer's influence

(E) list the challenges faced by black artists in contemporary society

15. In line 9, "unreserved" most nearly means

(A) vacant
(B) disrespectful
(C) available
(D) garrulous
(E) complete

16. The author mentions Waldo Frank and Sherwood Anderson (lines 14-15) as indications of the

(A) urgency with which Toomer courted a white readership
(B) fluctuating reputation Toomer had within the black community
(C) limited supply of published reviews of Toomer's first novel
(D) types of influences upon which Toomer drew in writing *Cane*
(E) appeal that Toomer had to both black and white readers

17. The author most directly supports the statement in lines 20-21 ("For many … inspiration") by citing

(A) influences from which Toomer drew inspiration
(B) the reception of Toomer's work by contemporary black critics
(C) lists of Toomer's most famous published works
(D) aspects of Toomer's art that showed a new way
(E) ways that Toomer's art addressed racial issues

18. In line 46, "These scraps" most directly refers to evidence that

(A) gives actual details of Toomer's biography
(B) paints a complete picture of Toomer's life
(C) frees literary historians to speculate
(D) reaffirms the messages found in Toomer's work
(E) depicts the state of contemporary race relations

19. the author discusses "race activism" (line 48) primarily to

(A) demonstrate that Toomer's racial attitudes were atypical
(B) praise the achievements of the Civil Rights movement
(C) refer to a major equality movement in American history
(D) give literary historians one reliable source of biographical information
(E) state that Toomer had no interest in contemporary race relations

20. In line 55, "taken" most directly emphasizes which aspect of Toomer's approach to race issues?

(A) His disapproval of broad social changes
(B) His ability to play both sides of an issue
(C) His focus on smaller matters
(D) His eagerness to fight for broader causes
(E) His reputation as a literary artist

21. In lines 58-69, the author emphasizes which point about Toomer?

(A) His contemporaries disparaged him for his cowering attitude toward social equality.
(B) His attitude toward race was rooted in private and philosophical concerns.
(C) His public attitude toward race differed sharply from his private views.
(D) His writings on race have a tendency to mislead literary historians.
(E) His commitment to racial equality influenced his political views on race.

22. In line 63, "black and white" most nearly means

- (A) faintly tinged
- (B) socially progressive
- (C) racially complex
- (D) hopelessly confused
- (E) reductively simple

23. Which resource, if it existed, would be most helpful for the task described in lines 72-75 ("Unfortunately … artist")?

- (A) Accurate information about the progress of social equality in the United States
- (B) Toomer's personal diary or autobiography
- (C) Records of household income kept by Toomer's wives
- (D) Writings by other black authors from the 1920s
- (E) Statements from later authors about the importance of Toomer's influence

24. The final phrase in lines 77-79 ("if … own") primarily emphasizes which of the following points?

- (A) Toomer hid the details of his race from those in his family and hometown.
- (B) Toomer identified as white at the end of his life to distance himself from Civil Rights.
- (C) Those in the Civil Rights movement were correct to dismiss Toomer as a counterproductive force.
- (D) Toomer had more advanced views than most African American authors from the 1920s.
- (E) Toomer's personal views on race remain complex even in our own day.

NO TEST MATERIAL ON THIS PAGE.

SECTION 3
Time — 25 minutes
24 Questions
(25–39)

Directions: For each question in this section, select the best answer from among the choices given and fill in the corresponding circle on the answer sheet.

Each sentence below has one or two blanks, each blank indicating that something has been omitted. Beneath the sentence are five words or sets of words labeled A through E. Choose the word or set of words that, when inserted in the sentence, best fits the meaning of the sentence as a whole.

Example:

Hoping to ------- the dispute, negotiators proposed a compromise that they felt would be ------- to both labor and management.

   (A) enforce . . useful
   (B) end . . divisive
   (C) overcome . . unattractive
   (D) extend . . satisfactory
   (E) resolve . . acceptable

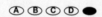

25. Unlike the other holiday travelers who argued impatiently, Francisco remained -------, quietly waiting for his turn at the ticket counter.

   (A) delighted   (B) tranquil   (C) confused
   (D) anxious   (E) brusque

26. It is possible a cryptologist could have ------- the unique markings in the coded message, but to us they were -------.

   (A) unscrambled . . accessible
   (B) obstructed . . concealed
   (C) interpreted . . indecipherable
   (D) deciphered . . straightforward
   (E) deflected . . provided

27. In spite of the health department's massive efforts to annihilate it, the deadly virus pandemic -------.

   (A) ebbed   (B) eradicated   (C) escalated
   (D) inflamed   (E) abridged

28. The ------- of diverse Scottish clans is represented by the vast number of official tartan cloths, where every different style and color of plaid represents a unique clan -------.

   (A) plethora . . transmission
   (B) dearth . . separation
   (C) devotion . . personality
   (D) variety . . textile
   (E) abundance . . identity

29. For Carlos, any dairy products he ate after his bout of food poisoning were instantly nauseating; cheese and yogurt, therefore, were ------- to him.

   (A) delectable   (B) nutritious   (C) abhorrent
   (D) expeditious   (E) assuaging

The passages below are followed by questions based on their content; questions following a pair of related passages may also be based on the relationship between the paired passages. Answer the questions on the basis of what is <u>stated</u> or <u>implied</u> in the passage and in any introductory material that may be provided.

Questions 30-31 are based on the following passage.

The immune system, science students are taught, has a goal: to protect and defend. The various levels of the immune system are the ranks of officers stationed around the sensitive and valuable treasure of the human body: to discourage those who would do harm, to safeguard from those who get too close, and to fight against those who get in. The barrier system is the beat officer that keeps bacteria and viruses from entering the body; the innate immune system is the detective seeking out pathogens that do get into the body; the adaptive immune system is the special forces unit that tailors defense tactics to each specific pathogen in order to destroy it. By providing various levels of defense, the immune system effectively protects the human body from the multitude of harmful microbes that assault it each day.

30. The primary purpose of the passage is to

(A) imply that good health is similar to a good police force
(B) illustrate the different roles of the immune system
(C) emphasize the dangers of improper hygiene
(D) criticize criminals for their actions
(E) explain the ranking system for law enforcement

31. In the passage, the author makes use primarily of

(A) hyperbole
(B) dramatic irony
(C) foreshadowing
(D) extended analogy
(E) satire

Questions 32-33 are based on the following passage.

A financial adviser mentored by Steven Kerrigan taught all of his employees to emulate Mr. Kerrigan's style of customer service. "Always be honest with your clients," he
Line told them. "Even if the advice isn't quite what the clients want
5 to hear, or it contradicts what someone else has promised them. Be thorough with your assessment, so you can give your clients solid advice. If your clients trust you, they will stay with you. If you don't do a thorough assessment, though, and your advice is based on empty promises, your clients may be
10 happy at first with the promises you've made, but you will lose them when they find you haven't been honest. If you're not going to do it right, don't do it."

32. The financial adviser suggests that the most important professional relationships are

(A) built on a foundation of trust
(B) profitable for both the client and the adviser
(C) assessed thoroughly by both parties
(D) centered around hefty promises
(E) formed from the same model for each client

33. According to the passage, Kerrigan's style of honesty even when it's not necessarily good news will benefit the advisers by

(A) earning them large payoffs from happy clients
(B) validating their work in the field
(C) creating solid connections with clients
(D) allowing them to promise clients great things
(E) increasing their word-of-mouth business

Questions 34-39 are based on the following passages.

The following passages were adapted from two novels published in 2012. The hockey team the Montreal Canadiens is known in French by the nickname "les Habitants."

Passage 1

Antoine couldn't stand his favorite hockey announcer's replacement, who spoke of his Montreal Canadiens as if they were at once a collection of the greatest and worst players of all time. The timbre of his voice flew around as erratically as the puck itself, bouncing and careening from one end to the other. The stuff of legend, he said. Some of the greatest moments in the history of sports. We are back, *les Habitants,* and this will be the new stuff of history. He had the smooth, too-perfect voice of a game-show announcer or a salesman, Antoine felt—he made you wary with his sales pitch, even if it was something you already wanted. Give it a try, he seemed to say. Put your faith in me.

Antoine couldn't let go of the old announcer, Pierre—a good French-Canadian name, not like this interloper's, Jack or Jimmy. Pierre was even-toned, almost dull. He sounded like a pedantic schoolteacher—he stood in front of a class, not modifying his tone whether the students were listening or not. Pierre had been around so long that it seemed almost that he'd never be replaced, but now he was. His relationship to the players was one of cold familiarity, one of Antoine's favorite features of the broadcast, as if Pierre could assess them as the flawed men that they were. In interviews with the players, Pierre could lecture them on their poor efforts, or he could praise them in the faint terms that wouldn't allow for inflated egos. Antoine looked forward to hearing him every game, always sure to get a good honest reporting of the game from a true expert. Antoine hoped that Pierre's new job, with a team in Florida, would be the calm respite that a man such as Pierre deserved, but such comfort was by no means certain.

Passage 2

Though we might not think of them that way, the best teachers, parents, and hockey announcers are actually pretty similar; their job is to educate, of course, but to do so in the face of anything or anyone, whether punishingly dull or wildly exciting. Whether they've got a classroom of rowdy students, a crying child in a crowded place, or a bench-clearing brawl, dispassionate action is the name of the game. "I'm sorry you feel that way," a teacher might say, "but the principal is waiting for you," but that even tone might just as well come from a parent in the face of an insolent child or from Dan Schantz the hockey announcer commentating on a blowout loss. All of them let you know that, rain or shine, at least someone is keeping it together.

Dan always starts the games with one of his cool, obvious observations: "It's a cold one here in Winnipeg, folks, and a heck of a night to watch a hockey game." He'll add, "Our team has no easy victory on its hands tonight." No matter who the opposing team is, Dan's there to tell us not to take a win for granted. But then, lest his even temper be too sobering, he adds, "But our boys will take care of business tonight if they can just keep a few key things in mind." And, like a coach, he'll add, "We're going to focus on fundamentals. We want to play good defense, and the goals will come. Keep their puck out of the net, and ours will find a way in." I love Dan's honest, simple take on the game. When things go well, it almost seems like the players can hear him. Hockey's an exciting game, so why try to ramp it up with a bunch of broadcaster's tricks?

---

34. In context, the phrase "bouncing and careening" (line 5) primarily serves to demonstrate Antoine's

 (A) scorn for the poor acoustics in a hockey arena
 (B) love of the excitement involved in tracking a hockey game
 (C) sarcastic attitude toward hockey announcers in general
 (D) basic disapproval of the new hockey announcer's style
 (E) inability to focus on the puck during hockey games

35. The author of Passage 2 would most likely view the observation in lines 10-11, Passage 1 ("He ... wanted"), as

 (A) surprising, because hockey announcers and salesmen are so dissimilar to one another
 (B) distasteful, because it suggests that the two authors have different levels of respect for hockey announcers
 (C) bizarre, because salesmen are typically less prone to overstatement than hockey announcers
 (D) agreeable, because the two share similar attitudes toward how hockey announcers should broadcast
 (E) amusing, because hockey announcers do not generally major in business in college

36. Passage 1 serves as evidence that the assertion in lines 30-34, Passage 2 ("Though … exciting"), is

(A) untrue in some cases
(B) folksy and hackneyed
(C) no longer applicable
(D) purposefully misleading
(E) unnecessarily pessimistic

37. The author of Passage 2 uses the word "dispassionate" (line 36) to describe action that is

(A) firm but unemotional
(B) unloving but persuasive
(C) disdaining but accurate
(D) calm but unsure
(E) educating but dull

38. The author of Passage 2 would consider Pierre (Passage 1) to be

(A) obviously motivated by business goals
(B) a good representative of a type of hockey announcer
(C) novel but unduly dismissed by listeners
(D) a type of announcer that should be removed from hockey
(E) unaware of the contemporary trends in broadcasting

39. In Passage 2, the author's attitude toward Dan Schantz is best described as one of

(A) unfettered disapproval
(B) complete lionization
(C) measured approval
(D) affected ambivalence
(E) sarcastic irritation

Questions 40-48 are based on the following passage.

The following excerpt is adapted from a 1985 book on the role of storytelling in human understanding.

We love to spin yarns, to tell tales, to chronicle events.
If we get even a few details about someone, we'll start to
connect those details into some kind of narrative about that
Line person. We want any nearby dots to be connected. Effect with
5 no cause, correlation with no causation: we can't assimilate
these ideas because they don't have that narrative structure.
Our minds want stories, even if those stories need to be
twisted and mangled into existence.

This is how we give order to the chaotic world around
10 us. Take any messy, complicated historical event, something
like the American Civil War: a bloody and long conflict, and
hopelessly complex when taken in isolation. Historians and
onlookers alike have spent over a century debating the causes,
the effects, and the place of this event in the ongoing plot of
15 American history. Neuroscientists have referred to a "need
for narrative," both as an explanation for the popularity of
fiction and for how people interact with one another. In the
grander scheme, the need for narrative may inform the way
we understand ourselves. We'll take anything conclusive as
20 long as it's consistent.

Personality is one of life's great mysteries. It is too large;
it has too many components; it has too many omissions.
It changes all the time, from day to day or hour to hour,
and there are times that it can seem we've got multiple
25 personalities at once. Because it is too many things to
manage, we turn personality into a single narrative, a single
"me" or "you." I need my friend Jack to be the brainy one; I
need my husband to be the comforting one; I need my parents
to be my sources of strength. Understanding them as I do,
30 as the stories that they are, I simply forget whenever they
do something that doesn't make narrative sense. It makes
sense that in the earliest literary and historical texts we have,
the main characters are defined by their cardinal attributes.
Whether Odysseus is characterized by his bravery, Penelope
35 by her devotion, or Oedipus by his tragic love, these complex
characters are made into simpler, more consistent wholes on
the strength of narrative.

In all eras of history, literature and art have been
filled with "characters," whether the symbolic, allegorical
40 characters of the Bible or the subjects of contemporary
biographical film. In the early twentieth century, the very
notion of "consistent" stories broke down, and characters
became less rigidly defined as a result. Suddenly, amid
a cultural shift away from religious certainty, one's
45 environment, one's historical era, one's family history
could all come to bear on the maze of human personality.
Psychologists began to spend entire careers studying human
personalities, but for all these changes, the goal was still the
same: contain the human experience, find the story that can

50 encapsulate all of human complexity. If the human personality
seems more complex, then the method of storytelling needs to
be changed accordingly. Our need for narrative will not allow
us to abandon storytelling altogether. Because after all that
has come before us, and all that will come later, if we're not
55 part of the big story, what are we?

40. In line 1, "yarns" most nearly means

 (A) strings
 (B) tapestries
 (C) writings
 (D) narratives
 (E) tails

41. The author implies that "nearby dots to be connected"
(line 4) are details that

 (A) are part of the simplicity of the meaning of life
 (B) create exciting patterns and repetitions
 (C) do not exist in the real world
 (D) different personalities understand in different
     ways
 (E) may not be connected outside the human mind

42. The author uses the phrase "twisted and mangled"
(lines 7-8) in order to

 (A) chastise readers for accepting simple solutions
 (B) show the historical roots of a human response
 (C) identify why humans prefer certain types of
     personality
 (D) underline the need for a particular preference
 (E) admire humans' ability to understand difficult
     subjects

43. In context, the reference to "the ongoing plot" (line 14)
serves to emphasize the

 (A) historical interest in conspiracy theories
 (B) challenge in uncovering historical mysteries
 (C) perceived relatedness of historical events
 (D) human talent for creating fictional stories
 (E) smaller stories within large historical events

44. The phrase "In the grander scheme" (lines 17-18) serves as a transition between a discussion of

(A) historical events and literary texts
(B) a contested theory and scientific certainty
(C) a neuroscientist's view and a psychologist's critique
(D) a general theory and a specific application
(E) a confessional memoir and a historical narrative

45. Based on information presented in lines 38-55, which of the following would most likely be the title of a study of human personality in the twentieth century?

(A) *The Tragic Flaw in Human Personality*
(B) *Who We Are In Three Easy Steps*
(C) *The Mirror and the Labyrinth of Personality*
(D) *The Role of the American Civil War in History*
(E) *You Are a Good Person!*

46. The author refers to a "cultural shift" (line 44) to help account for

(A) the historically consistent understandings of personality
(B) psychologists' desires to do away with storytelling
(C) the primary supply of contemporary popular fictional stories
(D) a general human distrust of psychological theories
(E) the broad historical change in attitudes toward personality

47. In line 49, "contain" most nearly means

(A) hold
(B) understand
(C) imprison
(D) restrain
(E) comprise

48. Which of the following best captures the main idea in lines 54-55 ("Because … we?")?

(A) Our historical era is just as important as other past eras.
(B) Most stories we tell ourselves have deep historical roots.
(C) People in the future will tell themselves different stories from the ones we tell ourselves.
(D) History is ultimately very similar to writing fiction or poetry.
(E) Life as we know it would be much different without the need for narrative.

Directions: For this section, solve each problem and decide which is the best of the choices given. Fill in the corresponding circle on the answer sheet. You may use any available space for scratchwork.

1. If y is divisible by 2, 4, and 5, what is the least possible integer value of y ?

   (A)   8
   (B)   10
   (C)   20
   (D)   40
   (E)   50

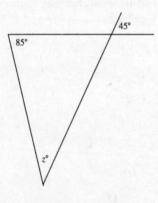

2. What is the value of z in the figure above?

   (A)   50
   (B)   45
   (C)   40
   (D)   35
   (E)   30

3. Of 45 books on a shelf, $\frac{1}{5}$ are biographies. If 3 of the biographies are <u>not</u> about women, how many of the biographies are about women?

(A) Five
(B) Six
(C) Seven
(D) Eight
(E) Nine

4. For some positive integer t, if $t^2 = 16$, what is the value of $(t-1)^2$?

(A) −5
(B) −3
(C) 3
(D) 4
(E) 9

5. If the sum of a and $3a$ is less than the sum of $5b$ and $-b$, which of the following must be true?

(A) $a < 0$
(B) $b < 0$
(C) $a < b$
(D) $a = -b$
(E) $b = 0$

$$A = \{1, t, 7\}$$
$$B = \{2, t, 6\}$$

6. If the average (arithmetic mean) of set A is 4, what is the average of set B ?

(A) 4

(B) $4\frac{1}{3}$

(C) 5

(D) $5\frac{2}{3}$

(E) 6

$$\sqrt{p^2 + 55} = 9$$

7. If the equation above is satisfied by the positive number p, what is the value of p, rounded to the nearest integer?

(A) 4
(B) 5
(C) 6
(D) 7
(E) 8

8. In the xy-plane, the coordinates of point F are $(-1, -3)$ and the coordinates of point G are $(-1, 0)$. If G is the midpoint of $\overline{FH}$, what are the coordinates of point H ?

(A) $(1, -3)$
(B) $(0, -3)$
(C) $(-1, 3)$
(D) $(-1, 6)$
(E) $(-3, 0)$

WOMEN'S RING SIZES (in millimeters)

Ring Size	Ring Diameter is greater than	But less than or equal to
5	$15\frac{2}{3}$ millimeters	$16\frac{1}{6}$ millimeters
$5\frac{1}{2}$	$16\frac{1}{6}$ millimeters	$16\frac{1}{2}$ millimeters
6	$16\frac{1}{2}$ millimeters	$16\frac{2}{3}$ millimeters
$6\frac{1}{2}$	$16\frac{2}{3}$ millimeters	$16\frac{5}{6}$ millimeters
7	$16\frac{5}{6}$ millimeters	$17\frac{1}{3}$ millimeters

9. According to the table above, if a woman's ring diameter is $16\frac{3}{4}$ millimeters what is her ring size?

(A) 5
(B) $5\frac{1}{2}$
(C) 6
(D) $6\frac{1}{2}$
(E) 7

10. If the equation $y = \dfrac{x-1}{x}$ is true for all positive integer values of x, what could be the value of y ?

(A) $\dfrac{1}{6}$
(B) $\dfrac{1}{3}$
(C) $\dfrac{3}{7}$
(D) $\dfrac{4}{5}$
(E) $\dfrac{7}{6}$

11. If $p < 6$ and $q < 12$, which of the following must be true?

    I. $p + q < 18$
    II. $q - p > 6$
    III. $2p = q$

(A) I only
(B) II only
(C) III only
(D) I and II
(E) I and III

13. Each of the blocks in a toy bin is either red, blue, or yellow. The number of yellow blocks is 3 more than the number of red blocks, and the number of blue blocks is 2 times the number of yellow blocks. Which of the following could be the total number of blocks in the toy bin?

(A)   7
(B) 10
(C) 14
(D) 15
(E) 17

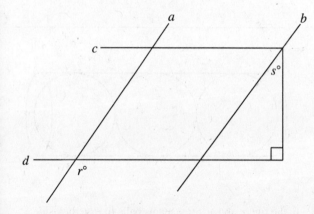

12. In the figure above, $a \parallel b$, $c \parallel d$, and $r = 140$. What is the value of s ?

(A) 30
(B) 40
(C) 45
(D) 50
(E) 60

$$j(x) = \sqrt{x} + 1$$
$$k(x) = (j(x))^3$$

14. If the above functions are defined for all values of x, what is the value of $k(4)$?

(A)   2
(B)   4
(C)   8
(D) 20
(E) 27

TYPES OF BUSINESS IN A TOWN

Business Type	Percent of Total Stores
Restaurant	41
Clothing store	20
Shoe store	17
Toy store	10
Bookstore	7
Jewelry store	5

15. The chart above shows the types of businesses in a certain town as a percent of the total number of businesses in the town. If there are 100 clothing stores, how many more book stores are there than jewelry stores?

(A) 10
(B) 15
(C) 25
(D) 35
(E) 105

16. Triangle ABC lies in the xy-plane such that vertex A is at $(m, 2n)$ and vertex B is at $(2m, 4n)$, where m and n are both positive. Which of the following is the equation of the line containing side $\overline{AB}$?

(A) $y = \dfrac{m}{n}x$

(B) $y = \dfrac{n}{m}x$

(C) $y = \dfrac{m}{n}x + m$

(D) $y = \dfrac{2n}{m}x$

(E) $y = \dfrac{2n}{m}x + n$

17. Amy's closet contains shoes of different styles and colors. If all the boots in Amy's closet are black, which of the following statements about the shoes in the closet must be true?

   I. If a shoe is not a boot, then it is not black.
  II. If a shoe is black, it is a boot.
 III. If a shoe is not black, it is not a boot.

(A) I only
(B) II only
(C) III only
(D) I and II
(E) II and III

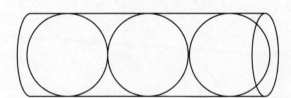

18. In the figure above, three tennis balls fit exactly inside a tube, just touching the top, bottom, and sides of the tube. If the diameter of each tennis ball is d, what is the volume of the tube in terms of d ?

(A) πd^2

(B) $2\pi d^2$

(C) $\dfrac{3}{4}d^3$

(D) πd^3

(E) $3\pi d^3$

19. How many positive four-digit integers have a 7 in the hundreds place, a 1 in the tens place, a prime number in the ones place, and exactly one of the digits equal to 2 ?

(A) 10
(B) 11
(C) 12
(D) 13
(E) 14

20. Side $\overline{TU}$ in isosceles triangle TUV is shorter than the other two sides. If the degree measure of $\angle V$ is divisible by 10, what is the smallest possible measure of $\angle T$?

(A) 40
(B) 45
(C) 50
(D) 60
(E) 65

SECTION 4
Time — 25 minutes
18 Questions
(21–38)

Directions: For this section, solve each problem and decide which is the best of the choices given. Fill in the corresponding circle on the answer sheet. You may use any available space for scratchwork.

Reference Information

$A = \pi r^2$
$C = 2\pi r$

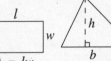
$A = lw$

$A = \frac{1}{2} bh$

$V = lwh$

$V = \pi r^2 h$

$c^2 = a^2 + b^2$

Special Right Triangles

The number of degrees of arc in a circle is 360.

The sum of the measures in degrees of the angles of a triangle is 180.

---

21. If $p + 3 = 12$ and $p - q = 5$, what is the value of q ?

(A) 4
(B) 6
(C) 9
(D) 10
(E) 20

A is the set of even integers.
B is the set of multiples of 9.
C is the set of the factors of 60.

22. Which of the following is a member of both sets A and B, but not of set C ?

(A) 6
(B) 9
(C) 12
(D) 15
(E) 18

TISHA'S WORKOUTS FOR 10 DAYS

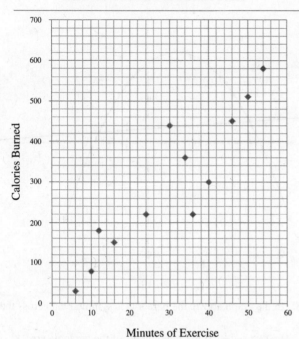

Calories Burned

Minutes of Exercise

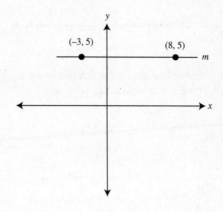

23. In the scatter plot above, Tisha's time for each of 12 workouts is plotted against the number of calories burned during that workout. During how many workouts did Tisha exercise for more than 25 minutes and burn more than 400 calories?

(A) Two
(B) Three
(C) Four
(D) Five
(E) Six

24. In the *xy*-coordinate plane above, line *m* passes though points (–3, 5) and (8, 5) as shown. Line *p* (not shown) is perpendicular to line *m* and passes through point (3, 8). Which point lies on both line *m* and line *p* ?

(A) (8, 3)
(B) (6, 5)
(C) (5, 8)
(D) (3, 8)
(E) (3, 5)

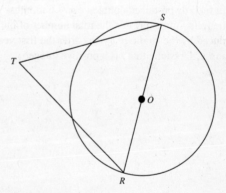

25. In the figure above, *O* is the center of the circle and points *R* and *S* lie on the circle. If △*RST* is equilateral with a perimeter of 54, what is the circumference of the circle?

(A) 81π
(B) 54π
(C) 36π
(D) 27π
(E) 18π

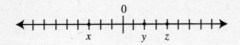

26. On the number line above, the tick marks are equally spaced. If $y + z = 2$, what is the value of x ?

(A) $-\dfrac{1}{2}$

(B) -1

(C) $-1\dfrac{1}{4}$

(D) $-1\dfrac{1}{3}$

(E) $-1\dfrac{1}{2}$

---

27. A certain recording studio produced 1 hit record in its first year of business. After the first year, the total number of hit records produced doubled every 6 months. Which of the following expresses the total number of hit records produced by the studio in t **years** after the first year of business? (Assume that t is a positive integer.)

(A) 2^{2t}

(B) t^6

(C) $2t$

(D) $\dfrac{2^t}{2}$

(E) $2^{\frac{t}{2}}$

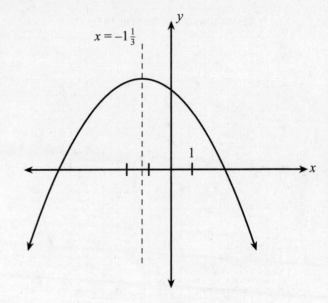

28. In the graph above, the parabola is symmetrical across the line $x = -1\dfrac{1}{3}$. If the x-intercepts of the parabola are $(-5, 0)$ and $(m, 0)$, what is the value of m ?

(A) $\dfrac{2}{3}$

(B) $1\dfrac{1}{3}$

(C) $1\dfrac{2}{3}$

(D) $2\dfrac{1}{3}$

(E) 3

Directions for Student-Produced Response Questions

Each of the remaining 10 questions requires you to solve the problem and enter your answer by marking the ovals in the special grid, as shown in the examples below. You may use any available space for scratch work.

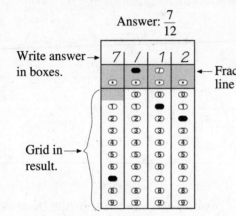

Answer: $\frac{7}{12}$

Write answer → in boxes.

← Fraction line

Grid in → result.

Answer: 2.5

← Decimal point

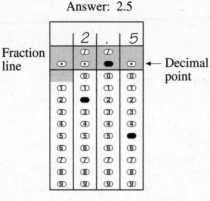

Note: You may start your answers in any column, space permitting. Columns not needed should be left blank.

- Mark no more than one circle in any column.

- Because the answer sheet will be machine-scored, **you will receive credit only if the circles are filled in correctly.**

- Although not required, it is suggested that you write your answer in the boxes at the top of the columns to help you fill in the circles accurately.

- Some problems may have more than one correct answer. In such cases, grid only one answer.

- No question has a negative answer.

- **Mixed numbers** such as $3\frac{1}{2}$ must be gridded as 3.5 or 7/2. (If [3 | 1 | / | 2] is gridded, it will be interpreted as $\frac{31}{2}$, not $3\frac{1}{2}$.)

- **Decimal Answers:** If you obtain a decimal answer with more digits than the grid can accommodate, it may be either rounded or truncated, but it must fill the entire grid. For example, if you obtain an answer such as 0.6666..., you should record your result as .666 or .667. **A less accurate value such as .66 or .67 will be scored as incorrect.**

Acceptable ways to grid $\frac{2}{3}$ are:

$x, y, 36, 108, ...$

29. The first term of the sequence above is x. If each term after the first is three times the previous term, what is the value of x ?

30. The price P, in dollars, of a certain stock m months after it was bought is given by the equation $P(m) = 125{,}000\left(\dfrac{1}{5}\right)^{\frac{m}{3}}$. What is the price, in dollars, of the stock 15 months after it was bought? (Disregard the $ sign when gridding in your answer.)

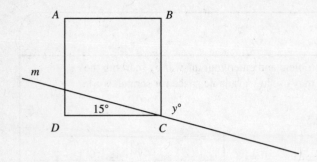

31. In the figure above, if *ACBD* is a square and line *m* passes through point *C*, what is the value of *y* ?

32. A bag of 40 marbles contains only marbles that are either red or blue. If the probability of choosing a red marble is 5 out of 8, how many blue marbles are in the bag?

33. The base of triangle *A* is three times that of triangle *B* and the height of triangle *A* is two times that of triangle *B*. If triangle *A* has an area of 120, what is the area of triangle *B* ?

34. Sue and David together own 57 hamsters. If David owns 5 more than 3 times the number of hamsters that Sue owns, how many hamsters does Sue own?

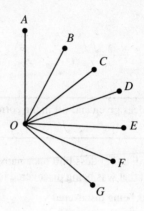

35. In the figure above, $\overline{EO}$ bisects $\angle COG$, $\overline{CO}$ bisects $\angle AOE$, $\overline{BO}$ bisects $\angle AOC$, and $\overline{FO}$ bisects $\angle EOG$. The measure of $\angle COG$ is what fraction of the measure of $\angle AOF$?

36. If the reciprocal of a number is greater than the square of that number, what is one possible value for the number?

37. The appendix of a certain book starts on page 153 and contains 7 sections. The sections are consecutive, and each section is exactly five full pages. No section shares a page with any other section. On what page is the last page of the appendix?

38. If $\dfrac{r}{s} = \dfrac{5}{6}$ and $\dfrac{s}{t} = \dfrac{2}{9}$, what is the value of $\dfrac{r}{t}$?

SECTION 5
Time — 30 minutes
39 Questions
(1–39)

Directions: For each question in this section, select the best answer from among the choices given and fill in the corresponding circle on the answer sheet.

The following sentences test correctness and effectiveness of expression. Part of each sentence or the entire sentence is underlined; beneath each sentence are five ways of phrasing the underlined material. Choice A repeats the original phrasing; the other four choices are different. If you think the original phrasing produces a better sentence than any of the alternatives, select choice A; if not, select one of the other choices.

In making your selection, follow the requirements of standard written English; that is, pay attention to grammar, choice of words, sentence construction, and punctuation. Your selection should result in the most effective sentence—clear and precise, without awkwardness or ambiguity.

EXAMPLE:

Bobby Flay baked his first cake <u>and he was thirteen years old then</u>.
(A) and he was thirteen years old then
(B) when he was thirteen
(C) at age thirteen years old
(D) upon the reaching of thirteen years
(E) at the time when he was thirteen

1. An opener for 1999's *Geniuses, Savants, and Prodigies* conference, <u>the piano was first played by David Helfgott when he was five years old</u>.

   (A) the piano was first played by David Helfgott when he was five years old
   (B) the first playing of the piano by David Helfgott was when he was five years old
   (C) David Helfgott began playing the piano when he was five years old
   (D) David Helfgott, who began playing the piano at five years old
   (E) David Helfgott, who first played the piano when he was five years old

2. The dodo bird, a flightless bird once native to the island of Mauritius, <u>that was being discovered</u> in 1598.

   (A) that was being discovered
   (B) with its discovery
   (C) discovered
   (D) having been discovered
   (E) was discovered

3. The stock market crashed heavily in 1929, <u>the initiating thereby of</u> an economic depression that devastated the nation.

   (A) the initiating thereby of
   (B) thereby initiating
   (C) it initiated thereby
   (D) which thereby made it initiate
   (E) thereby it initiated

4. Determined to finish the game despite the rain, <u>the football team's fight for the trophy was impressive</u>.

   (A) the football team's fight for the trophy was impressive
   (B) the football team fought impressively for the trophy
   (C) the trophy for which the football team impressively fought
   (D) the trophy was what the football team impressively fought for
   (E) the football team's impressive fight was for the trophy

5. <u>Being only a thousandth of a millimeter wide, even when produced by the largest spiders, are cobwebs</u>, delicate strands that are five times stronger than steel strands of the same thickness.

   (A) Being only a thousandth of a millimeter wide, even when produced by the largest spiders, are cobwebs,
   (B) Even when produced by the largest spiders, cobwebs, they are only a thousandth of a millimeter wide,
   (C) Cobwebs, while being barely a thousandth of a millimeter wide, even when produced by the largest spiders,
   (D) Only a thousandth of a millimeter wide, even when produced by the largest spiders, cobwebs are
   (E) Though only a thousandth of a millimeter wide, even when produced by the largest spiders, cobwebs as

6. *The Coronation of Napoleon*, by Jacques-Luis David, <u>an awe-inspiring and enormous painting that covers</u> nearly 650 square feet.

(A) an awe-inspiring and enormous painting that covers

(B) is an awe-inspiring and enormous painting that covers

(C) which is an awe-inspiring and enormous painting covering

(D) who created an awe-inspiring and enormous painting that covers

(E) awe-inspiring as an enormous painting that covers

7. The new phone cost almost nothing <u>after deducting the rebate</u> from its original price.

(A) after deducting the rebate
(B) following the deducting of the rebate
(C) of the deducting of the rebate
(D) since the deducting of the rebate
(E) after the rebate was deducted

8. <u>Tsar Nicholas II's violent dictatorship resulted in them eventually revolting against his brutality</u>.

(A) Tsar Nicholas II's violent dictatorship resulted in them eventually revolting against his brutality.

(B) Violent dictatorship, practiced by Tsar Nicholas II, eventually resulted in their revolting against his brutality.

(C) Tsar Nicholas II's violent dictatorship led to an eventual revolt against his brutality.

(D) Tsar Nicholas II dictated violently, which is why many eventually revolted against his brutality.

(E) They revolted against his brutality and it was because of the violent dictatorship of Tsar Nicholas II.

9. <u>Lindsay was needing to buy a new car, she went to the local car dealership to do that</u>.

(A) Lindsay was needing to buy a new car, she went to the local car dealership to do that.

(B) Needing to buy a new car, Lindsay went to the local car dealership.

(C) Having gone to the car dealership, buying a new car was what Lindsay needed.

(D) Going to the car dealership was Lindsay, where she needed to buy a new car.

(E) Lindsay went to the car dealership, she needed to buy a new car.

10. <u>The detectives identifying the criminal, they</u> were determined to catch the man who stole the jewelry.

(A) The detectives identifying the criminal, they
(B) To identify the criminal, the detectives
(C) The detectives identified the criminal, they
(D) Identifying the criminal, was why the detectives
(E) Having identified the criminal, the detectives

11. <u>Wanting more responsibility and to increase their monthly earnings,</u> many employees volunteer to work overtime.

(A) Wanting more responsibility and to increase their monthly earnings,

(B) More responsibility and an increase in their monthly earnings are wanted by

(C) To want more responsibility and increase their monthly earnings is why

(D) While wanting more responsibility and an increase in their monthly earnings, then

(E) Wanting more responsibility and an increase their monthly earnings,

12. The diverse works of Igor Stravinsky <u>ranges</u> from Russian ballets to neoclassical compositions and chamber works.

   (A) ranges
   (B) having ranged
   (C) range
   (D) that range
   (E) ranging

13. Many authors of the 1920s wrote novels that included so much symbolism <u>that the works are often difficult to comprehend; such symbolism</u> obscures, rather than clarifies, the author's main point.

   (A) that the works are often difficult to comprehend; such symbolism
   (B) that the works, being often difficult to comprehend and symbolizing
   (C) and the works are often difficult to comprehend, and they symbolize
   (D) being often difficult to comprehend, such work symbolizes and
   (E) that their works are often difficult to comprehend and symbolizing

14. In 1917 the Anti-Saloon League urged that the sale, production, and transportation of alcohol <u>being banned in the United States, thus initiating</u> the movement that led to the Prohibition.

   (A) being banned in the United States, thus initiating
   (B) should be banned in the United States for initiating
   (C) have a ban in the United States, which initiated
   (D) be banned in the United States, thus initiating
   (E) ought to be banned in the United States for initiating

15. <u>Charlemagne was crowned in 768 A.D. as King of the Franks, he was</u> the oldest son of Pepin the Short and Bertrada of Laon.

   (A) Charlemagne was crowned in 768 A.D. as King of the Franks, he was
   (B) In 768 A.D. they crowned Charlemagne as King of the Franks, having been
   (C) Charlemagne, in 768 A.D. crowned as King of the Franks, and he was
   (D) Crowned in 768 A.D. as King of the Franks, Charlemagne was
   (E) Charlemagne, in 768 A.D. he was crowned as King of the Franks, was

16. <u>Light bulbs generate their light</u> when a filament in its center is heated to a high temperature until the filament glows.

   (A) Light bulbs generate their light
   (B) A light bulb generates light
   (C) A light bulb's light, generated
   (D) The light bulb generates their light
   (E) The light of light bulbs are generated

17. Local restaurant critics consider the baked haddock at the new seafood restaurant on Main Street <u>as being able to be considered</u> among the worst they have ever tasted.

   (A) as being able as to be considered
   (B) that it is
   (C) to be able to be considered
   (D) to be
   (E) as to be

18. Ernest Hemingway, who began his career as a journalist for *The Kansas City Star*, <u>and created a concise writing style that was different from that of any other American writer</u> of his day.

(A) and created a concise writing style that was different from that of any other American writer

(B) would create a writing style that was different from any other American writer

(C) and would create a writing style that was different from any other American writer

(D) created a concise writing style that was different from that of any other American writer

(E) created a concise writing style that was differing with the style created by any other American writer

19. <u>The crusaders of the Middle Ages, according to historians, succeeded not in gaining access to Jerusalem, but only to leave</u> a trail of devastation in their wake as they devastated Mediterranean ports and fought among themselves.

(A) The crusaders of the Middle Ages, according to historians, succeeded not in gaining access to Jerusalem, but only to leave

(B) The crusaders of the Middle Ages, according to historians, succeeded not to gain access to Jerusalem, but only in leaving

(C) The crusaders of the Middle Ages, according to historians, succeeded not in gaining access to Jerusalem, but only in leaving

(D) According to historians the crusaders of the Middle Ages succeeded not in gaining access to Jerusalem but only to leave

(E) According to historians the crusaders of the Middle Ages, they did not succeed in gaining access to Jerusalem but instead they left

20. The <u>reputations of either of the shows appears to be well-merited</u>.

(A) The reputations of either of the shows appears to be well-merited.

(B) Either of the shows appears to have merited their reputation.

(C) Either of the shows appear to have merited the reputation.

(D) Either of the shows appears to have merited its reputation.

(E) The reputation of either of the shows appears to be well-merited.

The following sentences test your ability to recognize grammar and usage errors. Each sentence contains either a single error or no error at all. No sentence contains more than one error. The error, if there is one, is underlined and lettered. If the sentence contains an error, select the one underlined part that must be changed to make the sentence correct. If the sentence is correct, select choice E. In choosing answers, follow the requirements of standard written English.

EXAMPLE:

The other players and her significantly improved
      A   B   C

the game plan created by the coaches. No error
                    D   E

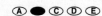

21. Abigail must choose between the upscale bistro
              A   B

downtown or eating at the diner across the street from her
            C   D

house. No error
       E

22. Each of the faculty members is allowed to use one lab
                                A

and three computers per semester to further any research
                                        B

project that they find interesting. No error
    C   D   E

23. Becoming a successful doctor involves not only
    A   B

compassion for others and also years of study. No error
                    C   D   E

24. The bank robberies committed by outlaws Bonny and
                       A

Clyde in a reputed safe part of the country surprised
            B   C

many locals and captured the interest of the nation.
                  D

No error
E

25. When he wrote his first treatise on emotions, René

Descartes confidently asserted on his ability to
                      A

provide deeper insight into the topic than had
        B   C

any previous philosopher. No error
        D   E

26. When a talented chef prepares a meal, they create
                        A   B

what many view as a work of art that both
    C

surprises and delights. No error
    D   E

27. The statements produced by the landlord indicate that the
                                            A

tenants who moved into the apartment next door is
            B   C

being increasingly disruptive on a regular basis. No error
    D   E

28. In 1692, Robert Calef argued that those convicted in the
                        A

Salem witch trials, many of them respected members of
                    B   C

the community, had been either unfairly imprisoned or
                            D

hanged. No error
        E

29. If you often interrupt James, one should recognize that he
            A   B

may become annoyed because he considers such behavior
    C   D

impolite. No error
          E

30. In response to Nelson Mandela's imprisonment for
$\underset{\text{A}}{\underline{\text{}}}$

sabotage and attempts to overthrow the South African

government, Mandela's supporters, many of whom

were members of the African National Congress,

have attempted to threaten governmental authority
$\underset{\text{B}}{\underline{\text{have attempted}}}$ $\underset{\text{C}}{\underline{\text{to threaten}}}$

themselves in 1990. No error
$\underset{\text{D}}{\underline{\text{themselves}}}$ $\underset{\text{E}}{\underline{\text{No error}}}$

31. Cave paintings found in Spain, $\underset{\text{A}}{\underline{\text{many of which}}}$ feature

large wild animals and tracings of human hands, $\underset{\text{B}}{\underline{\text{are}}}$

the remnants of a type of communication
$\underset{\text{C}}{\underline{\text{the remnants}}}$

long since abandoned. No error
$\underset{\text{D}}{\underline{\text{long since abandoned.}}}$ $\underset{\text{E}}{\underline{\text{No error}}}$

32. Neither the coach nor the team $\underset{\text{A}}{\underline{\text{were}}}$ prepared for

the opposing side's surprising strategy and

$\underset{\text{B}}{\underline{\text{Therefore both suffered}}}$ a loss that $\underset{\text{C}}{\underline{\text{no one}}}$ $\underset{\text{D}}{\underline{\text{would have}}}$

predicted. $\underset{\text{E}}{\underline{\text{No error}}}$

33. The cumulus cloud, $\underset{\text{A}}{\underline{\text{which appears}}}$ at low altitudes,

$\underset{\text{B}}{\underline{\text{is known}}}$ for having a puffy structure that $\underset{\text{C}}{\underline{\text{causes them to}}}$

form $\underset{\text{D}}{\underline{\text{interesting shapes.}}}$ $\underset{\text{E}}{\underline{\text{No error}}}$

34. $\underset{\text{A}}{\underline{\text{In contrast to}}}$ the game of Go, $\underset{\text{B}}{\underline{\text{in which pieces}}}$ cannot be

moved once $\underset{\text{C}}{\underline{\text{they have been placed}}}$ on the board,

$\underset{\text{D}}{\underline{\text{chess pieces}}}$ can move in a variety of different directions.

$\underset{\text{E}}{\underline{\text{No error}}}$

Questions 35-39 are based on the following passage.

(1) People are rarely grateful for the things that they have until after they lose them. (2) After that what takes places is compelling them realize the value of their friends, family, and possessions, and hopefully, to gain greater appreciation for the truly important things in life.

(3) One novel illustrates this point in an especially effective manner. (4) *The Prince and the Pauper* is a work of fiction written in 1881 by Mark Twain. (5) This book demonstrates the lesson through the story of Tom Canty, a poor boy from London. (6) In this book, Tom changes places with Prince Edward, whom he resembles very closely. (7) At first, Tom imagines that life as a wealthy prince will be perfect, but he soon discovers that the court customs and rules are more complicated than he had thought, and he longs to return to his family and even to the poverty of his former life. (8) When he finally does return home, he is appreciative of the few things that he does have and no longer envies those who only appear to have happiness.

(9) When we lose someone dear to us, or an important object, and then grow in appreciation for that person or thing, we are learning the same lesson that Tom learned. (10) It is possible to recognize the value of those who love us before we lose them. (11) Many people believe that Prince Edward is a more engaging character than Tom. (12) However, this is a lesson that some learn only after it is too late. (13) Instead, they spend their whole lives longing for their own "prince" with whom they can trade places. (14) They fail to acknowledge just how fortunate they already are. (15) Like Tom before he met Prince Edward, they imagine that wealth is the key to happiness, and overlook the fact that many of the happiest people who have lived have been those who possessed relatively little.

35. In context, which of the following is the best version of the underlined section of sentence 2 (reproduced below)?

    After that what takes places is often compelling them to realize the value of their friends, family, and possessions, and hopefully, to gain greater appreciation for the truly important things in life.

    (A) (As it is now)
    (B) After that, however, they are often compelled
    (C) Such a tragedy then occurs that often compels them
    (D) You are often compelled
    (E) Then what occurs is the person will often be compelled

36. In context, which of the following is the best way to combine sentences 4 and 5 (reproduced below)?

    The Prince and the Pauper is a work of fiction written in 1881 by Mark Twain. This book demonstrates the lesson through the story of Tom Canty, a poor boy from London.

    (A) *The Prince and the Pauper* is a work of fiction written in 1881 by Mark Twain, and it demonstrates the lesson through the story of Tom Canty, a poor boy from London.
    (B) *The Prince and the Pauper*, a work of fiction written by Mark Twain in 1881, demonstrates this lesson through the story of Tom Canty, a poor boy from London.
    (C) The story of the poor London boy Tom Canty, which demonstrates the lesson; *The Prince and the Pauper* is a work of fiction written by Mark Twain in 1881.
    (D) The story of Tom Canty is a work of fiction written in 1881 by Mark Twain, a poor boy from London, *The Prince and the Pauper* demonstrates the lesson.
    (E) *The Prince and the Pauper* is a work of fiction written by Mark Twain in 1881, demonstrating the lesson through the story of poor London boy Tom Canty.

37. Which of the following, if added after the second paragraph, would most improve the essay?

   (A) A paragraph detailing what Tom missed from his home in London and why those things were more important to him than the wealth he enjoyed in Prince Edward's court.

   (B) A paragraph explaining why the court customs in Prince Edward's court were more intricate than those of surrounding courts.

   (C) A paragraph discussing the reason that Tom's family became poverty-stricken.

   (D) A paragraph outlining the literary devices that Mark Twain used to demonstrate how Tom gained an appreciation for his home in London.

   (E) A paragraph showing how Mark Twain learned to appreciate his family and friends before he lost them in death.

38. In context, which of the following is the best combination of sentences 13 and 14 (reproduced below)?

   Instead, they spend their whole lives longing for their own "prince" with whom they can trade places. They fail to acknowledge just how fortunate they already are.

   (A) Instead spending their lives longing for their own "prince" with whom they can trade places, one fails to acknowledge just how fortunate one already is.

   (B) After you stop longing for your own "prince" with whom you can trade places, you will acknowledge how fortunate you are.

   (C) Before you can acknowledge just how fortunate you are, you must instead stop longing for your own "prince" with whom you can trade places.

   (D) Instead, they spend their whole lives longing for their own "prince" with whom they can trade places and they have failed to acknowledge just how fortunate they already are.

   (E) Instead, they spend their whole lives longing for their own "prince" with whom they can trade places, and fail to acknowledge just how fortunate they already are.

39. Deleting which of the following sentences would improve the essay?

   (A) Sentence 3
   (B) Sentence 4
   (C) Sentence 8
   (D) Sentence 9
   (E) Sentence 11

DRILLS ANSWERS

Section 1		Section 2		Section 3		Section 4		Section 5			
1.	B	1.	C	25.	B	21.	A	1.	C	28.	E
2.	E	2.	A	26.	C	22.	E	2.	E	29.	B
3.	E	3.	B	27.	C	23.	C	3.	B	30.	B
4.	C	4.	E	28.	E	24.	E	4.	B	31.	E
5.	E	5.	C	29.	C	25.	E	5.	D	32.	A
6.	A	6.	A	30.	B	26.	B	6.	B	33.	C
7.	A	7.	B	31.	D	27.	A	7.	E	34.	D
8.	C	8.	C	32.	A	28.	D	8.	C	35.	B
9.	E	9.	D	33.	C	29.	4	9.	B	36.	B
10.	D	10.	D	34.	D	30.	40	10.	E	37.	A
11.	C	11.	A	35.	D	31.	105	11.	E	38.	E
12.	C	12.	D	36.	A	32.	15	12.	C	39.	E
13.	A	13.	E	37.	A	33.	20	13.	A		
14.	C	14.	E	38.	B	34.	13	14.	D		
15.	E	15.	A	39.	C	35.	$\dfrac{4}{5}$	15.	D		
16.	E	16.	D	40.	D	36.	$0 < n$	16.	B		
17.	D	17.	C	41.	E		< 1	17.	D		
18.	A	18.	C	42.	D	37.	187	18.	D		
19.	A	19.	B	43.	C	38.	$\dfrac{5}{27}$ or	19.	C		
20.	C	20.	E	44.	D			20.	D		
21.	B			45.	C		0.185	21.	C		
22.	E			46.	E			22.	D		
23.	B			47.	B			23.	C		
24.	E			48.	E			24.	B		
								25.	A		
								26.	B		
								27.	C		

You will find a detailed explanation for each question beginning on page 115.

Chapter 6
Drills: Answers and Explanations

Section 1

1. **B**   The sentence tells you the semester had been *challenging and stressful*, which would be a negative thing. *Since* is a change direction trigger, so you know the missing word will have something to do with the students getting a break from the school. Choice (B) makes the most sense.

2. **E**   Start with the second blank. Because Henry got a position *as a starter on the varsity team*, you know he's a good athlete. If his teammates are *second-string and jealous of his success*, we know they aren't as good as Henry. You can easily eliminate choice (B). Now that you know the teammates are *jealous*, go back to the first blank. The missing word must have something to do with them being jealous. *Envy* means *a feeling of discontent with another's advantage*, so choice (E) is the best answer.

3. **E**   The sentence tells you that Einstein is *one of the most famous scientists in the world*, so his winning the Nobel Prize would only increase that fame. The first blank must mean something like *increase or earn*, so you can eliminate choices (B), (C), and (D). Continuing with those same clues, the second blank must mean something like *fame* or *attention*. Between choices (A) and (E), choice (E) is the best answer.

4. **C**   The sentence gives you examples of the *black mamba snake's lethality*, so the missing word must mean something about being poisonous. *Virulent* means *venomous hostility*, so choice (C) is the best answer.

5. **E**   Because the reviewer *denounced* the acting, you know the missing word will be negative. The colon is a same direction trigger, so what follows gives you more information about the missing word. The actress's style is *flat* and *tedious*. Since *monotonous* means *lacking in variety or tediously unwavering*, choice (E) is definitely the best answer.

6. **A**   The definition of the missing word is included in this sentence: *speaking at inordinate length to obstruct a legislative assembly*. Choice (A), *filibustering*, is the word that matches that definition, so it is the correct answer.

7. **A**   Do the first blank first. A *wide-reaching enterprise* with a *monopoly on a market* is likely to drive up prices and take advantage of consumers. You can eliminate choices (D) and (E). In order to avoid the monopoly, it's necessary to have other businesses, or *competition*, in the market. Therefore, choice (A) is the best answer.

8. **C**   Do the second blank first. Because the first part of the sentence tells you that a *vast majority… are advantageous*, the blank that refers to *the preponderance* must also mean *advantageous*. Choices (B) and (D) can easily be eliminated. Then go back to the first blank. If you are trying to distinguish *pathogens* from bacteria that are advantageous, the first blank must be a negative word. The pathogens are not *helping the host (allies)*, nor are they *indicating the future (portent)*, so you can also eliminate choices (A) and (E). Choice (C) is the right answer.

9. **E** Both Locke and Hebb agree that environmental factors are important to human development. However, Locke believes that the environmental factors are the *only* influence, so you can eliminate choices (B) and (D). Hebb never mentions anything about *tabula rasa,* so you can eliminate choice (A). Neither mentions *government regulations* at all, so that one can also be eliminate, leaving you with choice (E), the right answer.

10. **D** Hebb uses the analogy to explain how the two ideas are *so tightly knitted, it's impossible to say which determines an individual's characteristics.* Be careful about choice (C). It looks good at first, but the question is asking about *nature* specifically, not the general meaning of the analogy. Choice (D) is the right answer.

11. **C** Locke felt that experience was the only way humans learn and develop. He said that we are born *blank slates* and that *our experiences must "write" who we are on our minds.* There are no innate characteristics. Choice (C) is the best answer.

12. **C** Passage 1 is a theory from a *seventeenth-century philosopher* and Passage 2 is the viewpoint of a *twentieth-century psychologist.* Eliminate choice (B), because the Passage 1 is not the *modern assumption.* Choice (D) is also wrong, because only one perspective is presented in Passage 1. There is no problem/solution, so also eliminate choice (E). Choice (C) is the right answer.

13. **A** Although the first few paragraphs detail Toomer's importance during the Harlem Renaissance, the end of the passage states that *Toomer's early literary output can be more thoroughly understood than his later personal life.* Choices (B) and (C) are disproven in the first paragraph, and choice (E) is disproven in the fourth paragraph. Choice (D) is also slightly off: it cannot be said that Toomer's essays were inconsistent, only that there were so few of them.

14. **C** Because these two paragraphs are particularly about Jean Toomer, choices (A) and (E) can be eliminated. Both paragraphs are concerned with how other artists and thinkers thought of Toomer, however, so the best answer must be (C).

15. **E** Because Braithwaite's review of *Cane* is so glowing, his praise can be described as *total* or *complete,* as in choice (E). All other choices provide alternate meanings of the word "unreserved," but they do not work in this context.

16. **E** The first paragraph states, *Toomer gained huge accolades from the white literary world as well, and well-known authors such as Sherwood Anderson and Waldo Frank considered him one of their own.* In this context, Sherwood Anderson and Waldo Frank are used as representatives of the *white literary world,* lending support to choice (E). Choice (A) cannot work because there is no indication that Toomer was courting this white readership, particularly not with any *urgency.*

17. **D** The sentence in question is the topic sentence of the second paragraph. It introduces the ideas that are to come. The paragraph goes on to say that Toomer *could incorporate influences from white as well as black artists, and he melded them into a new, innovative style that mixed poetry, prose, jazz, folklore, and spiritualism.* As in choice (D), these are aspects of Toomer's art that showed black and white artists alike a new *artistic freedom.*

18. **A** The sentence that directly precedes "These scraps" is as follows: *Toomer himself may not have thought of these marriages as interracial: particularly by the 1940s, Toomer insisted that his race was "American" and by the end of his life, he may have even identified as a white man.* The repetition of the word *may* shows the author's uncertainty as to Toomer's exact attitudes. "These scraps" must then refer to the scant biographical evidence that literary historians have in piecing together Toomer's later life, as suggested by choice (A).

19. **A** The fourth paragraph discusses the increase in *race activism*, though it says of Toomer, *By then, and until his death in 1967, Toomer was much more taken with local issues, and his main concern was with his church, the Friend's Society of Quakers, and the high school students whom he taught there.* In other words, Toomer was not as interested in race activism as were many of his African American contemporaries. In this sense, his views were atypical, as suggested by choice (A). Choice (E) offers a similar answer, but it is too extreme and is disproven by the quotation in the following paragraph. It was not that he had *no* interest in contemporary race relations but more that his interest was different.

20. **C** Pay careful attention to the sentence that contains the word in question: *By then, and until his death in 1967, Toomer was much more taken with local issues, and his main concern was with his church, the Friend's Society of Quakers, and the high school students whom he taught there.* "Taken with" in this context means "occupied with" or "interested in," and as the sentence then states, Toomer was much more interested in smaller, local problems than in national race problems.

21. **B** The topic sentence of this paragraph reads as follows: *If Toomer's early literary output can be more thoroughly understood than his later personal life, or his later racial identification, it can only be because Toomer himself wanted it to be so.* This sentence suggests that the paragraph itself will discuss Toomer's own attitudes, eliminating choices (A) and (D). We learn in earlier paragraphs that Toomer did not have a typical "commitment to racial equality," eliminating choice (E), and he did not contradict himself in public and private, eliminating choice (C). Only choice (B) reflects the actual content of the paragraph.

22. **E** As the quotation from Toomer demonstrates, he saw race as a more complex thing than mere black and white. We can deduce, then, that he would've found the contemporary debates far too simple, as choice (E) suggests. His own views were "racially complex," but "black and white" refers to the contemporary debates in which Toomer was not a participant, eliminating choice (C). We may consider his views "socially progressive," but the passage does not state that they are, so choice (B) must also be eliminated.

23.   **B**   The sentence before the one cited in the question reads as follows: *Because Toomer was such a truly great artist, literary historians will always long for more information about his life.* In other words, *literary historians would like more information about his life.* Among the answer choices, choice (B) would best supply this information.

24.   **E**   The full sentence in question reads as follows: *We should be wary of the rigid categories that Toomer fought against all his life, and if anything, perhaps Toomer's refusal to fit into these categories can help us to modify our own.* This sentence is a reference to our own contemporary views on race, which, the sentence suggests, Toomer might be able to help us *modify*, as paraphrased in choice (E). Although we may consider his views *more advanced*, the passage does not refer to them in this way, eliminating choice (D).

Section 3

25.   **B**   The sentence tells you that the *holiday travelers are arguing impatiently.* You have the change direction trigger of *unlike,* so you know the missing word must mean the opposite of that. Additionally, you know that Francisco was *quietly waiting. Tranquil* means *peaceful, calm, or quiet,* so choice (B) is the best answer.

26.   **C**   Do the first blank first. If there are *unique markings in a coded message,* a cryptologist would be able to *solve* or *decode* the message. Eliminate choices (B) and (E). The *but* is a change direction trigger, so if the cryptologist is able to decode the message, then the missing word would mean *not able to decode.* Eliminate choices (A) and (D), leaving choice (C) as the best answer.

27.   **C**   *The health department* is unleashing *massive efforts to annihilate,* which would make it seem like the department is stopping the pandemic. However, the *in spite of* trigger lets you know the word will actually be the opposite of that, so choice (C) is the best answer.

28.   **E**   Do the first blank first. The *diverse Scottish clans* are represented by a *vast number of tartan cloths,* so the missing word must mean *large number.* Eliminate choices (B) and (C). The second blank refers to the connection between the tartans and the clans themselves. It wouldn't make sense that the official tartans would represent a clan *transmission,* so eliminate choice (A). *Textile* looks like a good option since a tartan is a cloth, but the tartan *is* the cloth, not a representation of the cloth, so you can also eliminate choice (D). Choice (E) is the best answer.

29.   **C**   If the foods are *instantly nauseating,* they will be *disgusting* or *revolting.* Choice (C) is the best answer.

30.   **B**   Although there is an analogy in the passage connecting the immune system with the structure of law enforcement, that analogy is used to explain the parts of the immune system. The primary purpose of the passage is to describe that system. Choice (A) can be eliminated because the passage isn't discussing good health—it's simply discussing the parts of the immune system. For that same

reason, choice (C) can also be eliminated. Choice (D) is irrelevant, loosely tied to the law enforcement analogy, but just barely. Choice (E) connects back to the analogy, but it's not the primary purpose of the passage. Choice (B) is the best answer.

31. **D** The passage compares the immune system to a law enforcement structure, and then continues to make similar connections on a more granular level. This is an extended analogy, making choice (D) the best answer.

32. **A** The description of the style begins with *always be honest* and then continues with *even if* statements. This lets you know that the most important thing is the honesty. Although profits, assessments, and promises are all mentioned in the passage, it's the honesty that is the most important quality. Choice (A) is the best answer.

33. **C** At the end of the passage, Kerrigan says *you will lose them when they find you haven't been honest*. The honesty may or may not result in large payoffs, validated work, or word-of-mouth business, but the passage clearly makes the connection between honesty and solid client relationships. Choice (C) is the best answer.

34. **D** Antoine of Passage 1 does not approve of the new announcer, so his comparison of the announcer's voice to a hockey puck is unfavorable, eliminating choice (B). He is commenting on one specific announcer, which eliminates choice (C). Only choice (D) effectively captures Antoine's disapproving attitude.

35. **D** The line in Passage 1 offers Antoine's critique of the new announcer. Antoine's preferred announcer, Pierre, is *even-toned, almost dull*. The author of Passage 2 likes similar announcers, those whose announcing can be characterized by *dispassionate action*. Therefore, the author of Passage 2 would likely find Antoine's critique "agreeable," as suggested by choice (D). Choices (A), (B), and (E) should be eliminated because they take the simile from Passage 1 too literally.

36. **A** The author of Passage 1 describes two different announcers, Pierre and Jack/Jimmy. Pierre is the type of announcer described in the quoted lines from Passage 2. Jack/Jimmy, however, is not characterized by this kind of even-tempered commentary. Instead, *the timbre of his voice flew around as erratically as the puck itself*, and Jack/Jimmy's voice is described as *too-perfect*. Although there is some indication in Passage 1 that new announcers tend to be more animated, there is no such indication in Passage 2, which eliminates choice (C). Furthermore, although Antoine does not like the new hockey announcer, his general attitude cannot be described as "unnecessarily pessimistic," because it is not general enough to be so, which eliminates choice (E).

37. **A** Passage 2 draws an analogy between good hockey announcers and good parents and teachers. He stresses their ability to educate *in the face of anything or anyone, whether punishingly dull or wildly exciting*. He goes on to say, *All of them let you know that, rain or shine, at least someone is keeping it together*. The last sentence, particularly, indicates someone who is firm and not overtaken by emotional over-statements, as suggested in choice (A). Although part of choice (E), "educating," could work, there is no indication that all "dispassionate action" is dull, only that it can be when necessary.

38.   **B**   Antoine's preferred announcer, Pierre, is *even-toned, almost dull*. The author of Passage 2 likes similar announcers, those whose announcing can be characterized by *dispassionate action*. Therefore, Pierre could be a "good representative" of a certain type of hockey announcer, as suggested by choice (B). Although Pierre has been replaced, there is no indication, particularly not in Passage 2, that such a type of announcer would be "unaware" of the new type of announcer, which eliminates choice (E).

39.   **C**   The author of Passage 2 has a positive attitude toward Dan Schantz, so choices (A), (D), and (E) can be eliminated. Choice (B), however, is too extreme an expression of a positive attitude. Choice (C) is milder and more in keeping with the tone of the essay, so it is the best choice.

40.   **D**   The phrase *to spin yarns* appears in the first sentence, and it is reiterated in the later sentences in the paragraph, which refer to *some kind of narrative* and our minds wanting *stories*. While choices (A), (B), and (E) offer alternate meanings of the word *yarns*, only choice (D) works in this context.

41.   **E**   The metaphor of connecting dots appears in this context: *We want any nearby dots to be connected. Effect with no cause, correlation with no causation: we can't assimilate these ideas because they don't have that narrative structure.* In other words, even if these *dots* aren't connected, our minds want them to be and thus connect them, as choice (E) suggests. Although the connections may not exist in the real world, the passage does not imply that the details themselves do not exist, thus eliminating choice (C).

42.   **D**   The full sentence reads as follows: *Our minds want stories, even if those stories need to be twisted and mangled into existence.* In other words, we can have a difficult time creating stories, but we have the need nonetheless, as choice (D) suggests. The author does not reflect on whether this is a good or bad trait, thus eliminating choices (A) and (E). The discussion of history does not come until later in the passage, thus eliminating choice (B).

43.   **C**   The phrase appears in this context: *Historians and onlookers alike have spent over a century debating the causes, the effects, and the place of this event in the ongoing plot of American history. Neuroscientists have referred to a "need for narrative."* The passage as a whole is about narrative, and the word *plot* relates to narratives, suggesting that the history of the American Civil War is another one of these narratives, full of related events, as choice (C) indicates. Choice (B) cannot work because the *plot* referred to here is not that of a *mystery*, nor are any historical mysteries discussed. The author does not refer to this need for narrative as a special *talent*, thus eliminating choice (D).

44.   **D**   The first two paragraphs discuss the *need for narrative* in a general way, even citing the findings of neuroscientists and the work of historians. The third and fourth paragraphs focus more specifically on *personality*, which can be explained with a specific application of the general theory of the need for narrative. Choice (D) best captures this transition. The latter half does discuss literary texts, but not exclusively, and the first half is focused on much more than *historical* events, so choice (A) can be eliminated. Choice (C) cannot work because the "need for narrative" is ultimately a psychological concept that is discussed throughout the passage, and it is not critiqued.

45. C The early twentieth century is discussed in these lines: *In the early twentieth century, the very notion of "consistent" stories broke down, and characters became less rigidly defined as a result. Suddenly, amid a cultural shift away from religious certainty, one's environment, one's historical era, one's family history could all come to bear on the maze of human personality.* In other words, this era was characterized by complexity rather than simplicity, so any discussion of personality must be more complex than the titles in choices (A), (B), and (E). Choice (D) is off-topic. Only choice (C) adequately captures the complexity described in the passage.

46. E This shift *away from religious certainty* is discussed in these lines: *In the early twentieth century, the very notion of "consistent" stories broke down, and characters became less rigidly defined as a result. Suddenly, amid a cultural shift away from religious certainty, one's environment, one's historical era, one's family history could all come to bear on the maze of human personality.* In other words, personality had become a newly complex object with many things influencing it, as choice (E) suggests. Choice (A) cannot work because understandings of personality have not been consistent throughout history. Choice (D) does not work because there is no evidence in the passage that non-psychologists critique the theories of psychologists.

47. B The word *contain* appears in this sentence: *Psychologists began to spend entire careers studying human personalities, but for all these changes, the goal was still the same: contain the human experience, find the story that can encapsulate all of human complexity.* Use the second part of the sentence as a clue. The word *contain* must mean something like *find the story that can encapsulate*, and the closest approximation from this list of answer choices is choice (B). The other choices offer synonyms for the word *contain*, but they do not work in this particular context.

48. E The last sentence of a passage will typically offer some kind of summary of a passage, and this sentence does just that. The passage as a whole discusses the *need for narrative* in many aspects of life, including how we understand ourselves. The last sentence asks, rhetorically, *Because after all that has come before us, and all that will come later, if we're not part of the big story, what are we?* Choice (E) captures this basic idea well in suggesting that without *the big story,* our lives would be different. Although the last sentence does look to the future a bit, it does not make any claims about the stories that people in the future will tell themselves, thus eliminating choice (C). Also, while there are some implied comparisons between the "narrative" of history and that of fiction, these comparisons are not addressed in this final sentence, eliminating choice (D).

Section 2

1. C When asked for the value of a variable, Plug In the Answers (PITA). Starting with the least value, see if each answer is divisible by 2, 4, and 5. 8 is divisible by 2 and 4 but not by 5, so (A) can be eliminated. 10 is divisible by 2 and 5 but not by 4, so (B) can be eliminated. 20 is divisible by 2, 4 and 5, and it is the least number left on the list. Although 40 is also divisible by 2, 4, and 5, it is greater than 20, so (D) can be eliminated. Choice (C) is the credited response.

2. **A** The angle in the upper right of the triangle is opposite the 45° angle, so it is also 45°. A triangle has 180°, so $85 + 45 + z = 180$. Therefore, $130 + z = 180$, so $z = 50$. Choice (A) is the credited response.

3. **B** There are 45 books on the shelf, of which $\frac{1}{5}$ are biographies. $\frac{1}{5}(45) = 9$ biographies. 3 are <u>not</u> about women, and $9 - 3 = 6$, so 6 <u>are</u> about women. Choice (B) is the credited response.

4. **E** If $t^2 = 16$, take the square root of both sides to get $t = 4$. The value of t could also be -4, but the question states that t is positive. Now, plug $t = 4$ into the equation $(t - 1)^2$, which is $(4 - 1)^2 = (3)^2 = 9$. Choice (E) is the credited response.

5. **C** Translate the English into math. If $a + 3a < 5b + (-b)$, then $4a < 4b$. Divide both sides by 4, so $a < b$, and (C) is the credited response. Plugging in numbers for a and b would also work, as long as the sum of a and $3a$ is less than the sum of $5b$ and $-b$. Try $a = 2$ and $b = 3$. $a + 3a = 2 + 6 = 8$. $5b + (-b) = 15 + (-3) = 12$. $8 < 12$, which fits the requirement in the question. Therefore, (A), (B), (D), and (E) can be eliminated.

6. **A** For average problems, draw an average pie. Set A has 3 numbers and an average of 4. Put those numbers in the lower left and lower right spots, respectively, as shown below. To get the total, multiply 3 by 4, which is 12.

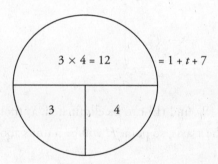

Therefore, $1 + t + 7 = 12$, $t + 8 = 12$, and $t = 4$. Now, plug $t = 4$ into set B. The total of set B is $2 + 4 + 6 = 12$. Draw another average pie, filling in the total and the number of things.

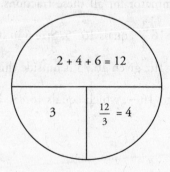

Total ÷ number of things = average, so $12 ÷ 3 = 4$. Therefore, choice (A) is the credited response.

7.   **B**   When the question asks for a specific value, use PITA. For choice (C), $p = 6$. $\sqrt{6^2 + 55} = \sqrt{36 + 55}$ $= \sqrt{91} = 9.54$. This value is more than the 9 in the equation, so (C) can be eliminated. Choices (D) and (E) are even larger than 6 and will yield answers larger than 9.54, so (D) and (E) can be eliminated as well. For choice (B), $p = 5$. $\sqrt{5^2 + 55} = \sqrt{25 + 55} = \sqrt{80} = 8.94$. This is very close to 9, so (B) is the credited response.

8.   **C**   For coordinate geometry questions, start with a sketch of the given information. Now, sketch in the location of point H. It will be above point G, with a negative x-coordinate and a positive y-coordinate, as shown below.

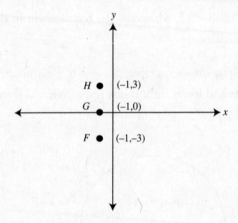

Based on the sketch, (A), (B), and (E) can be eliminated, as those are not in the correct quadrant. Point F is 3 units below the x-axis, so point H will be 3 units above the x-axis. Therefore, (C) is the credited response.

9.   **D**   The chart contains a lot of numbers with weird fractions, so start by ballparking. If the women's ring diameter is $16\frac{3}{4}$, it is larger than $16\frac{1}{2}$, so (A) and (B) can be eliminated. Now, rather than try to find a common denominator for all these fractions, convert each remaining number into decimals. The given value of $16\frac{3}{4}$ equals 16.75. Size 6 in (C) goes from $16\frac{1}{2}$, which equals 16.5, to $16\frac{2}{3}$, which equals 16.67. The given 16.75 is outside this range, so (C) can be eliminated. Size $6\frac{1}{2}$ in (D) goes from 16.67 to $16\frac{5}{6}$, which equals 16.83. The given 16.75 is in this range, so (D) is the credited response.

10. **D** With variables in the question, the best approach is to Plug In. PITA would mean a lot of algebraic manipulation to solve the equation for x. To answer this question, it is easier to plug in integer values of x. If $x = 1$, $y = \dfrac{1-1}{1} = \dfrac{0}{1} = 0$. This is not one of the fractions in the answer choices, so try the next integer value for x. If $x = 2$, $y = \dfrac{2-1}{2} = \dfrac{1}{2}$. This is also not one of the fractions in the answer choices, so keep going until one works. If $x = 3$, $y = \dfrac{3-1}{3} = \dfrac{2}{3}$. If $x = 4$, $y = \dfrac{4-1}{4} = \dfrac{3}{4}$. If $x = 4$, $y = \dfrac{5-1}{5} = \dfrac{4}{5}$. This is the value in (D), making (D) the credited response.

11. **A** When given ranges for variables but not actual values, plug in some numbers. If $p = 5$ and $q = 11$, $p + q = 5 + 11 = 16$, which is less than 18. Since case I is true for these numbers, it cannot be eliminated at this point. $q - p = 11 - 5 = 6$, which is not less than 6. Therefore, case II is false, and (B) and (D) can be eliminated. $2p = 2(5) = 10$, which is not equal to 11. Therefore, case III is false, and (C) and (E) can be eliminated. Choice (A) is the credited response.

12. **D** If line a is parallel to line b, then the big angle created by the intersection of lines b and d will be equal to $r°$, which equals 140°. There are 180° in a line, so the big angle and the small angle formed by this intersection must add up to 180°. Thus, the angle in the lower left of the triangle equals 40°, since $180 - 140 = 40$. There are 180° in a triangle, so $40 + 90 + s = 180$. Therefore, s equals 50°, and (D) is the credited response.

13. **E** This question seems like a good candidate for PITA, since it is asking for a specific value. However, the total is based on three different kinds of blocks, the numbers for which are based on other quantities. Therefore, start plugging in different values for the number of red blocks. If there is only 1 red block, there will be 4 yellow blocks, as the number of yellow is 3 more than the number of red. There are 2 times as many blue as yellow blocks, so there will be 8 blue blocks. The total number of blocks equals $1 + 4 + 8 = 13$. This is the smallest possible total, so (A) and (B) can be eliminated, since they are less than 13. If there are 2 red blocks, there will be 5 yellow blocks and 10 blue blocks. The total number of blocks equals $2 + 5 + 10 = 17$, so (E) is the credited response.

14. **E** For multiple functions, plug the x-value given into the correct function. For this problem, that means $k(4) = (j(4))^3$. Now, bring in the other function, plugging in the same x-value, to get $k(4) = (j(4))^3 = \left(\sqrt{4} + 1\right)^3$. This equals $(2 + 1)^3 = 3^3$, so $k(4) = 27$ and (E) is the credited response.

15.   **A**   The chart indicates that 20 percent of the businesses in town are clothing stores, and the question states that there are 100 clothing stores. Use this information to calculate the total number of businesses in town. $100 = \frac{20}{100} \times \text{Total}$. Solve this equation for the total by multiplying both sides by $\frac{100}{20}$, yielding a total of 500 businesses. Now use this total to calculate the number of bookstores and jewelry stores. For bookstores, the number equals $\frac{7}{100} \times 500 = 35$. For jewelry stores, the number equals $\frac{5}{100} \times 500 = 25$. The difference between the two numbers is 10, so (A) is the credited response.

16.   **D**   With variables in the answer choices, Plug In. If $m = 3$ and $n = 5$, point A is at (3, 10) and point B is at (6, 20). The slope can be found with any two points, and the slope formula is $\frac{y_2 - y_1}{x_2 - x_1}$. The slope of this line is $\frac{20 - 10}{6 - 3}$ or $\frac{10}{3}$. Plug m and n into the given in the answer choices to see which one has a slope equal to $\frac{10}{3}$. Choice (A) is $y = \frac{3}{5}x$, which has the wrong slope, so it can be eliminated. Choice (B) is $y = \frac{5}{3}x$, so it can be eliminated. Choice (C) is $y = \frac{3}{5}x + 3$ and can be eliminated. Choice (D) is $y = \frac{10}{3}x$ and (E) is $y = \frac{10}{3}x + 5$. A quick sketch of the two points and the line containing them will show that it goes through the origin. Therefore, there should be no y-intercept and the credited response is (D). Another option would be to plug one of the points, such as (3, 10), into the two remaining equations. Choice (D) becomes $10 = \frac{10}{3}(3)$, which is true and the credited response. Choice (E) becomes $10 = \frac{10}{3}(3) + 5$, which is false, so (E) can be eliminated.

17.   **C**   This is a logic question, so check each statement to determine if it is necessarily true about the shoes. Case I states that if a shoe is not black, then it is not a boot. The question only stated that boots were all black, but there could be other black shoes, such as sandals or sneakers. Therefore, I is not necessarily true, so (A) and (D) can be eliminated. Case II has the same problem – other types of shoes could also be black. Therefore, (B) and (E) can be eliminated. Only case III is true, so (C) is the credited response.

18.   **C**   The volume of a cylinder is the product of the area of the circular bottom, $A = \pi r^2$, and the height, h, so $V = \pi r^2 h$. Given the variable d for the diameter of one ball, plug in a number for d, such as $d = 4$. Therefore, the radius of the cylinder is 2. The height is made up of three balls, or $3d$, so the height is 12. Plug these values into the formula for volume, which yields $\pi(2^2)(12) = 48\pi$, the

target number. Now plug $d = 4$ into the answer choices to see which is equal to the target number. Choice (A) is 16π, which is not equal to 48π, so (A) can be eliminated. Choice (B) is $2\pi(16)$ or 32π and can also be eliminated. Choice (C) is $\frac{3}{4}\pi(64)$ or 48π, which is the target answer. Check out (D) and (E) to make sure they can be eliminated. Choice (D) is 64π and (E) is $3\pi(64)$ or 192π. Both of these can be eliminated, so (C) is the credited response.

19. **B**   The best way to tackle this problem is to just start listing out numbers that fit the requirements, since the greatest possible number of choices from the answers is 24. It is important to be systematic, though, so no numbers that work are left off the list. For the hundreds place, the number must be a 7, and the tens place must be a 1. The last digit must be a prime number, so it could be 2, 3, 5, or 7. There must be at least one 2 in the number, so start by assuming that the last digit is 2.

Since there is now a 2 in the 4-digit number, the first digit can be any number 1 through 9. The 4-digit numbers that fit the requirements in this scenario are 1,712; 3,712; 4,712; 5,712; 6,712; 7,712; 8,712; and 9,712.

If the last digit was not a 2, then the first digit must be a 2. Since there is now a 2 in the 4-digit number, the last digit can be any of the three remaining prime numbers – 3, 5, or 7. The 4-digit numbers that fit the requirements in this scenario are 2,713; 2,715; and 2,717. With 8 options in the first scenario and 3 options in the second, there are 11 total possible numbers, so (B) is the credited response.

20. **E**   Given a geometry problem with no figure, draw one. The question states that side $\overline{TU}$ is shorter than the other two sides. So draw an isosceles triangle with a base slightly shorter than the two equal legs, as shown below.

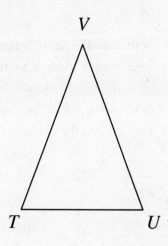

Now, with a picture for reference, it is time to PITA. Choice (C) gives a measure of 50° for $\angle T$. This will also be the measure for $\angle U$, since isosceles triangles have two equal angles. There are 180° in a triangle, so there are 80° left for $\angle V$. This makes $\angle V$ larger than the other two angles, so side $\overline{TU}$ would be longer than the other two sides. Therefore, (C) can be eliminated. Since $\angle V$ needs to be smaller, $\angle T$ and $\angle U$ need to be larger, so (A) and (B) can also be eliminated. Choice (D) makes $\angle T$ equal to 60°, so $\angle U$ equals 60°, and there are 60° left for $\angle V$. The sides are all equal now, so $\overline{TU}$ still is not shorter than the other sides. Choice (D) can be eliminated, and (E) is the credited response.

Section 4

21.   A   In the first equation, subtract 3 from both sides to find that $p = 9$. Plug in 9 for p in the second equation: $9 - q = 5$. Subtract 9 from both sides of the equation, then divide by –1 to find that $q = 4$. The credited response is (A).

22.   E   First, list out the numbers in each set. For sets A and B, only list up to the highest answer choice, in this case 18. Set $A = \{2, 4, 6, 8, 10, 12, 14, 16, 18, ...\}$. Set $B = \{9, 18, ...\}$. Set $C = \{1, 2, 3, 4, 5, 6, 10, 12, 15, 20, 30, 60\}$. Now check the answers to see which number is a member of both sets A and B, but not of set C. 6 is in all three sets, so eliminate (A). 9 is only in set B, so eliminate (B). 12 is in sets A and C, but not in set B, so eliminate (C). 15 is only in set C, so eliminate (D). 18 is in both sets A and B but not in set C, so the credited response is (E).

23.   C   Make sure to read the labels on the axis of the chart. Draw a vertical line at the 25 minute mark, then draw a horizontal line at the 400 calories mark. Count the number of dots that are above and to the right of where those two lines meet. There are four dots. The credited response is (C).

24.   E   Start by drawing the point (3, 8). Then draw line p perpendicular to line m through point (3, 8). Use your eye to determine where the lines intersect. All the points on line m have a y value of 5 and all the points on line p have an x value of 3. The lines will cross at point (3, 5). The credited response is (E).

25.   E   Geometry basics: Draw, Label, Formulas. The figure is drawn already. The triangle is equilateral so all of the sides are the same. Since the perimeter is 54, divide that by three to find the sides of the triangle are 18. Label the sides in the figure. To find circumference of the circle, write the circumference formula: $C = \pi d$. Notice that the side of the triangle is the diameter of the circle, so the diameter of the circle is also 18. Put that into the formula: $C = 18\pi$. The credited response is (E).

26. **B** "What is the value" with numbers in the answers…PITA! Normally you should start with choice (C) because it's in the middle, but it's an ugly number. It will be easier to start with (B) because it's a whole number. The question asks for x so start with choice (B) and plug in -1 for x. If $x = -1$ then each tick mark is $\frac{1}{3}$, which makes $y = \frac{2}{3}$ and $z = \frac{4}{3}$. Plug y and z into the equation to check. $\frac{2}{3} + \frac{4}{3} = \frac{6}{3} = 2$, which matches the question. The credited response is (B).

27. **A** Variables in the question and the answer choices: Plug In! Remember that t is in <u>years</u> and that the number of hit records doubles every <u>6 months</u>. Let's plug in 3 for t, which means that the number of hit records will double 6 times. Starting with 1 hit record, it doubles to 2 (6 months), then doubles to 4 (one year), then doubles to 8 (1 year 6 months), then doubles to 16 (2 years), then doubles to 32 (2 years 6 months), then doubles to 64 (3 years). So when $t = 3$, the target is 64. Plug 3 into each of the answer choices. Choice (A) is $2^{2\times3} = 2^6 = 64$, which matches the target. Remember to check all of the answers to be safe. The credited response is (A).

28. **D** Since the parabola is symmetrical across the line $x = -1\frac{1}{3}$, the x-intercepts are equidistant from the point $\left(-1\frac{1}{3}, 0\right)$. First find the distance from $\left(-1\frac{1}{3}, 0\right)$ to $(-5, 0)$ by subtracting the x-coordinates: $-1\frac{1}{3} - (-5) = \frac{-4}{3} + \frac{15}{3} = \frac{11}{3}$. The other x-coordinate is the same distance from $\left(-1\frac{1}{3}, 0\right)$, so add $\frac{11}{3}$ to find the other x-coordinate: $\frac{11}{3} + \left(-1\frac{1}{3}\right) = \frac{11}{3} - \frac{4}{3} = \frac{7}{3} = 2\frac{1}{3}$. The other x-intercept is $\left(2\frac{1}{3}, 0\right)$, so $m = 2\frac{1}{3}$. The credited response is (D).

29. **4** Since each term is three times the previous term, $y \times 3 = 36$ and, thus, $y = 12$. Then, $x \times 3 = 12$, and, thus, $x = 4$.

30. **40** It's safest to use the calculator on this question. Make sure to either do it in small steps and correct order of operations (PEMDAS) or be careful when typing the parentheses. To solve, plug in 15 for m in the equation: $P(m) = 125{,}000\left(\frac{1}{5}\right)^{\frac{15}{3}} = 125{,}000\left(\frac{1}{5}\right)^{5} = 125{,}000\left(\frac{1}{3{,}125}\right) = 40$.

31. **105** All the angles in a square are 90°. Since the small angle at point C is 15°, the large angle above it must be $90 - 15 = 75$. All straight lines have 180°, so $75 + y = 180$. Subtract 75 from both sides of the equation to find that $y = 105$.

32. **15** Recognize that the problem gives a relationship and a total value. Set up the ratio box. The actual total number of marbles is 40, so write that in the bottom right box. Probability is a "part to whole" relationship; on the Ratio row, write 5 for red and 8 for total.

	Red	Blue	Total
Ratio	5		8
Multiplier			
Actual			40

The Ratio row adds across, so write 3 for blue. Find that the multiplier from 8 to 40 is 5, which is the same multiplier for everything. Multiply to find that there are 25 red marbles and 15 blue marbles. The question asked for blue, so the answer is 15.

	Red	Blue	Total
Ratio	5	3	8
Multiplier	5	5	5
Actual	25	15	40

33. **20** Geometry basics: Draw, Label, Formulas. There's no figure, so draw the two triangles. Then write the area formula: $A = \frac{1}{2}bh$. The problem provides the area but neither the base nor height, so Plug In! For triangle A write $120 = \frac{1}{2}bh$, so $bh = 240$. Plug in numbers that work, such as $b = 12$ and $h = 20$. Since the base of triangle A is three times that of triangle B, divide the base of triangle A by 3 to get $\frac{12}{3} = 4$. Since the height of triangle A is two times that of triangle B, divide the height of triangle A by 2 to get $\frac{20}{2} = 10$. Now use the area formula again with the numbers of triangle B to find $A = \frac{1}{2}bh = \frac{1}{2}(4)(10) = 20$.

34. **13** Translate the English to Math. First translate "Sue and David together own 57 hamsters" to "$s + d = 57$". "David owns" translates to "$d =$", "5 more than" translates to "5 +", and "3 times the number of hamsters that Sue owns" translates to "$3 \times s$". Put it together to get $d = 5 + 3s$. Now substitute $5 + 3s$ for d in the first equation to get $s + (5 + 3s) = 57$. Simplify and solve: $4s + 5 = 57$, then $4s = 52$, then $s = 13$. Sue owns 13 hamsters.

35. $\frac{4}{5}$ Definition: "bisects" means "cuts in half." Since there are no numbers given, Plug In! Starting with the first given angle, plug in 40 for $\angle COG$. Since $\overline{EO}$ bisects $\angle COG$, both $\angle COE$ and $\angle EOG$ are 20. If $\overline{CO}$ bisects $\angle AOE$ then $\angle AOC$ and $\angle COE$ are equal, so they are both 20. If $\overline{BO}$

bisects $\angle AOC$ then $\angle AOB$ and $\angle BOC$ are equal, so they both equal 10. If $\overline{FO}$ bisects $\angle EOG$ then $\angle EOF$ and $\angle FOG$ are equal, so they both equal 10. Add the angles to find that $\angle COG = 40$ and $\angle AOF = 50$. Therefore $\dfrac{\angle COG}{\angle AOF} = \dfrac{40}{50} = \dfrac{4}{5}$.

36. **$0 < n < 1$**

This question is testing properties of numbers and exponents. Plug In to test what happens to different types of numbers. Try 1 first, because it's easy. The reciprocal of 1 is 1 and $1^2 = 1$. The reciprocal and the square of 1 are equal; neither is greater than the other so 1 is not a possible value. Now try something greater than 1, such as 3. The reciprocal of 3 is $\dfrac{1}{3}$ and $3^2 = 9$. Since $\dfrac{1}{3}$ is not greater than 9, this is not a possible value. Notice that the reciprocal got smaller and the square got bigger than the original number. This will be true for all numbers greater than 1. Now try again with a fraction less than 1, such as $\dfrac{1}{4}$. The reciprocal of $\dfrac{1}{4}$ is 4 and $\left(\dfrac{1}{4}\right)^2 = \dfrac{1}{16}$. Since 4 is greater than $\dfrac{1}{16}$, $\dfrac{1}{4}$ is one possible value. Any fraction between 0 and 1 will work. The reciprocal of a fraction between 0 and 1 will be greater than 1, and the square of a fraction between 0 and 1 will be a smaller fraction.

37. **187** This is a pattern question. Doing the quick calculation will likely lead to a trap answer. Be careful and list out the pattern. There are five pages in each section, so list 1, 2, 3, 4, 5. Then list the page numbers of each section. To save a little time, recognize the pattern. The last page of each section is 5 more than the last page of the previous section, so continue to add 5 until section 7. The last page is 187.

	1	2	3	4	5
Section 1	153	154	155	156	157
Section 2	158	159	160	161	162
Section 3	163	164	165	166	167
Section 4					172
Section 5					177
Section 6					182
Section 7					187

38. $\dfrac{5}{27}$ or 0.185

Variables! Plug In! The easiest numbers to choose are $r = 5$ and $s = 6$. Then plug $s = 6$ into the second equation to get $\dfrac{6}{t} = \dfrac{2}{9}$. Solve to find that $t = 27$. Therefore $\dfrac{r}{t} = \dfrac{5}{27}$.

Section 5

1. **C**   The phrase *An opener for 1999's "Geniuses, Savants, and Prodigies" conference* is a modifying phrase, so whatever comes immediately after the comma must be the person or thing described in the phrase. Since *the piano* did not serve as an opener, the original sentence contains a misplaced modifier. *David Helfgott* was the person who was *an opener,* so his name should appear immediately after the comma. Eliminate both choices (A) and (B). Choices (D) and (E) both place *David Helfgott* immediately after the comma, but because they use the word *who*, they both create incomplete sentences. Only choice (C) correctly fixes the misplaced modifier and does not introduce any new errors.

2. **E**   If you trim the fat and eliminate the descriptive phrase *a flightless dodo bird once native to the island of Mauritius*, you're left with *The dodo bird…that was being discovered in 1958*. The original sentence is incomplete, since the phrase *that was being discovered in 1958* serves as a descriptive phrase and does not contain a main verb. Choices (A), (B), (C), and (D) all repeat the original error since none of them turn the sentence into a complete thought. Only choice (E) fixes the error in the original sentence.

3. **B**   The second half of the sentence needs to modify the first half. As it's currently written, the second half of the sentence does not clearly state what did the initiating, and therefore does not modify the first half of the sentence. Eliminate choice (A). Choice (B) correctly modifies the first half of the sentence, and it contains no additional errors. Choices (C) and (E) both turn the second half of the sentence into complete thoughts. Since the first half of the sentence is also a complete thought, both choices (C) and (E) create comma splices, so eliminate them. Choice (D) is wordy and does not fix the error in the original sentence. The correct answer is (B).

4. **B**   The phrase *Determined to finish the game despite the rain* is a modifying phrase that must describe whatever appears immediately after the comma. Since the football team, and not the football team's fight, was determined, this sentence contains a misplaced modifier. Choices (A) and (E) repeat this error. Choices (C) and (D) also contain misplaced modifiers, since these choices make it seem as though the trophy, not the football team, was determined. Choice (B) fixes the error and does not introduce any new errors, so it is the correct answer.

5. **D** The original sentence uses the word *being*. Whenever possible, avoid choosing answers that use *being*, so eliminate choices (A) and (C). Choice (B) creates a fragment and unnecessarily uses the word *they*. Choice (D) does not use the word *being* and does not introduce any new errors, so choice (D) is the correct answer. Choice (E) removes the verb *are* and replaces it with *as*. Without the main verb, the sentence is incomplete, so choice (E) is not the correct answer.

6. **B** As the sentence is currently written, the phrase a*n awe-inspiring and enormous painting that covers nearly 650 square feet* modifies *Jacques-Luis David*. However, since *The Coronation of Napoleon,* not *David,* is a painting, the sentence contains a misplaced modifier. Choice (E) repeats this error, so you can eliminate choices (A) and (E). Choice (B) fixes the error by adding the verb *is*, so that the second half of the sentence is no longer a modifying phrase. The verb *is* refers back to *The Coronation of Napoleon,* so the intended meaning of the sentence is now clear. This choice does not introduce any new errors, so choice (B) is the correct answer.

7. **E** As the sentence is currently written, the new phone is the subject of the verb *deducting*. However, since the phone is not the person or thing doing the deducting, the sentence is incorrect as written, and you can eliminate choice (A). Choice (C) changes the meaning of the sentence by implying that the cost was somehow a fraction of the deduction, and is therefore incorrect. Choices (B) and (D) both use –ing verbs, whereas choice (E) does not. If possible, you generally want to eliminate –ing verbs, so choice (E) is the best choice.

8. **C** The pronoun *them* does not clearly refer to any other noun in the sentence. Therefore, this sentence contains a pronoun ambiguity error. Choices (A), (B), and (E) repeat the original error, and are therefore incorrect. Choice (C) is much more concise than choice (D), and is therefore the correct answer.

9. **B** This sentence incorrectly *uses was needing* rather than *needed*. Additionally, this sentence contains two complete thoughts joined by a comma, and is therefore a comma splice. Eliminate choice (A). Choice (E) repeats the comma splice error and is also incorrect. Choice (C) uses the modifying phrase *Having gone to the car dealership.* This phrase should modify whatever appears immediately after the comma. However, the word *buying* appears immediately after the comma in this case. Since the word *buying* cannot go anywhere, this choice contains a misplaced modifier. Choice (D) is passive, and incorrectly places the modifying phrase *where she needed to buy a new car* immediately after *Lindsay,* rather than after *car dealership.* Choice (B) fixes both of the errors in the original sentence and does not introduce any new errors, so choice (B) is the correct answer.

10. **E** The pronoun *they* is unnecessary and turns the first half of the sentence into a fragment. Therefore, choice (A) is incorrect. Choice (B) changes the intended meaning of the sentence by making it appear as though the detectives were determined to catch the criminal simply because they wanted to identify the criminal. Choice (D) similarly changes the meaning. In choice (C) the clause *The detectives identified the criminal* is a complete thought, and the clause *they were determined to catch the*

man who stole the jewelry is also a complete thought. Since this choice joins two complete thoughts with a comma, thus creating a comma splice, this choice is incorrect. Choice (E) fixes the error in the original sentence and does not introduce any new errors, so choice (E) is the correct answer.

11. E   The original sentence lists two things that employees want: *more responsibility* and *to increase their monthly earnings.* Since *responsibility* is a noun, and *increase* is a verb, and these two words are in a list, the list is not parallel. Therefore, choice (A) is incorrect. Choice (B) is passive, since the compound subject of the sentence is *more responsibility and an increase,* the verb is *are wanted,* and the employees, who are the people doing the action, are not the subject of the sentence. Choice (C) changes the meaning of the sentence by suggesting that the reason that many employees volunteer to work overtime is that they *want more responsibility.* Choice (C) is therefore incorrect. Choice (D) begins the sentence with *while.* However, this sentence does not contain two contrasting thoughts, and thus should not begin with *while.* Choice (E) fixes the error in the original sentence and does not introduce any new errors, so it is the correct answer.

12. C   The subject of the sentence is *works,* which is plural, and the verb is *ranges,* which is singular. Therefore, this choice has a subject-verb agreement error. Eliminate choice (A). Choices (B) and (E) change the verb to an *-ing* form and turn the sentence into a fragment. Choice (D) adds the word *that,* which would indicate that an additional thought should come after the phrase *that range from Russian ballets to neoclassical compositions and chamber works.* Choice (D) makes the sentence incomplete, and is therefore incorrect. Choice (C) fixes the subject-verb agreement error by making the verb plural, so choice (C) is the correct answer.

13. A   Choice (B) is disjointed and contains the word *being.* Whenever possible, avoid choosing answers that include the word *being.* Eliminate choice (B). Choice (D) also uses *being* and is incorrect. Choice (C) uses an unnecessary *and,* and is therefore a run-on. Choice (E) lists two facts about the authors' works: they are *difficult to comprehend* and *symbolizing obscures...the author's main point.* Since these two items are not in parallel form, this choice contains a parallelism error. Choice (A) correctly joins two complete thoughts with a semicolon and does not contain any additional errors. Choice (A) is the correct answer.

14. D   In the original sentence, *being banned* is an incorrect form of the verb. Remember to avoid the word *being* whenever possible. Eliminate choice (A). Do not use helping verbs such as *should* or *have* with verbs such as *urge* that communicate a wish or a command. Choices (B) and (C) both break this rule, and are therefore incorrect. Choice (E) changes the meaning by using the phrase *for initiating,* thus suggesting that the league suggested the ban for the purpose of initiating the movement. Choice (D) correctly uses the subjunctive voice, stating that the *Anti-Saloon League urged that the sale...be banned.* Choice (D) is the correct answer.

15. **D** The clause *Charlemagne was crowned in 768* A.D. *as King of the Franks* is a complete thought. The clause *he was the oldest son of Pepin the Short and Bertrada of Laon* is also a complete thought. Since this sentence links two complete ideas with a comma, this sentence contains a comma splice error. Eliminate choice (A). Choice (E) repeats this type of error by setting the complete thought *in 768 A.D. he was crowned King of the Franks* off by commas. Choice (B) uses the pronoun *they*, which does not clearly refer to any group of people mentioned in the sentence, and is therefore incorrect (C) uses a comma followed by the word *and*, and should therefore link two complete thoughts. However, since the first half of the sentence is a fragment, choice (C) is incorrect. Choice (D) fixes the original error in the sentence and does not introduce any new errors, so choice (D) is the correct answer.

16. **B** The singular pronoun *it* refers to the plural noun *bulbs*, so the original sentence has a pronoun agreement error. Choices (A) and (E) repeat the original error and thus are incorrect. Choice (C) turns the sentence into an incomplete thought and is therefore incorrect. Choice (D) uses the plural pronoun *their* to refer to the singular noun *bulb*, so choice (D) has a pronoun agreement error. Choice (B) fixes the error, and does not introduce any new errors, so choice (B) is the correct answer.

17. **D** This sentence uses the word *consider* twice, and therefore has a redundancy error. Choices (A) and (C) repeat this error, and are therefore incorrect. Choice (B) redundantly uses the word *it*, and is therefore incorrect Since *consider…as to be* is the wrong idiom, choice (E) is incorrect. Choice (D) fixes the original error in the sentence, and does not introduce any new errors, so choice (D) is the correct answer.

18. **D** The original sentence uses the conjunction *and*, therefore making the sentence incomplete. Eliminate choice (A). Choices (B) and (C) inappropriately change the verb to *would create*. They both also compare Hemingway's *writing style* to *any other American writer*. Since writing styles should be compared to other writing styles, rather that writing styles to writers, both of these choices also contain comparison errors. Choice (E) changes *was different* to *was differing*, and therefore uses the wrong form. Choice (D) corrects the error in the original sentence and does not introduce any new errors, so choice (D) is the correct answer.

19. **C** According to the sentence, crusaders did two things: *they succeeded not in gaining access…but to leave*. Since *gaining* and *to leave* are not in the same verb form, this sentence contains a parallelism error. Choices (A), (B), (D), and (E) all contain similar parallelism errors, and are therefore incorrect. Only choice (C) fixes the original error and does not introduce any new errors.

20. **D** In the original sentence, the subject is *reputations*, which is plural, but the verb is *appears*, which is singular. Therefore, this sentence contains a subject-verb agreement issue. Eliminate choice (A). Choice (B) changes the subject of the sentence to *either*, which is singular, but it later replaces *either* with the pronoun *their*, which is plural, so choice (B) is incorrect. Choice (C) uses the singular subject *either*, but changes the verb to *appear*, which is plural, so choice (C) is not the credited answer. Choice (E) does fix the original error but is written in passive voice. Choice (D) is the correct answer.

21. **C** Choice (C) contains two errors. First, this sentence uses *between...or*. The correct idiom is *between...and*. Therefore, this sentence contains an idiom error. Second, this sentence contains a parallelism error. There are two things Abigail must choose between: *the upscale bistro* and *eating at the diner*. In a correct version, Abigail can either choose between eating at the upscale bistro and eating at the diner, or she can choose between the upscale bistro and the diner, but she cannot choose between a bistro (a thing) and eating (an action).

22. **D** The subject of the sentence is *each*, which is singular. However, this sentence uses the pronoun *they*, which is plural, to replace the singular subject *each*. Thus, this sentence contains a pronoun agreement error. Additionally, since the pronoun should be the singular *he or she*, the verb *find*, which is plural, should be *finds*, which is singular. Choice (D) therefore contains two errors and is the correct answer.

23. **C** If you use the phrase *not only*, you must include the words *but also* later in the sentence. However, this sentence instead uses *and also*, and therefore contains an idiom error. Thus, choice (C) is the correct answer.

24. **B** In this sentence, the adjective *reputed* modifies the adjective *safe*. However, an adverb, not another adjective, should modify an adjective, so the sentence should say that the outlaws committed crimes in a *reputedly safe part of the country*. Choice (B) therefore contains an error and is the correct answer.

25. **A** Choice (A) contains an idiom error, since the verb *asserted* should not be paired with the preposition *on*. Correctly written, the sentence should say that *Descartes confidently asserted his ability*.

26. **B** The pronoun *they* is plural, but refers to the noun *chef*, which is singular, so choice (B) contains a pronoun agreement error. The correct answer is choice (B).

27. **C** The verb *is* is singular, but the subject of the verb is the plural noun *tenants*. Therefore choice (C) contains a subject-verb agreement error, which makes it the correct answer.

28. **E** The verb *argued* in choice (A) is in past tense and agrees with the subject, so there is no error in choice (A). In choice (B), *many of them* correctly refers back to those *those convicted*, so you can eliminate choice (B). Choice (C) uses the correct preposition and is therefore not the correct answer. Choice (D) properly pairs *either* with the conjunction *or*, so choice (D) does not contain an error. There are no errors in this sentence, so the correct answer is (E).

29. **B**   This sentence begins by using the pronoun *you*, but later incorrectly replaces that pronoun with *one*, rather than *you*. Thus, choice (B) is the correct answer.

30. **B**   Choice (B) uses the present perfect verb *have attempted*. The present perfect tense indicates that an action began in the past, and is still continuing today. However, the sentence indicates that the action occurred *in 1990*. Since the action occurred at one definite point in the past, the verb *have attempted* is in the wrong tense and should be in the simple past tense. Thus, choice (B) contains an error and is the correct answer.

31. **E**   Choice (A) correctly begins a modifier which describes *cave paintings*. Because *paintings* is plural, *many of which* agrees in number with *paintings*. The plural verb *are* in choice (B) agrees with the plural noun *paintings*, so choice (B) can be eliminated. Choice (C) correctly uses a plural noun, *remnants*, to refer back to the *paintings*, so you can eliminate choice (C). Choice (D) has no errors in verb tense. Because the sentence is correct as written, choice (E) is the correct answer.

32. **A**   In a sentence which uses the pairing *neither...nor*, the verb must agree with the last element in the list. In this case, the last element in the list is *team*, which is singular. However, the verb *were* is plural, so choice (A) contains a subject-verb agreement error.

33. **C**   Choice (C) uses the plural pronoun *them* to refer to the singular noun *cloud*. Therefore, choice (C) contains a grammatical error and is the correct answer.

34. **D**   This sentence compares two things: *the game of Go* and *chess pieces*. However, in order for the comparison to be parallel, the sentence must either compare *the game of Go* and *the game of chess*, or it must compare *Go pieces* and *chess pieces*. Therefore choice (D) contains a comparison error and is the correct answer.

35. **B**   This sentence uses the verb *is compelling*, which is in a tense that indicates continuous action. However, since this sentence discusses an action that should happen only once, rather than on a continuous basis, this sentence contains a verb tense error. Eliminate choice (A). Choice (C) changes the intended meaning of the sentence by suggesting that some form of tragedy must befall the people discussed in the sentence, so choice (C) is incorrect. Choice (D) incorrectly uses the pronoun *you* to refer to the *people* mentioned in the previous sentence, and thus contains a pronoun agreement error. Choice (E) uses the singular noun *person* to refer to the noun *people*, which is plural, so choice (E) contains a noun agreement error. Choice (B) fixes the error in the original sentence and does not introduce any new errors, so choice (B) is the correct answer.

36. **B**   Choice (A) combines the two sentences, but the conjunction *and* does not correctly connect the two thoughts since they are not directly related. Choice (B) is more concise than choice (A), and correctly joins the two sentences without introducing any new errors. Choice (C) connects the two thoughts using a semicolon. However, a semicolon should connect two complete thoughts. In this case, the first part of the sentence, which reads, *The story of the poor London boy Tom Canty, which demonstrates the lesson* is not a complete thought. Therefore, Choice (C) contains an error and is

not the correct answer. Choice (D) changes the intended meaning of the sentence by placing the phrase *a poor boy from London* immediately after *Mark Twain*, thus suggesting that Mark Twain, not Tom Canty, was the poor boy from London. Additionally, this sentence contains two complete thoughts joined by a comma, and thus contains a comma splice error. Choice (E) places the modifying phrase *demonstrating the lesson through the story of poor London boy Tom Canty* at the end of the sentence. This sentence changes the meaning so that it is unclear exactly what is demonstrating the lesson, and therefore contains a misplaced modifier error. Choice (B) is the only answer remaining and is therefore correct.

37. **A** The end of the second paragraph discusses the fact that Tom learns to appreciate the things that he does have, rather than envying what others have. However, the paragraph does not really explain how Tom learns this lesson, merely stating that life in the prince's court was more complicated than he had anticipated. Therefore, the author could strengthen his or her point by including more details about what caused Tom to miss and gain such appreciation for his home in London. Choice (A) correctly identifies the pieces of information missing from the second paragraph, and is the correct answer. While adding information about the ways in which the customs in Prince Edward's court were intricate might be helpful, the ways in which those customs relate to the customs in other courts is irrelevant to the topic. Therefore, choice (B) is not the correct answer. The paragraph and the essay as a whole do not relate to the reasons that Tom's family became poverty-stricken, but instead relate to how Tom learned to appreciate his life despite that poverty. Thus, choice (C) is not the correct answer. The second paragraph does relate to how Tom gained an appreciation for his home in London, but it does not relate to the literary devices that Mark Twain used to convey that lesson. Eliminate choice (D). Finally, the second paragraph focuses on Tom, rather than Mark Twain, so a discussion of Twain's life would be out of place at this point in the essay. Therefore choice (E) is incorrect.

38. **E** Choice (A) uses the singular pronoun *one* to replace the plural pronoun *they*, and therefore contains a pronoun agreement error. Both choices (B) and (C) inappropriately change the pronoun in the sentence to *you*, rather than *they*. Since the pronoun refers to *many people*, the pronoun *you* is incorrect, so you can eliminate choices (B) and (C). Choice (D) changes the present tense verb *fail* to the past perfect verb *have failed*. Since the rest of the verbs in the sentence are in the present tense, and the sentence does not call for a tense change, this choice contains a verb tense error. Choice (E) correctly joins the two sentences and does not introduce any new errors, so choice (E) is the correct answer.

39.   **E**   Sentence 3 provides a transition from the main topic of the essay to the example of *The Prince and the Pauper* and is therefore an important part of the first paragraph. Without sentence 4, readers would not know which book the author is discussing, so sentence 4 is also a critical part of the first paragraph. Sentence 8 demonstrates how the example of *The Prince and the Pauper* relates to the main topic of the essay, and is therefore necessary to the essay. Sentence 9 relates the example of the book back to the essay's thesis by showing how the example relates to people in general. Therefore, sentence 9 should remain in the essay. Sentence 10 links the idea in sentence 9 to the idea in sentence 12, and is therefore a valuable part of the essay. However, sentence 11 introduces irrelevant information. The previous sentence discusses the idea that it is possible to appreciate those who love us before we lose them, and the sentence that follows discusses the idea that few people actually learn this lesson before it is too late. Thus, sentences 10 and 12 discuss related ideas, but sentence 11, which points out that many believe that Tom is a more engaging character than Prince Edward, provides unnecessary information. The correct answer is choice (E).

Part IV
Practice Tests

Chapter 7
Practice Test 2

The Princeton Review

PSAT

R NAME:_____
nt)   Last   First   M.I.

NATURE:_____ DATE:_____ /_____ /_____

ME ADDRESS:_____
nt)   Number and Street
                                          E-MAIL:_____
ity   State   Zip

NE NO.:_____ SCHOOL:_____ CLASS OF:_____
nt)

IMPORTANT: Please fill in these boxes exactly as shown on the back cover of your text book.

SCANTRON F-17982-PRP P3 2803 628 5 4 3 2 1
© The Princeton Review, Inc.

5. YOUR NAME

First 4 letters of last name				FIRST INIT	MID INIT

TEST FORM
_____

DATE OF BIRTH

MONTH	DAY	YEAR
JAN		
FEB		
MAR		
APR		
MAY		
JUN		
JUL		
AUG		
SEP		
OCT		
NOV		
DEC		

3. TEST CODE

4. PHONE NUMBER

7. SEX
- MALE
- FEMALE

8. OTHER
1 A B C D E
2 A B C D E
3 A B C D E

1 READING

1 A B C D E   8 A B C D E   15 A B C D E   22 A B C D E
2 A B C D E   9 A B C D E   16 A B C D E   23 A B C D E
3 A B C D E   10 A B C D E   17 A B C D E   24 A B C D E
4 A B C D E   11 A B C D E   18 A B C D E
5 A B C D E   12 A B C D E   19 A B C D E
6 A B C D E   13 A B C D E   20 A B C D E
7 A B C D E   14 A B C D E   21 A B C D E

2 MATHEMATICS

1 A B C D E   8 A B C D E   15 A B C D E
2 A B C D E   9 A B C D E   16 A B C D E
3 A B C D E   10 A B C D E   17 A B C D E
4 A B C D E   11 A B C D E   18 A B C D E
5 A B C D E   12 A B C D E   19 A B C D E
6 A B C D E   13 A B C D E   20 A B C D E
7 A B C D E   14 A B C D E

3 READING

25 A B C D E   33 A B C D E   41 A B C D E
26 A B C D E   34 A B C D E   42 A B C D E
27 A B C D E   35 A B C D E   43 A B C D E
28 A B C D E   36 A B C D E   44 A B C D E
29 A B C D E   37 A B C D E   45 A B C D E
30 A B C D E   38 A B C D E   46 A B C D E
31 A B C D E   39 A B C D E   47 A B C D E
32 A B C D E   40 A B C D E   48 A B C D E

Use a No. 2 pencil only. Be sure each mark is dark and completely fills the intended oval. Completely erase any errors or stray marks.

4 MATHEMATICS

21 Ⓐ Ⓑ Ⓒ Ⓓ Ⓔ
22 Ⓐ Ⓑ Ⓒ Ⓓ Ⓔ
23 Ⓐ Ⓑ Ⓒ Ⓓ Ⓔ
24 Ⓐ Ⓑ Ⓒ Ⓓ Ⓔ

25 Ⓐ Ⓑ Ⓒ Ⓓ Ⓔ
26 Ⓐ Ⓑ Ⓒ Ⓓ Ⓔ
27 Ⓐ Ⓑ Ⓒ Ⓓ Ⓔ
28 Ⓐ Ⓑ Ⓒ Ⓓ Ⓔ

ONLY ANSWERS ENTERED IN THE OVALS IN EACH GRID AREA WILL BE SCORED.
YOU WILL NOT RECEIVE CREDIT FOR ANYTHING WRITTEN IN THE BOXES ABOVE THE OVALS.

Grid-in questions 29, 30, 31, 32, 33 (each with columns containing oval markings: ⁄ • ⓪ ① ② ③ ④ ⑤ ⑥ ⑦ ⑧ ⑨)

Grid-in questions 34, 35, 36, 37, 38 (each with columns containing oval markings: ⁄ • ⓪ ① ② ③ ④ ⑤ ⑥ ⑦ ⑧ ⑨)

5 WRITING SKILLS

1 Ⓐ Ⓑ Ⓒ Ⓓ Ⓔ
2 Ⓐ Ⓑ Ⓒ Ⓓ Ⓔ
3 Ⓐ Ⓑ Ⓒ Ⓓ Ⓔ
4 Ⓐ Ⓑ Ⓒ Ⓓ Ⓔ
5 Ⓐ Ⓑ Ⓒ Ⓓ Ⓔ
6 Ⓐ Ⓑ Ⓒ Ⓓ Ⓔ
7 Ⓐ Ⓑ Ⓒ Ⓓ Ⓔ
8 Ⓐ Ⓑ Ⓒ Ⓓ Ⓔ
9 Ⓐ Ⓑ Ⓒ Ⓓ Ⓔ
10 Ⓐ Ⓑ Ⓒ Ⓓ Ⓔ
11 Ⓐ Ⓑ Ⓒ Ⓓ Ⓔ
12 Ⓐ Ⓑ Ⓒ Ⓓ Ⓔ
13 Ⓐ Ⓑ Ⓒ Ⓓ Ⓔ

14 Ⓐ Ⓑ Ⓒ Ⓓ Ⓔ
15 Ⓐ Ⓑ Ⓒ Ⓓ Ⓔ
16 Ⓐ Ⓑ Ⓒ Ⓓ Ⓔ
17 Ⓐ Ⓑ Ⓒ Ⓓ Ⓔ
18 Ⓐ Ⓑ Ⓒ Ⓓ Ⓔ
19 Ⓐ Ⓑ Ⓒ Ⓓ Ⓔ
20 Ⓐ Ⓑ Ⓒ Ⓓ Ⓔ
21 Ⓐ Ⓑ Ⓒ Ⓓ Ⓔ
22 Ⓐ Ⓑ Ⓒ Ⓓ Ⓔ
23 Ⓐ Ⓑ Ⓒ Ⓓ Ⓔ
24 Ⓐ Ⓑ Ⓒ Ⓓ Ⓔ
25 Ⓐ Ⓑ Ⓒ Ⓓ Ⓔ
26 Ⓐ Ⓑ Ⓒ Ⓓ Ⓔ

27 Ⓐ Ⓑ Ⓒ Ⓓ Ⓔ
28 Ⓐ Ⓑ Ⓒ Ⓓ Ⓔ
29 Ⓐ Ⓑ Ⓒ Ⓓ Ⓔ
30 Ⓐ Ⓑ Ⓒ Ⓓ Ⓔ
31 Ⓐ Ⓑ Ⓒ Ⓓ Ⓔ
32 Ⓐ Ⓑ Ⓒ Ⓓ Ⓔ
33 Ⓐ Ⓑ Ⓒ Ⓓ Ⓔ
34 Ⓐ Ⓑ Ⓒ Ⓓ Ⓔ
35 Ⓐ Ⓑ Ⓒ Ⓓ Ⓔ
36 Ⓐ Ⓑ Ⓒ Ⓓ Ⓔ
37 Ⓐ Ⓑ Ⓒ Ⓓ Ⓔ
38 Ⓐ Ⓑ Ⓒ Ⓓ Ⓔ
39 Ⓐ Ⓑ Ⓒ Ⓓ Ⓔ

SECTION 1
Time — 25 minutes
24 Questions
(1–24)

Directions: For each question in this section, select the best answer from among the choices given and fill in the corresponding circle on the answer sheet.

Each sentence below has one or two blanks, each blank indicating that something has been omitted. Beneath the sentence are five words or sets of words labeled A through E. Choose the word or set of words that, when inserted in the sentence, best fits the meaning of the sentence as a whole.

Example:

Desiring to ------- his taunting friends, Mitch gave them taffy in hopes it would keep their mouths shut.

(A) eliminate   (B) satisfy   (C) overcome
    (D) ridicule   (E) silence

Ⓐ Ⓑ Ⓒ Ⓓ ●

1. Since the coach didn't want the opposing team to pick up her signals to the runner, she was careful to use the utmost -------.

    (A) athleticism   (B) discretion   (C) autonomy
        (D) credibility   (E) disparity

2. Recently unearthed drawings of spears, traps, and cudgels from ancient times show that ------- was necessary for each head of the household, thus making him the ------- of the provider of the family.

    (A) sporting . . epicenter
    (B) farming . . highlight
    (C) hunting . . embodiment
    (D) fishing . . enemy
    (E) running . . epitome

3. Hall of Fame baseball player Ty Cobb's skills as an athlete have never been questioned by those with knowledge of the game, even if his personal temperament has never been agreed upon: his few instances of kindness and generosity are often ------- by stories of uncontrollable -------.

    (A) highlighted . . irritability
    (B) rebutted . . charity
    (C) contradicted . . jealousy
    (D) overshadowed. . . irascibility
    (E) bequeathed . . ecstasy

4. The celebrity chef believed that originality was a far better attribute of good cooking than mere skill, consistently stating that diners much prefer ------- over -------.

    (A) innovation . . competence
    (B) enigma . . concord
    (C) novelty . . opulence
    (D) revolution . . craft
    (E) decadence . . mendacity

5. In contrast to what Ms. Banks expected from her students, Raphael was always ------- instead of punctual, and consistently disrespectful when he should have been -------.

    (A) mercurial . . grandiose
    (B) sluggish . . dutiful
    (C) tardy . . deferential
    (D) dilatory . . ornery
    (E) meticulous . . obedient

6. Rupert criticized the new film as too much of -------: it highlighted the origins of the story's characters without fully realizing their motivations or coming to a satisfying resolution.

    (A) a prelude   (B) a picaresque   (C) a roman a clef
        (D) an anachronism   (E) an epilogue

7. The films of the 1980s were considered clichéd and commercial, as opposed to those of the 1970s that were remembered as ------- and -------.

    (A) conventional . . derogatory
    (B) maverick . . ubiquitous
    (C) cinematic . . nonsalable
    (D) therapeutic . . superfluous
    (E) iconoclastic . . independent

8. The auto mechanic's ability to diagnose a vehicle's problem prior to inspection prompted his customers to describe him as -------.

    (A) prescient   (B) efficient   (C) vicarious
        (D) scintillating   (E) precocious

GO ON TO THE NEXT PAGE →

The passages below are followed by questions based on their content; questions following a pair of related passages may also be based on the relationship between the paired passages. Answer the questions on the basis of what is <u>stated</u> or <u>implied</u> in the passage and in any introductory material that may be provided.

Questions 9-10 are based on the following passage.

Even though he wasn't ready to write a full letter, or read a complete book in English yet, Samuel's understanding of his new land's language was strong enough to garner him a *Line* job in a local restaurant as a line cook. In fact, his limited
5 familiarity with the new language actually allowed him the benefit of not questioning certain restaurant lingo that he may have found strange if it was spoken in his familiar tongue. How, for example, would he be expected to react when told to "kill the chicken" or "drop the food" if both were spoken
10 in his native tongue without the knowledge of those phrases' acceptance as slang in English?

9. The author uses the phrases "kill the chicken" and "drop the food" (line 9) in order to

(A) emphasize the urgency for Samuel to learn English
(B) underscore the silliness in restaurant lingo
(C) highlight the benefits of Samuel's gradual integration of the English language
(D) criticize Samuel's inability to write a full English letter
(E) show Samuel's fascination with the restaurant industry

10. The passage indicates that Samuel's limited familiarity with English was considered

(A) advantageous
(B) debilitating
(C) satisfying
(D) humbling
(E) appetizing

Questions 11-12 are based on the following passage.

Sugar, once considered something we might treat ourselves with from time to time, has become so prevalent in modern society that its presence in food has expanded *Line* from the expected, such as candies and sweet drinks, to
5 the unexpected, such as breads and salad dressings. So widespread is sugar that our brains have now become programmed to perceive it as an addictive substance on par with that of many illegal narcotics. Scientists believe that most mammals, from rats to humans, are born with an
10 innate sensitivity to sweet food items. For most of our human existence, we have had minimal contact with sugar. Therefore, the growing abundance of sugar-laden foods over the past several decades has allowed our sweet receptors to trigger a reward signal to the brain so powerful that even our own
15 sense of self control may not be able to override it.

11. The author mentions "candies" and "breads" in lines 4-5 in order to

(A) show items that are commonly associated with sugar
(B) indicate the range of items that contain sugar
(C) caution against overfeeding children with sugar products
(D) argue that sugar is an ingredient in far too many foods
(E) criticize the use of sugar in abnormal foods

12. The passage suggests which of the following about sugar?

(A) It rivals illegal narcotics as the most addictive substance consumed by humans
(B) Rats and humans process sugar in the same way
(C) It is more prevalent in foods today than it was ten years ago
(D) It is an ingredient in most food products today
(E) People are sometimes powerless to avoid consuming sugar products

GO ON TO THE NEXT PAGE

Questions 13-24 are based on the following passage.

This passage is adapted from a 2009 book looking at Western (that is, European and American) attempts to modernize the Middle East and other regions.

The international history of the twentieth century is overflowing with Western projects to modernize the Middle East. The United States, and England to a lesser degree, have
ine tried to bring freedom to oppressed peoples throughout
5 the region, and as the word "freedom" implies, this was a philanthropic mission. President Bill Clinton, for example, is still praised for his role in Israeli-Palestinian peace talks, even as his other failures and accomplishments gained front-page news in the mid-1990s. His even-handed, mediating role
10 helped to save these warring states from total destruction. This attitude toward non-Western regions, the belief that the West's systems of government can help save the people of the Middle East, Africa, or Latin America, is a holdover from an imperial moment, when European nations conquered
15 these regions with militaries rather than diplomats. It may be time to start asking, however, whether Western systems of government are universally applicable. That is to say, perhaps the Western value of "freedom"—as it relates to markets, speech, and behaviors—is not one that is shared by
20 people outside the West. Unrest in the Middle East and other non-Western regions can only continue until new systems of governance begin to emerge from the regions themselves.

These modernization projects bear an eerie resemblance to the "civilizing missions" of European nations in the
25 nineteenth century. These missions always begin with the premise that those in non-Western nations are unable to govern themselves. In most cases, the result is little more than a large-scale, prolonged clash of cultures, in which prejudices toward the "poor souls" who can't take care of themselves
30 only become that much firmer in the minds of the un-self-conscious interlopers. The native peoples who are then forced to live under the new government's rule become extremely skeptical of it, as its supposed successes are measured by seemingly irrelevant metrics. Many of the great ancient and
35 historical societies come from these regions, but since the seventeenth century, these regions have been considered almost universally backward. This notion has persisted into contemporary politics, and in the United States, the idea that the U.S. is making the world safe for democracy is
40 common among both major political parties. As recently as 2003, in a war that was billed as one of self-defense, George W. Bush was promising Americans, "Helping Iraqis achieve a united, stable, and free country will require our sustained commitment."

45 Bush is the inheritor of a long tradition of this belief in the power of Western influence. This influence, though, has not been a pure force for good. While Western systems of government were created as responses to nation states and royal traditions, non-Western nations have their own set of
50 foundations and traditions. The earliest colonial governments in these non-Western regions were run by Westerners. But now that the colonial governments have been kicked out, a system of rule by the actual people who live in these non-Western nations must be something else.

55 To take one example, the name "Iraq" is not quite as applicable to all its citizens as the names "France," "Portugal," or "The United States" are in their own regions. For many Westerners, nationality is a given and ultimately trumps the more local identifications of town, city, or state. In Iraq, as
60 the Bush administration learned, religious distinctions are more meaningful than national similarities. Approximately 65 percent of those living in Iraq are Shia Muslims, but does this make it a Shia country? To an extent, maybe, but Sunni Muslims represent a powerful and vocal minority, and the
65 northern regions of Iraq comprise a semiautonomous region of a third group, the Kurds. The Western notions of nation-above-all and religious coexistence can't maintain in this and other countries because the value systems have developed so independently of these notions.

70 As in many other parts of the world, "Iraqi freedom" was defined by someone other than the Iraqis themselves. Western civilizing efforts have always been based on the unfortunate premise that non-Westerners cannot govern themselves, often on no other evidence than Westerners' firm belief in
75 the success of their own political systems. The refusal to accept that the basic principles of democracy and free-market capitalism may not be universally applicable has always compromised efforts at Western modernization because these efforts have lacked the appropriate local perspectives.
80 Certainly, Western nations are today more sensitive to cultural differences than they have ever been. It still remains to be seen, however, whether this new multicultural stance is a genuine change or a simple repackaging of an old product.

One lingering idea in all modernizing efforts is that
85 difference—whether among races, religions, or tribes—must be overcome. The idea goes that if a particular nation is going to be brought into the twentieth or twenty-first century, all its people must unite. But policymakers are increasingly forced to see that difference can be just as powerful as unity.
90 The West can bring its message of national unity, but it must be ready and willing to accept the differences in the to-be-modernized regions: a forced friendship is not likely to last very long.

GO ON TO THE NEXT PAGE

13. In the context of lines 1-3 ("The international … East"), the phrase "overflowing with" suggests that

    (A) modernization is a common subject of conversation for Middle Eastern visitors to the West
    (B) some Middle East countries have been subject to more modernization efforts than others
    (C) there have been many attempts by Western countries to modernize the Middle East
    (D) there are simply too many countries in the Middle East for historians to describe accurately
    (E) the Middle East is a populous region with a rich historical legacy

14. The author mentions Bill Clinton (line 6) primarily in order to

    (A) cite one person who represents a certain perspective
    (B) describe the rewards of one person's courage against difficult odds
    (C) state that those who have contributed to peace in the region come from a variety of backgrounds
    (D) show that Middle East peace was only one of Clinton's minor accomplishments
    (E) argue that this approach to Middle East issues is the correct one

15. According to the passage, it is worth asking "whether Western systems of government are universally applicable" (lines 16-17) because they

    (A) are too reliant upon ancient forms of non-Western government
    (B) refuse to recognize the accomplishments of diplomats like Bill Clinton
    (C) have as their only goal the introduction of Western goods into non-Western markets
    (D) may not be the most appropriate forms of government for those outside the West
    (E) deny the importance of having native peoples in high government positions

16. Which of the following best states how the peoples mentioned in line 31 feel about West-influenced governments?

    (A) They despise the governments because they are hopelessly corrupt.
    (B) They question the ability of their fellow citizens to govern them.
    (C) They disagree with how local money is being paid out to officials.
    (D) They doubt that the governments have delivered on all that they have promised.
    (E) They support the new regime because it represents a change from old ways.

17. According to the author, what has changed "since the seventeenth century" (lines 34-35)?

    (A) Native citizens are now in open conflict with Western-style governments.
    (B) Middle Eastern government officials look to the West for models of how to govern.
    (C) Regions that were once considered model civilizations are no longer thought of as ideals.
    (D) People in non-Western countries are not willing to compromise in a way that supports democracy.
    (E) Those who were once unable to govern themselves have been helped by those who have shown them how to govern.

18. The statement that Western influence "has not been a pure force for good" (line 47) suggests that the author, in general, believes that

    (A) people in the Middle East would prefer to have their fellow citizens in high government positions
    (B) people in the Middle East have not necessarily benefited from Western-style governments
    (C) voters in Middle East elections wish there were more candidates from the West
    (D) forms of democracy in the Middle East are more advanced than those in the West
    (E) Western policymakers did not expect voter turnout to be as low as it has been in Middle East elections

19. In line 58, "trumps" most nearly means

    (A) kicks out
    (B) performs
    (C) defeats by force
    (D) beautifies
    (E) is more important than

20. In line 67, "maintain" most nearly means

    (A) work
    (B) repair
    (C) hang
    (D) sit
    (E) build

GO ON TO THE NEXT PAGE

21. Which of the following, if true, would refute the claim made in lines 70-71 ("As ... themselves")

(A) The Western influence in the Middle East has not been able to overcome internal divisions among groups within Iraq.

(B) Many representatives from the Middle East have been crucial to developing the government systems that exist in the Middle East today.

(C) Contemporary styles of government in the Middle East can be traced back to principles developed in Europe in the late 1700s.

(D) Famous diplomats such as Bill Clinton have continued to offer guidance to those in the Middle East and elsewhere.

(E) The U.S. has ensured that Sunnis, Shias, and Kurds are equally represented in the Iraqi government.

22. Which of the following best describes the sentence in lines 80-81 ("Certainly ... been")?

(A) A response to critics of the author's own argument

(B) An idea developed further in other work by the author

(C) A tangent that the author considers necessary for his main point

(D) A concession that contemporary trends are not exclusively negative

(E) A restatement of the author's central claims

23. The author uses the phrase "repackaging of an old product" (line 83) primarily to

(A) outline an analogy for an ideal approach

(B) suggest the type of reformulation necessary for success

(C) express skepticism toward a certain transformation

(D) criticize the financial interests of Western governments

(E) admit that the Western approach has many benefits

24. The author would most likely consider which approach to be a new strategy for the formation of governments in the Middle East?

(A) Allowing Western governments to shape government policy in the Middle East

(B) Breaking down cultural barriers within countries to promote national unity

(C) Increasing the authority of government official to implement Western democracy

(D) Collaborating with local representatives to determine which style of government is best for a particular country

(E) Holding elections in the West to determine which officials should represent Middle East governments

STOP

If you finish before time is called, you may check your work on this section only.
Do not turn to any other section in the test.

SECTION 2
Time — 25 minutes
20 Questions
(1–20)

Directions: For this section, solve each problem and decide which is the best of the choices given. Fill in the corresponding circle on the answer sheet. You may use any available space for scratchwork.

Reference Information

$A = \pi r^2$ $A = lw$ $A = \frac{1}{2}bh$ $V = lwh$ $V = \pi r^2 h$ $c^2 = a^2 + b^2$

Special Right Triangles

The number of degrees of arc in a circle is 360.

The sum of the measures in degrees of the angles of a triangle is 180.

1. A spice merchant sells ground cinnamon for x dollars per ounce. At this rate, what is the cost of 3 ounces of cinnamon, in dollars, in terms of x ?

    (A) $\dfrac{1}{3}$

    (B) $\dfrac{x}{3}$

    (C) $\dfrac{3}{x}$

    (D) $3x$

    (E) 3

2. If 5.73×10^h equals 0.0573, what is the value of h ?

    (A) -2
    (B) -1
    (C) 1
    (D) 2
    (E) 3

GO ON TO THE NEXT PAGE

3. If $3a = 5$ and $2b = 9$, what is the value of $2(3a) + 4(2b)$?

(A) 32
(B) 45
(C) 46
(D) 58
(E) 66

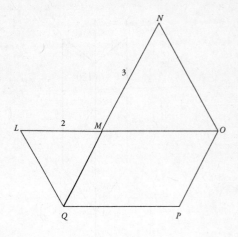

4. The sum of a and b is 18 and the sum of c, d, and e is 37, what is the average (arithmetic mean) of a, b, c, d, and e ?

(A) 8
(B) 11
(C) 18
(D) 20
(E) 22

5. In the figure above, triangles LMQ and MNO are equilateral. If $LM = 2$ and $MN = 3$, what is the perimeter of the parallelogram $MOPQ$?

(A) 3
(B) 4
(C) 5
(D) 8
(E) 10

6. If $13 - (x + y)^2 = 4$, which of the following could be the value of $(x + y)$?

(A) $-\sqrt{17}$
(B) -3
(C) $\sqrt{17}$
(D) 13
(E) 17

GO ON TO THE NEXT PAGE

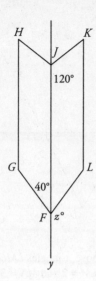

7. In the figure above, quadrilateral *FJKL* is the reflection of quadrilateral *FGHJ* about the line *y*. What is the value of *z* ?

(A)   20
(B)   80
(C)   120
(D)   140
(E)   160

8. The sum of 50° and ∠*p* is 180°. Which of the following angles could be ∠*p* ?

(A)

(B)

(C)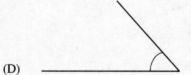

(D)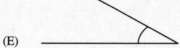

(E)

GO ON TO THE NEXT PAGE

9. If the number t is quadrupled, the result is the same as if 30 were added to t. What is the value of t ?

(A) 4

(B) $\dfrac{30}{7}$

(C) 5

(D) $\dfrac{15}{2}$

(E) 10

10. Jeff plans to screenprint all 70 T-shirts in his print shop to complete an order. He discovers that ten of the T-shirts he has in stock are the wrong size for this order, and one-third of the T-shirts he can print do not print correctly. How many correctly printed T-shirts does Jeff have for this order?

(A) 40
(B) 42
(C) 50
(D) 56
(E) 60

Creative Crafters Club

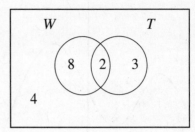

11. The 17 members of a crafting club are choosing a meeting night, with the availability of all members represented in the rectangular region of the figure above. Circular region W represents all members that can meet on Wednesdays, and circular region T represents all the members that can meet on Thursdays. If the numbers indicate how many people are in each of the separate categories, how many people in the club cannot meet on Thursday?

(A) 5
(B) 7
(C) 8
(D) 11
(E) 12

GO ON TO THE NEXT PAGE

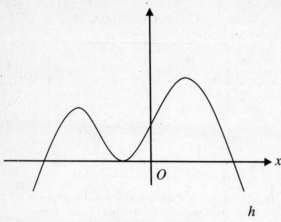

Note: Figure not drawn to scale.

12. A portion of the graph of the function h is shown in the figure above. For how many values of x shown in this portion does $h(x) = 0$?

(A) Four
(B) Three
(C) Two
(D) One
(E) Zero

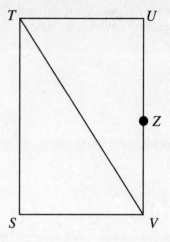

13. In the rectangle above, point Z is located so that $ZV + TV = ZU + TU$. If $SV = 15$ and $TV = 39$, what does ZV equal?

(A) 3
(B) 4
(C) 5
(D) 6
(E) 7

GO ON TO THE NEXT PAGE ➡

PRICES OF PUSHPIN PACKAGES

Brand	Price of Package	Pushpins in Package
Bob's Brass Tacks	$1.50	20
Pokey's Pushpins	$2.25	36
Thumbelina's Tacks	$2.50	42

14. The chart above indicates the brands of pushpins available at a certain office supply store. If Karen needs 100 pushpins to decorate her new bulletin board, what is the least amount she could spend on enough pushpins at this store?

   (A) $6.50
   (B) $6.75
   (C) $7.00
   (D) $7.25
   (E) $7.50

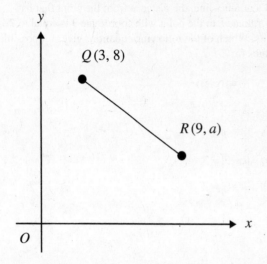

15. In the figure above, line segment $\overline{QR}$ has a slope of $-\dfrac{2}{3}$. What is the value of a ?

   (A) 2.5
   (B) 3
   (C) 3.5
   (D) 4
   (E) 4.5

GO ON TO THE NEXT PAGE

16. On a number line, the distance from the point that has coordinate k to the point with coordinate 3 is equal to 7 units. Which of the following equations gives all possible values for k ?

(A) $|k-10|=0$

(B) $|k-7|=3$

(C) $|k+7|=3$

(D) $|k-3|=7$

(E) $|k+3|=7$

17. The sum of all odd integers from 1 to 303, inclusive, is 23,104. What is the sum of all odd integers from 3 to 301, inclusive?

(A) 22,496
(B) 22,794
(C) 22,800
(D) 23,103
(E) 23,408

18. All values of c in which of the following intervals satisfy the inequality $\dfrac{1}{8c+2}<0$?

I. $-\dfrac{1}{4}<c-\dfrac{1}{6}$

II. $-\dfrac{2}{3}<c-\dfrac{1}{3}$

III. $-\dfrac{7}{8}<c-\dfrac{3}{8}$

(A) I only
(B) II only
(C) III only
(D) I and II
(E) II and III

GO ON TO THE NEXT PAGE

19. In the equation $f^g = 81$, where f and g are positive integers, how many different values of f are possible?

(A) Two
(B) Three
(C) Four
(D) Five
(E) More than five

20. In the xy-coordinate plane, the vertices of $\triangle MNO$ are point M (r, s), point N $(3r, 0)$, and the origin O. If r and s are positive numbers, what is the area of $\triangle MNO$, in terms of r and s ?

(A) $\dfrac{1}{2}rs$

(B) rs

(C) $\dfrac{3}{2}rs$

(D) $\dfrac{1}{2}r^3s$

(E) r^3s

STOP
If you finish before time is called, you may check your work on this section only.
Do not turn to any other section in the test.

SECTION 3
Time — 25 minutes
24 Questions
(25–48)

Directions: For each question in this section, select the best answer from among the choices given and fill in the corresponding circle on the answer sheet.

Each sentence below has one or two blanks, each blank indicating that something has been omitted. Beneath the sentence are five words or sets of words labeled A through E. Choose the word or set of words that, when inserted in the sentence, best fits the meaning of the sentence as a whole.

Example:

Hoping to ------- the dispute, negotiators proposed a compromise that they felt would be ------- to both labor and management.

(A) enforce . . useful
(B) end . . divisive
(C) overcome . . unattractive
(D) extend . . satisfactory
(E) resolve . . acceptable

Ⓐ Ⓑ Ⓒ Ⓓ ●

25. Stephen's new road bike was much more -------, even lighter, while his previous one was a ------- form of transportation.

(A) diminutive . . speedy
(B) compact . . bulky
(C) commonplace . . competent
(D) gargantuan . . immense
(E) durable . . mechanical

26. Since the supermarket would no longer ------- its deli meats properly, customers found it increasingly -------- to distinguish a strip steak from a pot roast.

(A) clean . . redundant
(B) label . . forthright
(C) display . . delectable
(D) tag . . complicated
(E) restock . . arduous

27. The folk singer wrote songs that showcased the human spirit in all its forms, always choosing to -------- the triumphant moments of one's life, as well as the sorrowful.

(A) undermine (B) articulate (C) personify
(D) contradict (E) underscore

28. The author's new work was considered by many critics to be a(n) ------- novel, since it used many elements and details that would have been out of place for this story's -------.

(A) anachronistic . . setting
(B) satirical . . medium
(C) subordinate . . rectitude
(D) archaic . . whimsy
(E) allegorical . . milieu

29. Reinhold was always backing down from his own arguments and deferring his point of view to that of others; he therefore was consistently known for his -------.

(A) autonomy (B) brevity (C) erudition
(D) tenacity (E) acquiescence

GO ON TO THE NEXT PAGE

The passages below are followed by questions based on their content; questions following a pair of related passages may also be based on the relationship between the paired passages. Answer the questions on the basis of what is <u>stated</u> or <u>implied</u> in the passage and in any introductory material that may be provided.

Questions 30-33 are based on the following passages.

Passage 1

The life of an obsessive sports fan is certainly not one of ease, nor one that I would want to foist upon others. The ability to explain, in detail, the rules of Australian football has not garnered me a legion of new friends and followers,
5 but the exact opposite in fact. Whenever I try to tell my family why a Wing T formation is preferable to a Double Back, I just see eyes roll. I've tried to integrate myself into the interests of my non-sports-fan friends, but even a recent book club discussion on Bernard Malamud's baseball classic
10 *The Natural* ended in despair when I monopolized the conversation on why lead character Roy Hobbs really should have been a switch hitter.

Passage 2

Would one begrudge a mechanic who knew everything about cars? Or a surgeon who knows every minute detail
15 about human anatomy? And yet sports fanatics who can tell you who played center field for the winning team of the 1974 World Series (it was Billy North, by the way) are met with a level of derision for our obsession that would stand in direct contrast with the revered professions mentioned above. It
20 probably has less to do with our superior knowledge of all things athletic than with the fact that we continually return to a well of knowledge with which we are already intimately familiar. We may be referred to as "obsessives" by some, but I welcome the term since it's better to be a master of one
25 domain than merely a spectator of many.

30. Both passages primarily focus on

(A) certain sports that are of interest to all fans
(B) particular hobbies that may be unhealthy
(C) some disdain from others for certain obsessions
(D) the elation felt by sports fans for talking about their interests
(E) the contempt sports fanatics feel towards those who know less than them

31. The "family" in passage 1, line 6 would probably view the "sports fanatics" of Passage 2, line 15 with

(A) marked agreement
(B) formal disgust
(C) sheer enthusiasm
(D) respectful consideration
(E) general disinterest

32. In line 4, "garnered" most nearly means

(A) given
(B) persuaded
(C) supplemented
(D) squandered
(E) displayed

33. Both passages make use of

(A) metaphor
(B) comparison
(C) personal experience
(D) hypothetical situations
(E) specific details

GO ON TO THE NEXT PAGE

Questions 34-42 are based on the following passages.

This passage, adapted from a short story, presents an 11-year-old girl, Sarah, her father, and her brother.

Daddy was seeing an awful lot of his new friend. One of the rooms in his house was all of a sudden full of her stuff; neither Sarah nor her brother was allowed in there anymore.
Line It had started with a few dinners and shopping trips, and now
5 it seemed that their father's friend basically lived in the house, even shifting around some furniture that had been in place for as long as Sarah could remember. Her name was Tess. She had a pretty face that seemed to change when she was wearing shiny makeup, and she seemed to have a different
10 scarf for every day of the year. And Sarah and her brother were still not sure how to act around her. She seemed to act so much like their mother, but she was not, after all, their mother. The easiest thing, Sarah had decided, would be to nod and smile politely and save the big talks for when she was alone
15 with Dad.

Then Tess became more insistent on having those big talks with Sarah and her brother. "Your dad and I" and "Me and your daddy" seemed to start every one of her sentences now. And eventually there was talk of "your new mommy"
20 and Tess's very old parents introduced themselves as "grandma and grandpa." Sarah and her brother had not been warned that these things were happening: they just happened. And on one Thursday afternoon, Tess picked Sarah up after school to take her shopping for a Junior Bridesmaid's dress.
25 Sarah watched out the window as they drove to the mall: "Bride?"

"We've decided to have all the bridesmaids in purple," said Tess. "Don't you think purple is a nice color in June?"

Sarah remembered the date from the morning
30 announcements at school. "But it's May."

"May, too. Purple's just a real nice color, don't you think?"

So Tess and Sarah chose the prettiest purple dress they could find: a maxi dress with small purple carnations sewn into the shoulders. Sarah had never worn that kind of fancy
35 dress before, but she had seen pictures of her mother and father from some years ago in which her mother had worn a very similar dress. And Sarah would wear her hair up with a carnation to match. She found herself talking easily to Tess about all of this. Tess said only, "I'm glad we're both excited."
40 In the coming weeks, though, Sarah was not to be so involved again. She was usually asked to watch her brother as her daddy and Tess met with planners, caterers, and decorators. How many guests would they have? What was the color scheme of the place? What kind of music should the
45 band play? Sarah's father sat back admiringly and let Tess make most of the decisions. Sarah had never seen him so calm—he was usually such an over-planner, barking orders at all within his sight.

Sarah was playing board games in the next room with
50 her brother, rolling the dice haphazardly, trying to hear the conversation between the adults. She wanted to walk in there and take a seat at the table with them. She remembered all the conversations at that same dinner table between her mother and father. Sarah was her brother's age then, those few weeks
55 before her mom went to the hospital. Then, until Tess came along, it was just Sarah, her dad, and her brother. Sarah didn't want whatever was happening to creep up on her like that again. She wanted to be at the table, calling whatever shots she could. Her father had told her back then what a big girl
60 she was, but he had actually explained so little.

"I want Sarah to walk down the aisle with me," said Tess. "Oh, you should just see the dress we bought the other day."

"Sarah honey, how does that sound to you?" her father asked, looking at her slyly.
65 Sarah didn't answer right away. She rolled the dice and moved her piece along the board slowly. He wanted her to help with the plans. She wanted to go upstairs and put the dress on right now. She was ready to walk down the aisle with Tess, her new mom.

34. In lines 1-3, the phrases "an awful lot" and "all of a sudden" help to emphasize Sarah's

(A) disapproval of her father's new girlfriend
(B) apathy toward her personal space being invaded
(C) wish that things could be as they once were
(D) unwillingness to accept a new person into her life
(E) surprise at a new development in her father's home

35. In line 5, "basically" suggests that

(A) Sarah's father bought his girlfriend a new house
(B) Sarah and her brother now live in the same room
(C) the house does not have all modern amenities
(D) Sarah invited Tess to live at the house
(E) Tess comes to the house very frequently

36. In context, "shifting around some furniture" (line 6) is best characterized as an example of

(A) one of many possible improvements that a homeowner can make
(B) something typically done by someone who lives in the house containing the furniture
(C) one of Sarah's biggest problems with her father's new girlfriend
(D) an aspect of home decorating in which Sarah is particularly interested
(E) the reason Tess is invited so often to the house

GO ON TO THE NEXT PAGE

37. In lines 17-21, the author uses quotation marks to emphasize

(A) an insult that Tess's family uses when referring to Sarah
(B) a joke between Sarah and her younger brother
(C) a slangy way of referring to family members
(D) a change in how people are referring to themselves
(E) a metaphorical way of describing a father's love

38. In line 26, "Bride?" primarily serves to suggest that Sarah

(A) cannot hear Tess over the noisy car
(B) is unaware of a planned future event
(C) is acting like she does not know any words
(D) resists the idea of having Tess as a mother
(E) refuses to pay attention when Tess talks to her

39. The questions in lines 43-45 ("How … play?") primarily serve to

(A) set up the scene in the next paragraph
(B) name specific topics of discussion
(C) demonstrate the depths of the disagreement
(D) suggest Sarah's continued exclusion
(E) create suspense in a reader who wants to know the answers

40. In line 47, the phrase "barking orders" is primarily used to suggest

(A) an organized plan
(B) a calm attitude
(C) a pet-like docility
(D) an aggressive approach
(E) an open discussion

41. In line 63, her father's question to Sarah suggests that he

(A) wishes Sarah would not invade his private moments with Tess
(B) resists the idea of getting married for a second time
(C) is aware that she is listening to the adult conversation
(D) will ask Sarah's brother to be one of his groomsmen
(E) wants Sarah to forget about her mother altogether

42. The passage as a whole suggests that Sarah wishes that, in her family's life, she were

(A) somewhere else
(B) away at school
(C) more involved
(D) getting married
(E) her brother's age

GO ON TO THE NEXT PAGE →

Questions 43-48 are based on the following passages.

Online education refers to courses that are not taken in a traditional classroom but via the Internet, with teachers and students working on computers. Both of the following passages were published in 2014.

Passage 1

Online education hasn't freed itself of all the connotations, both positive and negative, that anything "online" could have. It's imperfect and incomplete. Just because it is sponsored by revered schools doesn't mean it can't be full of all the
Line
5 silliness, inaccuracy, and distraction of any online browsing. We can't overlook, however, that it is a positive step in the direction of making higher education available to all. Online education, which might originally have been the province of companies just interested in selling degrees, now has its
10 own standards of rigor. On the other hand, online education is, as much as any other product, a child of the market. When faced with the accusation that college costs too much money, college administrators always have a response at the ready: that's why we're moving online, where lower costs for us
15 mean lower costs for the students!

So how successful have these online courses been? According to a 2013 study, 77 percent of academic leaders rate the learning outcomes in online education as the same or superior to those in face-to-face classes. According to the
20 survey, many leaders still consider low retention rates to be the biggest roadblock to the growth of online education. It's hard to know how these numbers would translate to face-to-face classes because those classes are typically so much smaller. Perhaps the problem is deeper. Maybe "online"
25 education is not such a new development: those students who are in face-to-face classes are not required to do their homework in Internet-free areas, and most students can browse the Internet freely in class. The Internet is already everywhere, and the undetected outcome may be lowered
30 educational standards in general. Online education isn't perfect yet. It might, however, be the only real way for educators to adapt to our new web-centric mode of existence. Perhaps online education will be the wave of the future because it's the one mode that will be able to balance the
35 "education" part with the much more powerful cultural tide of the "online."

Passage 2

Whatever its negative implications, online education is no longer something we can choose to ignore. Thirty-two percent of higher-education students now take at least one
40 class online, and the percentage who take two or more is not much lower. Even for courses that are not taught purely online, as many as 70 percent of instructors say that online learning is critical to their long-term teaching strategies. Though our initial response may be one of panic, things
45 are not so revolutionarily bad as they might seem. Online education certainly has its benefits. (77 percent of instructors rank online courses nearly as high as face-to-face courses in terms of learning effectiveness.) And the belief that online education must necessarily be a diluted form of the "real
50 thing" is simply misguided conservatism. The "real thing," after all, had its own set of problems long before online education came along, and while students may be truant or distracted from online courses, they are just as likely to be so in face-to-face courses.

55 The online education model is not only less expensive and more convenient than traditional educational models, it's also—like so much else in the culture today—excitingly multifaceted. Imagine an online physics course. A basic unit on mechanics will give you not just a sheet of formulas and
60 a list of problems but also interactive games with mini-labs, links to outside sources for extra help, and online chats with TAs and professors. For traditional educators, the risk of online education is not that it doesn't teach the material but that it teaches too much material and floods students with
65 so many stimuli and so much information that they end up learning nothing at all.

43. The first sentence of Passage 1 implies that online education

(A) is overly inexpensive
(B) is fashionable but ineffective
(C) has both good and bad aspects
(D) is declining in popularity
(E) has replaced traditional education

44. The sentence in lines 11-15 ("When … students") serves primarily to

(A) mock the speech of administrators
(B) set up the anecdote that follows
(C) expand the idea in an earlier sentence
(D) provide incentives to buy a product
(E) express concern over a trend

GO ON TO THE NEXT PAGE

45. Like the author of Passage 1, the author of Passage 2 most likely thinks of face-to-face education as

(A) collaborative and able to incorporate many media
(B) the last hope for aspiring professionals
(C) an outmoded way of relaying information
(D) exclusive to those who can afford it
(E) susceptible to compromising influences

46. As it is used in line 49, "diluted" most nearly means

(A) split
(B) flooded
(C) moistened
(D) purer
(E) weakened

47. The author of Passage 1 would most likely view the point made in lines 50-54, Passage 2 ("The ... courses"), as

(A) essentially correct
(B) bullishly wrongheaded
(C) exceedingly respectful
(D) subtly heavy-handed
(E) unreasonably cruel

48. Both passages cite the 77 percent statistic in order to make a point about

(A) widespread disapproval
(B) perceived effectiveness
(C) academic methodologies
(D) traditional models
(E) learning objectives

STOP

If you finish before time is called, you may check your work on this section only.
Do not turn to any other section in the test.

SECTION 4
Time — 25 minutes
18 Questions
(21–38)

Directions: For this section, solve each problem and decide which is the best of the choices given. Fill in the corresponding circle on the answer sheet. You may use any available space for scratchwork.

<table>
<tr><td rowspan="4">Notes</td></tr>
<tr><td>1. The use of a calculator is permitted.</td></tr>
<tr><td>2. All numbers used are real numbers.</td></tr>
<tr><td>3. Figures that accompany problems in this test are intended to provide information useful in solving the problems. They are drawn as accurately as possible EXCEPT when it is stated in a specific problem that the figure is not drawn to scale. All figures lie in a plane unless other wise indicated.</td></tr>
</table>

4. Unless otherwise specified, the domain of any function f is assumed to be the set of all real numbers x for which $f(x)$ is a real number.

$A = \pi r^2$ $A = lw$ $A = \frac{1}{2}bh$ $V = lwh$ $V = \pi r^2 h$ $c^2 = a^2 + b^2$

$C = 2\pi r$

Special Right Triangles

The number of degrees of arc in a circle is 360.

The sum of the measures in degrees of the angles of a triangle is 180.

$$t < 6$$
$$16 < 4t$$

21. If t is an integer that satisfies the inequalities above, what is the value of t ?

(A) 2
(B) 3
(C) 4
(D) 5
(E) 6

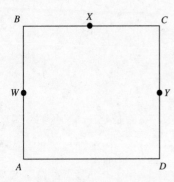

22. In the figure above, *ABCD* is a square. If *W* is the midpoint of *AB*, *X* is the midpoint of *BC*, and *Y* is the midpoint of *CD*, which of the following is NOT equal to *BC* ?

(A) *AD* + *AW*
(B) *AW* + *XC*
(C) *CD*
(D) *DY* + *BW*
(E) *AD* + *CY* − *AW*

GO ON TO THE NEXT PAGE

$$6 + 4z = 20$$

23. How many values for z satisfy the equation above?

(A) Zero
(B) One
(C) Two
(D) Three
(E) More than three

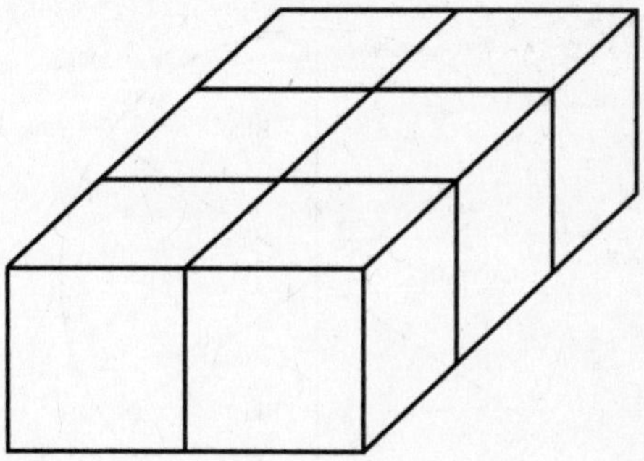

25. In the figure shown above, the large rectangular solid has been divided into 6 congruent cubes. If the face of each cube has an area of 3 square inches, what is the total surface area of the rectangular solid, in square inches?

(A) 22
(B) 33
(C) 50
(D) 66
(E) 132

24. If $10 < s^3 < 12$ and $\sqrt{t} = s$, which of the following could be the value of t ?

(A) 2
(B) 4
(C) 5
(D) 8
(E) 20

26. If $\dfrac{y}{x}$ is negative and $x > 0$, which of the following is negative?

(A) x^3
(B) y^2
(C) $-y$
(D) $2x$
(E) y

GO ON TO THE NEXT PAGE ⟩

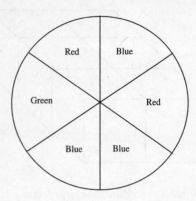

Note: Figure not drawn to scale.

27. The sectors of the circular dart board shown in the figure above are each painted one of three colors: blue, green, or red. The probability that a thrown dart that hits the dart board will land in a red sector is $\frac{1}{4}$. If the central angle of each red sector has degree measure r, what is the value of r ?

(A) 30
(B) 45
(C) 55
(D) 60
(E) 90

x	$g(x)$	$h(x)$
0	−4	2
1	2	3
2	3	0
3	1	1
4	0	4

28. Several values of the functions g and h are shown in the table above. For which of the following values of x is $g(x) = h(1)$?

(A) 0
(B) 1
(C) 2
(D) 3
(E) 4

GO ON TO THE NEXT PAGE

Directions for Student-Produced Response Questions

Each of the remaining 10 questions requires you to solve the problem and enter your answer by marking the ovals in the special grid, as shown in the examples below. You may use any available space for scratch work.

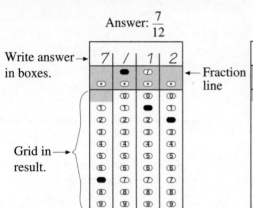

Answer: $\frac{7}{12}$

Write answer → in boxes.

Fraction line

Answer: 2.5

Decimal point

Grid in → result.

Note: You may start your answers in any column, space permitting. Columns not needed should be left blank.

- Mark no more than one circle in any column.

- Because the answer sheet will be machine-scored, **you will receive credit only if the circles are filled in correctly.**

- Although not required, it is suggested that you write your answer in the boxes at the top of the columns to help you fill in the circles accurately.

- Some problems may have more than one correct answer. In such cases, grid only one answer.

- No question has a negative answer.

- **Mixed numbers** such as $3\frac{1}{2}$ must be gridded as

  3.5 or 7/2. (If $\boxed{3\ 1\ /\ 2}$ is gridded, it will be

  interpreted as $\frac{31}{2}$, not $3\frac{1}{2}$.)

- **Decimal Answers:** If you obtain a decimal answer with more digits than the grid can accommodate, it may be either rounded or truncated, but it must fill the entire grid. For example, if you obtain an answer such as 0.6666..., you should record your result as .666 or .667. **A less accurate value such as .66 or .67 will be scored as incorrect.**

Acceptable ways to grid $\frac{2}{3}$ are:

x	$-\frac{1}{2}$	$-\frac{2}{3}$	-1	-2
y	-12	-9	-6	-3

29. For each pair (x, y) in the table above, $x = \dfrac{k}{y}$, where k is a constant. What is the value of k?

30. For each chore Kevin completes, his mother gives him 8 dollars. If Kevin's mother gave him less than 1,500 dollars for doing chores last month, what is the <u>greatest</u> possible number of chores Kevin could have completed last month?

GO ON TO THE NEXT PAGE ⇒

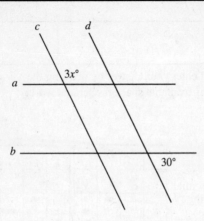

31. In the figure above, $a \parallel b$ and $c \parallel d$. What is the value of x ?

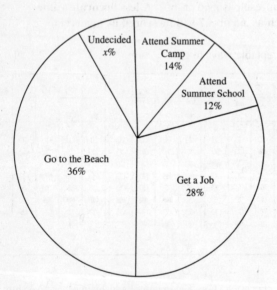

What will you do during your summer vacation?

Survey of 600 High School Juniors

32. In a survey, 600 high school juniors each selected one of six responses to the question "What will you do during your summer vacation?" The results are shown in the circle graph above. How many of the high school juniors selected a response other than "Go to the beach?"

33. If the area of circle P is 121π, what is the diameter of circle P ?

If 12 and 9 are factors of z,
then 12×9 is a factor of z.

34. If z is a positive integer less than 120, what is one possible value of z that proves the statement above false?

GO ON TO THE NEXT PAGE

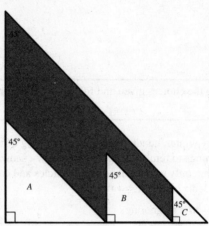

37. How many integers between 100 and 1,000 have at least one digit that is a four?

35. The figure above shows three small right triangles inside one large right triangle. If the area of triangle *A* is 18, the area of triangle *B* is 8, and the area of triangle *C* is 2, what is the area of the shaded region?

38. Ben and Carl left school at the same time and each drove directly to his own house. Ben drove an average speed of 20 miles an hour, and Carl drove an average speed of 15 miles per hour. Ben and Carl arrived at their respective houses at the same time. If Ben drove 15 miles further than Carl did, how far, in miles, did Ben drive?

36. If $\dfrac{a}{b} = \dfrac{4}{5}$ and $\dfrac{a}{c} = \dfrac{1}{15}$, then $\dfrac{b}{c} =$

STOP
If you finish before time is called, you may check your work on this section only.
Do not turn to any other section in the test.

SECTION 5
Time — 30 minutes
39 Questions
(1–39)

Directions: For each question in this section, select the best answer from among the choices given and fill in the corresponding circle on the answer sheet.

The following sentences test correctness and effectiveness of expression. Part of each sentence or the entire sentence is underlined; beneath each sentence are five ways of phrasing the underlined material. Choice A repeats the original phrasing; the other four choices are different. If you think the original phrasing produces a better sentence than any of the alternatives, select choice A; if not, select one of the other choices.

In making your selection, follow the requirements of standard written English; that is, pay attention to grammar, choice of words, sentence construction, and punctuation. Your selection should result in the most effective sentence—clear and precise, without awkwardness or ambiguity.

EXAMPLE:

Bobby Flay baked his first cake <u>and he was thirteen years old then</u>.
(A) and he was thirteen years old then
(B) when he was thirteen
(C) at age thirteen years old
(D) upon the reaching of thirteen years
(E) at the time when he was thirteen

1. The Great Wall of China, <u>which was built to protect the Chinese Empire from invasion, and it extends</u> over more than 13,000 miles.

   (A) which was built to protect the Chinese Empire from invasion, and it extends
   (B) was built to protect the Chinese Empire from invasion, it extends
   (C) built to protect the Chinese Empire from invasion, therefore extending
   (D) which was built to protect the Chinese Empire from invasion, extends
   (E) it was built to protect the Chinese Empire from invasion, extending

2. Every winter, hundreds of <u>drivers ignoring</u> official warnings to remain at home while heavy snow is falling, only to crash into other vehicles and cause major accidents on the highway.

   (A) drivers ignoring
   (B) drivers ignore
   (C) drivers in their ignoring
   (D) drivers who ignore
   (E) drivers, when ignoring

3. Walking the moon's surface for slightly more than two hours, <u>numerous photos were taken by Neil Armstrong and Buzz Aldrin of Little West Crater</u>.

   (A) numerous photos were taken by Neil Armstrong and Buzz Aldrin of Little West Crater
   (B) numerous photos of Little West Crater were taken by Neil Armstrong and Buzz Aldrin
   (C) photos of Little West Crater, many of them were taken by Neil Armstrong and Buzz Aldrin
   (D) Neil Armstrong and Buzz Aldrin took, of Little West Crater, numerous photos
   (E) Neil Armstrong and Buzz Aldrin took numerous photos of Little West Crater

4. Chiropractic methods of treatment, once commonly criticized by many in the medical field, <u>appear to be gaining</u> general acceptance among health care professionals.

   (A) appear to be gaining
   (B) although gaining
   (C) but they appear to have gained
   (D) will appear to have gained
   (E) but gaining

GO ON TO THE NEXT PAGE ⟶

5. The largest and most diverse rainforests in the world <u>is</u> found in the South American Amazon Basin, which includes regions belonging to nine different nations.

(A) is
(B) that are
(C) are
(D) having been
(E) were

6. After the Curies discovered radium in 1898, this element became known for its damaging effects upon humans, <u>some are</u> mutated cells, ulcers, and cancer.

(A) some are
(B) those effects include
(C) they are
(D) such as
(E) among them was

7. Though most famous for her relationship with Beatles singer John Lennon, <u>the important contributions of Yoko Ono include her work in</u> art, peace, and AIDS outreach programs.

(A) the important contributions of Yoko Ono include her work in
(B) Yoko Ono has been an important contributor to
(C) Yoko Ono's important contributions include her work in
(D) the important contributions of Yoko Ono would have been her work in
(E) the works of Yoko Ono are important contributions to

8. Genghis Khan united many nomadic tribes of northeast Asia in the early thirteenth <u>century and founded</u> the Mongol Empire.

(A) century and founded
(B) century, who founded
(C) century and to found
(D) century, he also founded
(E) century and founding

9. When a teacher cares about her classes, she prepares <u>for them carefully, and often late at night, which demonstrated that they were important</u> to her.

(A) them carefully, and often late at night, which demonstrated that they were important
(B) it carefully, often late at night, and this demonstrates that it is important
(C) it carefully, often late at night, so it demonstrates that it is important
(D) them carefully, often late at night, which demonstrates that it is important
(E) for them carefully, often late at night, thereby demonstrating that they are important

10. Rebekah chose a wedding date, discovered that it was a date that most of her invited guests could not attend, <u>and it was postponed</u> until the following Saturday.

(A) and it was postponed
(B) she then postponed it
(C) postponing it
(D) then postpone it
(E) and then postponed it

11. Ludovic built <u>a house of cards that was enormous but simultaneously it was very fragile as well</u>.

(A) a house of cards that was enormous but simultaneously it was very fragile as well
(B) an enormous house of cards, it was simultaneously very fragile
(C) a house of cards that was enormous and as well simultaneously very fragile
(D) an enormous but very fragile house of cards
(E) an enormous and simultaneously very fragile house of cards

GO ON TO THE NEXT PAGE

12. As the autumn wore on, the temperatures <u>start to drop</u> below freezing on a regular basis.

    (A) start to drop
    (B) started to drop
    (C) start dropping
    (D) have started dropping
    (E) are beginning to drop

13. Walkway Over the Hudson, originally a railroad bridge and <u>part of the Poughkeepsie Bridge Route, now used by locals as a pedestrian walkway.</u>

    (A) part of the Poughkeepsie Bridge Route, now used by locals as a pedestrian walkway
    (B) part of the Poughkeepsie Bridge Route, which is now used by locals as a pedestrian walkway
    (C) part of the Poughkeepsie Bridge Route, is now used by locals as a pedestrian walkway.
    (D) It was part of the Poughkeepsie Bridge Route, being used today by locals as a pedestrian walkway
    (E) used today by locals as a pedestrian walkway, and it was once part of the Poughkeepsie Bridge Route

14. The gecko's feet are <u>different than other lizards</u> such as the iguana or the Komodo dragon.

    (A) different than other lizards
    (B) different than those of other lizards
    (C) different than other lizards' feet
    (D) unlike seeing other lizards
    (E) unlike other lizards

15. The biologist observed the similarities between the results of his own experiments <u>with what resulted from Watson and Crick's</u> experiments more than sixty years previously.

    (A) with what resulted from Watson and Crick's
    (B) with Watson and Crick's
    (C) and also Watson and Crick's
    (D) and those of Watson and Crick's
    (E) and Watson and Crick's

16. <u>By planning to arrive early to the concert is why</u> Carl was confident that he would be able to find a seat right in front of the stage.

    (A) By planning to arrive early to the concert is why
    (B) His planning to arrive early to the concert ended in that
    (C) Due to his plan of arriving early to the concert,
    (D) Because he planned to arrive early to the concert,
    (E) He planned to arrive early to the concert is the reason

17. Nikola Tesla was a remarkable scientist not only because he made numerous contributions towards the fields of x-ray imaging and <u>radio but he patented</u> more than 300 inventions.

    (A) radio but he patented
    (B) radio, he also patented
    (C) radio, but also because he patented
    (D) radio but because he patented also
    (E) radio but he also patented

GO ON TO THE NEXT PAGE

18. Alzheimer's disease causes memory loss and <u>confusion; for instance, those affected frequently forget</u> the names of close friends and relatives.

   (A) confusion; for instance, those affected frequently forget

   (B) confusion, forgetting, as for instance,

   (C) confusion; for instance, often forgetting

   (D) confusion, a for instance is when they forget

   (E) confusion, often forgetting, for instance

19. In 1505, Michelangelo started building Pope Julius II's <u>tomb but never finishing it to his satisfaction, perhaps because he was constantly distracted by other tasks.</u>

   (A) tomb but never finishing it to his satisfaction, perhaps because he was constantly distracted by other tasks

   (B) tomb, however, it was never finished to his satisfaction, perhaps because he was constantly distracted by other tasks

   (C) tomb, although distracted, perhaps, by other tasks, it was never completed to his satisfaction

   (D) tomb, he never finished it to his satisfaction however, perhaps because he was constantly distracted by other tasks

   (E) tomb, but, perhaps because he was distracted by other tasks, he never completed the tomb to his satisfaction

20. The claims made by the witnesses, particularly the statements of the victim, <u>has convinced the jury that the defendant is guilty and returned</u> a verdict of guilty.

   (A) has convinced the jury that the defendant is guilty and returned

   (B) have convinced the jury to return

   (C) has created so much conviction among the jury that it has returned

   (D) have convinced the jury, returning

   (E) have so convinced the jury that they have returned

GO ON TO THE NEXT PAGE

The following sentences test your ability to recognize grammar and usage errors. Each sentence contains either a single error or no error at all. No sentence contains more than one error. The error, if there is one, is underlined and lettered. If the sentence contains an error, select the one underlined part that must be changed to make the sentence correct. If the sentence is correct, select choice E. In choosing answers, follow the requirements of standard written English.

EXAMPLE:

The other players and her significantly improved
   A   B   C

the game plan created by the coaches. No error
             D   E

21. The insurance company has given an extension of the
                             A

payment deadline to seniors, but the benefits of this

extension having been outweighed by a rise in the
               B   C

company's charges. No error
   D   E

22. While Mathilde was generally not one to complain, her
    A   B   C

and Tiffany decided to go to the manager to report the
                          D

salesman's inappropriate behavior. No error
                 E

23. When the Impressionists began violating the accepted
     A

academic rules of painting, they have been received
                            B

by art critics with disapproval rather than with
  C   D

enthusiasm. No error
        E

24. Mao Zedong, a Chinese communist revolutionary
                 A

which was responsible for commanding the Red Army
           B

during its battle with Chiang Kai-Shek,
      C

eventually became the founding father of the People's
          D

Republic of China. No error
          E

25. In anticipation of winter, the grey squirrel has hidden nuts
       A

and seeds throughout the area to ensure its food source

during the colder months and preventing other competing
                      B

species from consuming all of the available food.
     C   D

No error
 E

26. According to historians, the ancient Mayans' knowledge

of both mathematics as well as astronomy was far beyond
               A   B

that of other civilizations of the same time period.
  C   D

No error
 E

GO ON TO THE NEXT PAGE ➤

27. Jeremy, <u>whose</u> entire life was focused on his career,
           A

responded at his mother's suggestion <u>that he marry</u>
          B   C

<u>by laughing</u> and going back to work. <u>No error</u>
       D   E

28. The prevalence <u>of crime</u> within neighborhoods <u>located</u>
                A   B

within the city center <u>have</u> increased dramatically in the
       C   D

last twenty years. <u>No error</u>
                     E

29. His parents <u>having</u> convinced Claude <u>that</u> to attend
        A   B   C

college at the university nearest his hometown would

<u>be both</u> inexpensive and convenient. <u>No error</u>
       D   E

30. The driver <u>changed</u> lanes <u>on</u> the icy road as <u>quick</u> as he
               A   B   C

could when the car in front of him began <u>sliding wildly</u>
                                              D

into the ditch. <u>No error</u>
                   E

31. One claim that conspiracy theorists <u>make</u> <u>to explain</u>
              A   B

sightings of unidentified flying objects near Area 51 <u>is</u>
                                                   C

that such objects <u>are</u> actually <u>alien aircrafts</u>. <u>No error</u>
                       D   E

32. Amy, <u>whose</u> volleyball skills I have always <u>respected</u>,
            A   B

understands better than <u>I</u> how to properly spike and <u>serve</u>
                           C   D

the ball. <u>No error</u>
               E

33. While hiring mall security guards <u>is</u> actually an effective
                                     A

means <u>in protecting</u> customers, such guards are
              B

often <u>dismissed by the public</u> <u>as powerless</u>. <u>No error</u>
            C   D   E

34. After choosing <u>a location, menu, and band</u> for the
                     A

wedding reception that they <u>would have</u>, Josh and Carla
                               B

<u>calculated</u> that their reception would be less expensive
       C

than their <u>friends</u>. <u>No error</u>
                D   E

GO ON TO THE NEXT PAGE →

> **Directions:** The following passage is an early draft of an essay. Some parts of the passage need to be rewritten.
>
> Read the passage and select the best answers for the questions that follow. Some questions are about particular sentences or parts of sentences and ask you to improve sentence structure or word choice. Other questions ask you to consider organization and development. In choosing answers, follow the requirements of standard written English.

Questions 35-39 are based on the following passage.

(1) Since prehistoric times, painters have been creating portraits of celebrities, nobility, and other notable individuals. (2) The talents of some painters have proven to be particularly well-suited to the task of portrait painting. (3) John Singer Sargent, for example. (4) All of his portraits have been displayed in famous museums such as the Metropolitan Museum of Art in New York City and the National Gallery in London. (5) Of these, *The Lady with the Rose* is considered his best loved and most widely exhibited work.

(6) The task of accurately capturing not just the photographic likeness, but also the inner essence of the subject, is a challenging one. (7) In proper portrait painting, the subject's mouth should remain relatively neutral, not smiling openly or frowning, so the artist must find ways to convey expression through the eyes and eyebrows. (8) Faced with this difficulty, Paul Cézanne focused on capturing a single moment in time, and would sometimes take hours to complete a single brush stroke. (9) He frequently required as many as 150 sittings from his subjects, spending hours on a single feature. (10) Doing this proved worthwhile: his *Portrait of Louis-Auguste Cézanne, Father of the Artist, reading 'l'Evénement* was displayed at the prestigious Paris Salon.

(11) Subjects are often dissatisfied with their portraits, especially if they feel that their best features have not been emphasized or if they do not feel as if the painting does not convey the proper image of their persona. (12) When Sargent's *Portrait of Madam X* aroused scandal due to its subject's pose and dress, the reaction caused the sitter, Amélie Gautreau, to reject the painting. (13) Nevertheless, when it comes to portrait painting, a flattering portrayal will not ensure the subject's approval. (14) As a portrayal of George Washington, John Trumbull's portrait *General George Washington* was rejected by the committee that had commissioned it. (15) Trumbull was a respected painter whose *Declaration of Independence* was used on the two-dollar bill.

35. What is the best version of the underlined portions of sentences 3 and 4 (reproduced below)?

    John Singer Sargent, for example. All of his portraits have been displayed in famous museums such as the Metropolitan Museum of Art in New York City and the National Gallery in London

    (A) (No change)
    (B) All of John Singer Sargent's portraits, for example, have
    (C) There is John Singer Sargent, for example. His portraits have all
    (D) For example, John Singer painted many portraits, and all of them have
    (E) John Singer Sargent, for example, whose portraits have all

36. Which of the following, if placed at the beginning of sentence 6 (reproduced below), would provide the most effective transition between the first and second paragraphs?

    The task of accurately capturing not just the photographic likeness, but also the inner essence of the subject, is a challenging one.

    (A) Although portrait painters have been popular for centuries,
    (B) Because of the focus on photographic accuracy,
    (C) With such demand from subjects,
    (D) But no matter how attractive a person is,
    (E) It may require time to become a skilled painter, but

37. In context, which of the following is the best revision of the underlined section of sentence 10 (reproduced below)?

    Doing this proved worthwhile: his Portrait of Louis-Auguste Cézanne, Father of the Artist, Reading 'l'Evénement *was displayed at the prestigious Paris Salon.*

    (A) (No change)
    (B) Painting Impressionist works
    (C) His effort had
    (D) That has eventually
    (E) This meticulousness

GO ON TO THE NEXT PAGE →

38. Which of the following sentences would best be placed at the beginning of paragraph 3, before sentence 11?

(A) Some portrait artists have become quite famous.
(B) We may not always realize how the length of time required to a paint quality portrait.
(C) Most of us have seen portraits hanging in museums.
(D) Some portraits have not been so well received.
(E) There are a number of instances that show this to be true.

39. In context, which of the following is the best version of the first underlined portion of sentence 14 (reproduced below)?

As a portrayal of George Washington, John Trumbull's portrait General George Washington *was rejected by the committee that had commissioned it.*

(A) (No change)
(B) Following
(C) Even though it complimented
(D) With its presentation of
(E) Arguably an accurate portrayal

STOP

If you finish before time is called, you may check your work on this section only.
Do not turn to any other section in the test.

PRACTICE TEST 2 ANSWERS

Section 1		Section 2		Section 3		Section 4		Section 5			
1.	B	1.	D	25.	B	21.	D	1.	D	31.	E
2.	C	2.	A	26.	D	22.	A	2.	B	32.	E
3.	D	3.	C	27.	E	23.	B	3.	E	33.	B
4.	A	4.	B	28.	A	24.	C	4.	A	34.	D
5.	C	5.	E	29.	E	25.	D	5.	C	35.	B
6.	A	6.	B	30.	C	26.	E	6.	D	36.	A
7.	E	7.	D	31.	E	27.	B	7.	B	37.	E
8.	A	8.	A	32.	A	28.	C	8.	A	38.	D
9.	C	9.	E	33.	E	29.	6	9.	E	39.	C
10.	A	10.	A	34.	E	30.	187	10.	E		
11.	B	11.	E	35.	E	31.	50	11.	D		
12.	E	12.	B	36.	B	32.	384	12.	B		
13.	C	13.	D	37.	D	33.	22	13.	C		
14.	A	14.	A	38.	B	34.	36 or 72	14.	B		
15.	D	15.	D	39.	B	35.	44	15.	D		
16.	D	16.	D	40.	D	36.	$\frac{1}{12}$ or .083	16.	D		
17.	C	17.	C	41.	C			17.	C		
18.	B	18.	E	42.	C	37.	252	18.	A		
19.	E	19.	B	43.	C	38.	60	19.	E		
20.	A	20.	C	44.	C			20.	B		
21.	B			45.	E			21.	B		
22.	D			46.	E			22.	C		
23.	C			47.	A			23.	B		
24.	D			48.	B			24.	B		
								25.	B		
								26.	A		
								27.	B		
								28.	D		
								29.	B		
								30.	C		

You will find a detailed explanation for each question beginning on page 185.

SCORING YOUR PRACTICE PSAT

Critical Reading

After you have checked your answers against the answer key, you can calculate your score. For the two Critical Reading sections (Sections 1 and 3), add up the number of correct answers and the number of incorrect answers. Enter these numbers on the worksheet on the next page. Multiply the number of incorrect answers by .25 and subtract this result from the number of correct answers. Then round this to the nearest whole number. This is your Critical Reading "raw score." Next, use the conversion table to convert your raw score to a scaled score.

Math

Calculating your Math score is a bit trickier, because some of the questions have five answer choices (for these, the incorrect answer deduction is .25), and some are Grid-Ins (which have no deduction for wrong answers).

First, check your answers to all of the problem-solving questions on Sections 2 and 4. For Section 2 and questions 21–28 of Section 4, enter the number of correct answers and the number of incorrect answers into the worksheet on the next page. Multiply the number of incorrect answers by .25 and subtract this result from the number of correct answers. For questions 29–38 of Section 4, the Grid-In questions, simply enter the number of correct answers. Now, add up the totals for both types of math questions to give you your total Math raw score. Then you can use the conversion table to find your scaled score.

Writing Skills

The Writing Skills section should be scored just like the Critical Reading sections. Add up the number of correct answers and the number of incorrect answers from Section 5, and enter these numbers on the worksheet on the next page. Multiply the number of incorrect answers by .25 and subtract this result from the number of correct answers. Then round this to the nearest whole number. This is your Writing Skills raw score. Next, use the conversion table to convert your raw scores to scaled scores.

WORKSHEET FOR CALCULATING YOUR SCORE

Critical Reading

	Correct	**Incorrect**

A. Sections 1 and 3 _____ – (.25 × _____) =

A

B. Total rounded Critical Reading raw score

B

Math

	Correct	**Incorrect**

C. Sections 2 and 4—Problem Solving _____ – (.25 × _____) =

C

D. Section 4—Grid-Ins _____ =

D

E. Total unrounded Math raw score (C + D)

E

F. Total rounded Math raw score

F

Writing Skills

	Correct	**Incorrect**

Section 5 _____ – (.25 × _____) =

Total rounded Writing Skills raw score

SCORE CONVERSION TABLE

Math Raw Score	Math Scaled Score	Critical Reading Raw Score	Critical Reading Scaled Score	Writing Skills Raw Score	Writing Skills Scaled Score
38	80	48	80	39	80
37	77	47	80	38	80
36	74	46	78	37	78
35	72	45	76	36	77
34	70	44	74	35	76
33	68	43	72	34	74
32	66	42	71	33	73
31	65	41	69	32	71
30	64	40	68	31	69
29	62	39	67	30	68
28	61	38	66	29	66
27	60	37	64	28	65
26	59	36	63	27	63
25	58	35	62	26	62
24	57	34	62	25	60
23	55	33	61	24	59
22	54	32	60	23	57
21	53	31	59	22	56
20	52	30	58	21	55
19	51	29	57	20	54
18	50	28	56	19	52
17	48	27	55	18	51
16	47	26	54	17	50
15	46	25	54	16	49
14	45	24	53	15	48
13	44	23	52	14	46
12	43	22	51	13	45
11	42	21	50	12	44
10	41	20	49	11	43
9	40	19	48	10	41
8	39	18	47	9	40
7	38	17	46	8	39
6	36	16	45	7	37
5	35	15	44	6	36
4	34	14	43	5	35
3	32	13	42	4	33
2	30	12	41	3	32
1	29	11	40	2	31
0	26	10	39	1	30
		9	38	0	29
		8	37		
		7	36		
		6	34		
		5	33		
		4	32		
		3	30		
		2	29		
		1	27		
		0	25		

Chapter 8
Practice Test 2:
Answers and
Explanations

Section 1

1. **B**   Since the coach *didn't want the opposing team to pick up her signals*, she therefore wanted to keep them secret. "Secretive" would be a good word to put in the blank. Eliminate choice (A), which is a trap since this sentence deals with sports. Choices (C), (D), and (E) do not match "secretive," so choice (B) is the best answer.

2. **C**   Start with the first blank. The clues of *spears, traps, and cudgels* are typically involved with hunting, so eliminate everything except choices (C) and (D). Now work the second blank. Since the sentence says that this activity *was necessary for the head of the household*, the second blank should be something like "symbol" or "prime example." Eliminate choice (D) since it doesn't match. Choice (C) is the correct answer.

3. **D**   Start with the second blank. The sentence states that *his personal temperament has never been agreed upon*, so you know there is a disagreement about Ty Cobb. Since there are clues stating he had instances of *kindness and generosity*, find something for the second blank that is the opposite of those traits. Eliminate everything but choices (A) and (D) since *irritability* and *irascibility* are both opposites of the clues. Since it's clear that he has different *temperaments*, the first blank should indicate that his bad behavior stands in opposite of his good behavior. The first blank should be something that means "goes against." Eliminate choice (A) since *highlighted* does not fit. Choice (D), *overshadowed*, is the correct answer.

4. **A**   Since the *chef believed that originality was a far better attribute of good cooking than mere skill*, the first blank will need something that mirrors *originality* and the second blank will need to match *skill*. Start with the first blank and eliminate everything but choices (A) and (C). Now work with the second blank. Eliminate choice (C) because *opulence* means "extravagance," and is therefore incorrect. Choice (A) is the correct answer.

5. **C**   Since Raphael was always in contrast with what *Ms. Banks expected from her students*, look for opposites of the clues. Start with the first blank, which needs to be the opposite of *punctual*. Eliminate everything except choices (B) and (C) since *sluggish* means "slow" and could fit the blank. The second blank needs to be the opposite of *disrespectful*. Both *dutiful* (which means "obedient") and *deferential* (which means "respectful") are possibilities, but the combination of words in choice (C) is a better fit, so eliminate choice (B). Choice (C) is the correct answer.

6. **A**   The clue here is that the film looks only at the *origins of the story's characters*. Therefore, the blank should be something that means "beginning." Choice (A) fits the blank, since *prelude* means "beginning." *Picaresque* means "humorous adventure," so eliminate choice (B). *A Roman a clef* is "historical fiction," so eliminate choice (C). *An anachronism* is something that is "out of place" while *an epilogue* is the opposite of beginning, so get rid of both choices (D) and (E). Choice (A) is the correct answer.

7.   **E**   Since the sentence contrasts *the films of the 1980s*, which *were considered clichéd and commercial*, with *those of the 1970s*, the words for the two blanks will be the opposites of each other. The first blank should be the opposite of *clichéd*, so look for something that means "not clichéd" or "original." Eliminate everything but choices (B) and (E). The second blank needs to be the opposite of *commercial*, so look for something that means "not intended for a mass market." Eliminate choice (B) since *ubiquitous* means "abundant." Choice (E) is the correct answer.

8.   **A**   The clue here is that the auto mechanic can figure out a problem *prior to inspection*, so therefore we need a word in the blank that means "having foresight or being able to see in the future." Choice (A) matches these words well. *Scintillating* is sometimes used to describe intelligence, but it means "shining brightly," so eliminate choice (D). Choice (B) means "working well," so eliminate it. Choice (C) means to "experience through watching others," and choice (E) describes children with "advanced abilities beyond their age," so eliminate them. Choice (A) is the correct answer.

9.   **C**   The main idea in this passage is that Samuel's limited English skills were actually good for him in his current job, since he didn't question some of the odd phrases used in the kitchen. Therefore, the author uses those phrases in order to portray Samuel's limited English as helpful. Eliminate choice (A), since this is not mentioned. Choice (B) seems like it could work, but the author is not placing any emphasis on whether or not the phrases are silly. Choice (C) seems to match the prediction, so keep it. Choices (D) and (E) are not mentioned, so eliminate them. Choice (C) is the correct answer.

10.   **A**   Since it's stated that Samuel's lack of English skills actually helped him in his current job, the correct answer will be something that means "helpful." Choice (A) fits, so keep it. Choice (B) is negative, so eliminate it. Choice (C) is a positive word, but the passage never mentions whether Samuel likes his job, so eliminate it. Choice (D) doesn't mean "helpful," while choice (E) is a trap answer since it's associated with food, so eliminate both answers. Choice (A) is the correct answer.

11.   **B**   The author states at the beginning of the passage that sugar, once considered a common ingredient of sweet foods such as *candies*, has also become common in more *unexpected* foods, such as *breads and salad dressings*. So the correct answer should show how sugar is part of such a wide range of foods. Choice (A) is only half right, since bread is not commonly associated with sugar. Choice (B) is a good match, so keep it. Choice (C) doesn't work since the author isn't expressing *caution* and choice (E) doesn't work since the author doesn't *criticize* the use of sugar. Choice (D), while it may seem to fit the author's main idea, is too extreme. Choice (B) is the correct answer.

12.   **E**   The question states that the author suggests something about sugar, so find an answer that is definitely true based on the passage. Choice (A) is incorrect since the passage never states that sugar or narcotics are the most addictive substances. Choice (B) doesn't work since the passage never states that the humans and rats process foods in the same way and choice (D) can be eliminated since *most* is too extreme. Choice (C) seems okay, except the passage only states that sugar has become

more widespread over the past several decades, so there is no evidence to suggest that there is more now than exactly 10 years ago. Choice (E), the correct answer, is true because it is stated in the last sentence.

13.   **C**   The word "overflowing" suggests that there have been many *Western projects to modernize the Middle East.* This is a fairly general statement, so the specifics in choices (A) and (B) cannot be supported. Choices (D) and (E) do not address these *Western projects* at all, so they too can be eliminated.

14.   **A**   The sentence in which Bill Clinton appears reads as follows: *President Bill Clinton, for example, is still praised for his role in Israeli-Palestinian talks,* and a few sentences later, the author goes on to say, *This attitude toward non-Western regions, the belief that the West's systems of government can help save the people of the Middle East....* Therefore, it can be inferred that Bill Clinton is a representative of *this attitude,* as choice (A) suggests. The author goes on to criticize this attitude, so choices (B), (D), and (E) can be eliminated. Choice (C) can also be eliminated because Clinton is the only example given.

15.   **D**   Another way of saying *universally applicable* would be "appropriate to all." The author is stating in these lines that Western styles of government may not be appropriate for all people, especially those outside the West, as choice (D) indicates. The author goes on to suggest a need for more non-Western perspectives, therefore eliminating choices (A), (B), and (E). Choice (C) is too extreme in its use of the word *only,* so it can be eliminated. Choice (D) remains as the correct answer.

16.   **D**   The relevant lines state the following: *The native peoples who are then forced to live under the new government's rule become extremely skeptical of it, as its supposed successes are measured by seemingly irrelevant metrics.* The key words here are *extremely skeptical,* which agree most closely with choice (D) and disagrees with choice (E). The information in the passage is not specific enough to support choices (B) or (C). Choice (A) is too extreme in its use of the word *despise,* so it can be eliminated.

17.   **C**   The relevant lines state the following: *Many of the great ancient and historical societies come from these regions, but since the seventeenth century, these regions have been considered almost universally backward.* In other words, these regions were once considered "great" but are now considered "backward," as choice (C) suggests. These lines do not address contemporary governments, which eliminates all other choices.

18.   **B**   This paragraph discusses the influence of George Bush and others, suggesting that this influence has not been a good one, as choice (B) suggests. The lines do not contain specific support for the other choices, so (A), (C), (D), and (E) can be eliminated.

19.   **E**   Cross out the word in the context and replace it with your own: *For many Westerners, nationality is a given and ultimately _____ the more local identifications of town, city, or state.* A word like *supersedes* or *replaces* would work here, in which case only choice (E) comes close. The other choices may represent other meanings for the word *trumps,* but they do not work in this context.

20. **A** Cross out the word in the context and replace it with your own: *The Western notions of nation-above-all and religious coexistence can't _____ in this and other countries because the value systems have developed so independently of these notions.* Some word like *apply* or *function* would work here, in which case only choice (A) comes close. The other choices may represent other meanings for the word *maintain*, but they do not work in this context.

21. **B** This question asks for a statement that would *refute* the author's claim in the lines, *As in many other parts of the world, "Iraqi freedom" was defined by someone other than the Iraqis themselves.* Any statement that would suggest that Iraqis or some other group had a role in defining their own government systems would refute this claim, so choice (B) provides the best refutation. Choices (A), (C), (D), and (E) all support the author's central claim that the West has had a too-powerful influence in the region.

22. **D** The author writes for the most part about the negative effects of Western influence in the Middle East, but the lines, *Certainly, Western nations are today more sensitive to cultural differences than they have ever been,* suggest that this influence may be improving. Choice (D) reflects this concession and slight change of tone. It does not reflect the author's broader point, however, which eliminates choices (A), (B), (C), and (E).

23. **C** The relevant sentence says the following: *It still remains to be seen, however, whether this new multicultural stance is a genuine change or a simple repackaging of an old product.* In this case, the *simple repackaging* is contrasted with *a genuine change.* The author is therefore skeptical that this new approach is a *genuine change,* as suggested in choice (C). The author does not hope for this *simple repackaging,* eliminating choice (A), (B), and (E). Choice (D) takes the word *product* too literally.

24. **D** The author argues throughout the passage that the influence of the West has been too strong in the Middle East and that there needs to be more local influence in government policy. Choice (D) best reflects this main idea. Choices (A), (C), and (E) go against this goal. Choice (B) is also an example of a Western ideal, so it too can be eliminated.

Section 2

1. **D** Given variables in the answer choices, Plug In. If x = 2 ounces of cinnamon, at $3 per ounce, the cost would be $6. This is the target answer, so check the answer choices to see which one equals 6. Choices (A) and (E) can be eliminated, since those numbers are not 6. Choice (B) equals $\frac{2}{3}$, which does not equal 6 and can be eliminated. Choice (C) equals $\frac{3}{2}$, which does not equal 6 and can be eliminated. Choice (D) is 3(2), which does equal 6. Choice (D) is the credited response.

2. **A** When asked for the value of a variable, Plug In the Answers (PITA). Start with choice (C), and plug in 1 for h. The equation becomes $5.73 \times 10^1 = 5.73 \times 10 = 57.3$. This is too big, so eliminate (C). Choices (D) and (E) will also be too big, so eliminate those as well. For choice (A), the equation is $5.73 \times 10^{-2} = 5.73 \times 0.01 = 0.0573$. Therefore choice (A) is the credited response.

3. **C** This seems like a Plugging In problem, because of the variables, or like one in which solving for a and b would help. However, the question asks for a value in terms of $3a$ and $2b$, quantities which are already given. Therefore, $2(3a) + 4(2b)$ becomes $2(5) + 4(9) = 10 + 36 = 46$. Choice (C) is the credited response.

4. **B** To solve average questions, draw an average pie. The total goes in the top space. In this problem, though the individual numbers are unknown, the total for $a + b + c + d + e$ equals the sum of a and b plus the sum of c, d, and e. Therefore, Total = $18 + 37 = 55$. Place this number in the top space and the number of things, which is 5, in the lower left space.

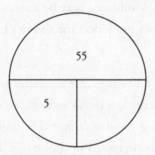

The average is the total divided by the number of things. In this case, that is $55 \div 5 = 11$, so (B) is the credited response.

5. **E** If triangle LMQ is an equilateral triangle and $LM = 2$, then $MQ = 2$ as well. For this same reason, if $MN = 3$, then $MO = 3$ as well. Opposite sides of a parallelogram are equal, so side OP of $MOPQ$ is equal to 2 and side PQ is equal to 3. Therefore, the perimeter of parallelogram $MOPQ$ is $3 + 2 + 3 + 2 = 10$, and (E) is the credited response.

6. **B** When the question asks for a specific value and there are numbers in the answers, Plug In the Answers. Start with choice (C), and plug in $\sqrt{17}$ for the expression $(x + y)$ in the equation. This gives us $13 - (\sqrt{17})^2 = 4$, which is $13 - 17 = -4$. Choice (C) is wrong, so let's try choice (B) and plug in -3 for the expression $(x + y)$. $13 - (-3)^2 = 4$, which translates to $13 - 9 = 4$. Since this is true, (B) is the credited response.

7. **D** The question does not indicate that the figure is "not drawn to scale," so start by ballparking. The angle with measurement $z°$ is obtuse, so (A) and (B) can be eliminated. Since quadrilateral *FJKL* is the reflection of quadrilateral *FGHJ*, $\angle JFL$ will have the same measurement as $\angle GFJ$, which is 40°. Line *y* is a straight line, so the measurement of $\angle JFL$ plus $z°$ equals 180°. Therefore, $z = 140$, so (D) is the credited response. The information that $\angle FJK$ equals 120° is a distraction and is not necessary to solve this problem.

8. **A** If $50 + p = 180$, then $p = 130°$. Therefore, $\angle p$ is obtuse, so the acute angles in (C), (D), and (E) can be eliminated. Of the two remaining angles, (B) appears to be just greater than 90°, whereas (A) looks to be in between 90° and 180°. Choice (A) is closer is 130°, so (A) is the credited response.

9. **E** When asked for a specific value and given numbers in the answer choices, PITA. Start with (C) and assume that $t = 5$. When 5 is quadrupled, or multiplied by 4, the result is 20. When 30 is added to 5, the result is 35. These results are not the same, so (C) can be eliminated. A greater number than 5 is needed to bring the two results closer together; eliminate choices (A) and (B). Choice (D) contains a fraction that is more difficult to plug in, so try (E). When 10 is quadrupled, the result is 40. When 30 is added to 10, the result is also 40, so (E) is the credited response.

10. **A** If Jeff has 70 shirts total but 10 are the wrong size, he only has 60 shirts that he can print for this order. One-third of those 60 shirts, or 20 of them, do not print correctly. This leaves 40 shirts that are correctly printed, making (A) the credited response.

11. **E** There are 17 total members in this crafting club. All of them can either meet on Thursday or they <u>cannot</u> meet on Thursday. To find how many of them <u>cannot</u> meet on Thursday, add up every member outside the Thursday region. This includes the 4 members who cannot meet either Wednesday or Thursday and the 8 members who can only meet Wednesday but not Thursday. $4 + 8 = 12$ members who <u>cannot</u> meet on Thursday.

Alternatively, the same result can be achieved by subtracting the number that <u>can</u> meet on Thursday from the total number of members. In this case, the number of members that can meet on Thursday include the 2 who can also meet on Wednesday plus the 3 who can only meet on Thursday, or 5 of the members. Subtract these 5 from the total 17 to get 12 who <u>cannot</u> meet on Thursday.

Either way, the result is 12, and (E) is the credited response.

12. **B** When dealing with graphs of functions, $f(x)$ or $h(x)$ is the y value for any given x. The question asks how many values of x make $h(x) = 0$, so draw a line on the graph at $y = 0$. This is also the x-axis of the xy-coordinate plane. The number of points of intersection between the graph of $h(x)$ and the line drawn will be the number of values for which x makes $h(x) = 0$.

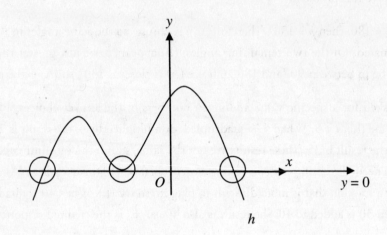

There are three points of intersection, so (B) is the credited response.

13. **D** When asked for a specific value, PITA. First, though, the figure needs to be labeled and the lengths of all sides determined. Start by labeling the given lengths on the figure. Since it is a rectangle, opposite sides are equal, so label those as well. Also, find the length of *UV*, either by using the Pythagorean Theorem or the fact that these triangles are the 5:12:13 Pythagorean triple with each side multiplied by 3. Therefore, *UV* equals 36.

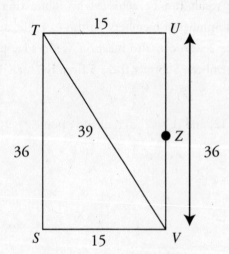

With the figure labeled, it is time to PITA. Start with (C), and plug in 5 for ZV. If $ZV = 5$, then $ZU = 31$, since $UV = 36$. Now check if $ZV + TV = ZU + TU$ by plugging in the values for each segment. This becomes $5 + 39 = 31 + 15$ or $44 = 46$. This is not true, so (C) is not the correct value and can be eliminated. A larger number is needed for ZV to make the left side of the equation larger, so eliminate (A) and (B) as well. For (D), $ZV = 6$ and $ZU = 30$. $ZV + TV = ZU + TU$ becomes $6 + 39 = 30 + 15$ or $45 = 45$. This is true, so (D) is the credited response.

14. **A** From the chart, it is difficult to determine which brand of pushpins is the cheapest per pin. For each brand, take the cost and divide by the number of pins to get the cost per pin. For Bob's, this is $\frac{1.50}{20} = \$0.075$ per pin. For Pokey's, this is $\frac{2.25}{36} = \$0.0625$ per pin. For Thumbelina's, this is $\frac{2.50}{42} = \$0.0595$ per pin. Thumbelina's are the lowest price per pin and the best value, so Karen should start with those. If she buys 2 packages of Thumbelina's at \$2.50 each, she will spend \$5.00 for 84 pushpins. She needs 100 pushpins total, so she still needs 16. To spend the least amount of money, she should get one package of Bob's, since those have at least as many as she needs at the lowest cost. This adds another \$1.50 to her total spending, bringing it to \$6.50. Choice (A) is the credited response.

15. **D** When asked for a specific value and given numbers in the answer choices, PITA. Starting with (C), plug the value for a into the slope formula: $\frac{y_2 - y_1}{x_2 - x_1}$ or $\frac{a - 8}{9 - 3}$. For (C), the slope is $\frac{3.5 - 8}{9 - 3} = \frac{-4.5}{6}$. This is not equal to $-\frac{2}{3}$, so (C) can be eliminated. The value in (C) yielded a slope that was too small, so a bigger value of a is needed. Therefore, (A) and (B) can also be eliminated. For (D), the slope is $\frac{4 - 8}{9 - 3} = \frac{-4}{6} = -\frac{2}{3}$, so (D) is the credited response.

16. **D** The question describes a number line, so draw one to make the numbers easier to visualize. Mark the point with coordinate 3 and then the two points that sit at a distance of 7 from that point.

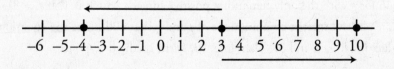

Therefore, the two numbers at a distance of 7 from the point 3 are −4 and 10. Plug these numbers for k into the expressions in the answer choices to determine which one is true. Choice (A) is $|-4-10| = 0$, or $|-14| = 0$. This is not true, so (A) can be eliminated without checking if 10 will make the equation true.

Choice (B) is $|-4-7| = 3$, or $|-11| = 3$. This is not true, so (B) can also be eliminated. Choice (C) is $|-4+7| = 3$, or $|3| = 3$. This is true, so check if 10 makes the equation true. $|10+7| = |17|$, which is not equal to 3, so (C) can be eliminated. Choice (D) is $|-4-3| = 7$, or $|-7| = 7$. This is true, so check if 10 makes the equation true. $|10-3| = 7$, or $|7| = 7$. This is also true, so (D) is the credited response.

17. **C** The question gives the sum of the odd integers from 1 to 303, and then it asks for the sum of fewer numbers. Therefore, the answer must be less than 23,104, so (E) can be eliminated. The numbers that are not to be included in the answer sum are 1 and 303. Subtract these from 23,104 to get the new sum. $23{,}104 - 1 = 23{,}103 - 303 = 22{,}800$. Choice (C) is the credited response.

18. **E** To determine if the intervals satisfy the inequality, pick a value from each one and plug it in for c into the equation. For case I, try $c = -\frac{1}{5}$. The inequality becomes $\dfrac{1}{8(-\frac{1}{5})+2} = \dfrac{1}{-\frac{8}{5}+2} = \dfrac{1}{-\frac{8}{5}+\frac{10}{5}} = \dfrac{1}{\left(\frac{2}{5}\right)}$. This is not less than 0, so case I is not true. Choices (A) and (D) can be eliminated, as they contain case I. For case II, plug in $c = -\frac{1}{2}$. The inequality becomes $\dfrac{1}{8(-\frac{1}{2})+2} = \dfrac{1}{-4+2} = \dfrac{1}{-2}$. This is less than 0, so case II satisfies the inequality. Choice (C) can be eliminated, as it does not contain case II. For case III, plug in $c = -\frac{5}{8}$. The inequality becomes $\dfrac{1}{8(-\frac{5}{8})+2} = \dfrac{1}{-5+2} = \dfrac{1}{-3}$. This is less than 0, so case III is also true, and (E) is the credited response.

19. **B** When asked for the number of values that are possible for a variable, start Plugging In, following the requirements of the question. The first positive integer is 1, and there is no integer power to which 1 can be raised that will make it equal 81. The same is true if $f = 2$. If $f = 3$, it could be raised to the 4th power to yield 81. In fact, if 81 is broken down into prime factors, the only one is 3. Therefore, trying only multiples of 3 can save time. If $f = 6$, there is no integer power to which it can be raised that will make it equal 81. If $f = 9$, it could be raised to the 2nd power to yield 81. At this point, the values possible for g are getting very small. Rather than plugging in for f, now try plugging in for g with the only remaining positive integer, which is 1. If $f^1 = 81$, then $f = 81$. There are no more positive integer combinations of f and g that will make the equation true, so there are only 3 values for f: 3, 9, and 81. Therefore, (B) is the credited response.

20. **C** When the question has variables in the answer choices, Plug In. Pick values for *r* and *s*, such as *r* = 2 and *s* = 8 With these values, point *M* is now at (2, 8) and point *N* is at (6, 0). Draw a sketch of these points in the coordinate plane and the triangle they form with the origin.

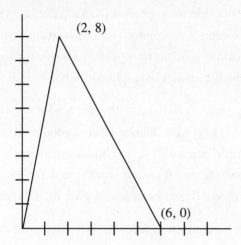

To find the area of the triangle, write out the formula: $A = \frac{1}{2}bh$ and plug in known values. The base is 6 and the height is 8, so the area is $\frac{1}{2}(6)(8)$ or 24. This is the target number. Now plug *r* = 2 and *s* = 8 into the answer choices to see which matches this target number. Choice (A) is $\frac{1}{2}(2)(8)$, which equals 8. This is not the target answer, so (A) can be eliminated. Choice (B) is (2)(8) or 16, so it can also be eliminated. Choice (C) is $\frac{3}{2}(2)(8)$, which equals 24. This is the target answer, but the remaining answers must be checked before selecting (C). Choice (D) is $\frac{1}{2}(2^3)(8)$, which equals 32, so (D) can be eliminated. Choice (E) is $(2^3)(8)$, which equals 64, so (E) can be eliminated. Choice (C) is the only one remaining and is the credited response.

Section 3

25. **B** Start with the first blank. Since *Stephen's new road bike* is described as *lighter*, look for a word that means *lighter*. Eliminate everything but choices (A) and (B). Since his new bike is *lighter*, his previous bike would have been "heavy." Eliminate choice (A) since *speedy* is irrelevant. Choice (B) is the correct answer.

26. **D** Start with the second blank. Since the sentence states that the deli doesn't do something *properly* anymore, it must be "difficult" to *distinguish a strip steak from a pot roast*. Eliminate everything but choices (D) and (E). Next, check the first blank. Since it's difficult to distinguish the meats, they

must not be "labeled" properly. *Restock* doesn't match "labeled," so eliminate choice (E). Choice (D) is the correct answer.

27. **E** Since the folk singer *showcased the human spirit in all its forms,* look for a word similar to "emphasize" that would fit the blank. Eliminate choices (A) and (D) since these are the opposite of emphasize. Choice (B) means to "express coherently," which doesn't quite fit. Eliminate choice (C) since it means to "give human qualities to ideas or concepts." Choice (E) works, since *underscore* means to "show importance to," which is similar to emphasize. Choice (E) is the correct answer.

28. **A** Start with the first blank. Since it's stated that the *new work* has many *elements that are out of place,* look for a word that means *out of place.* Choice (A) is a good match for *out of place* and choice (D), which means "old fashioned," could also fit, so eliminate choices (B), (C), and (E). Next, check the second blank. Since *elements or details are out of place,* look for a word similar to "context" for the second blank. Eliminate choice (D) since *whimsy* doesn't fit. Choice (A) is the correct answer.

29. **E** The sentence tells us that *Reinhold was always backing down from his own arguments and deferring his point of view,* so fill in the blank with something like "giving in to others." Eliminate choices (A) and (C) since both mean the opposite of the clue. Choice (B) means "brief" and choice (D) means "persistence," so eliminate them. Choice (E) matches the clue, therefore it is the correct answer.

30. **C** The correct answer to this question must address both passages, so be wary of answers that are one-sided. Eliminate choice (A) since *all fans* is extreme. Choice (B) also doesn't work since neither passage ever states that sports fanaticism is *unhealthy.* Choice (C) could work since Passage 1 mentions that the author's family's *eyes roll* whenever he would talk about sports, and the author of Passage 2 mentions that his knowledge is *met with derision.* Eliminate choices (D) and (E) since both *elation* and *contempt* are too strong. Choice (C) is the correct answer.

31. **E** The author of Passage 1 sees his family's *eyes roll* when he talks about sports, and the *sports fanatics* in Passage 2 are similar to the author of Passage 1, so the family would not be interested in the view of the *sports fanatics* of Passage 2. Choices (A), (C), and (D) all indicate some form of acceptance, so eliminate them. Choice (B) is too extreme. Choice (E) fits well and is therefore the correct answer.

32. **A** This is a vocabulary in context question, so cross out the word in question and replace it with another word. Since knowing the *rules of Australian football* seems to be something only the author cares about, we can replace garnered with "gained" or "accumulated." Only choice (A) fits, so it is the correct answer.

33. **E** The correct answer to this question must address both passages, so be wary of answers that are one-sided. Choice (A) is incorrect since it doesn't apply to either passage. Eliminate choices (B) and (D) since only Passage 2 makes any sort of *comparison* or *hypothetical situation.* Passage 1 makes use of *personal experience,* but Passage 2 does not, so eliminate choice (C). Choice (E) fits because Passage

1 refers to *why a Wing T formation is preferable to a Double Back* and Passage 2 mentions *who played center field for the winning team of the 1974 World Series*. Choice (E) is the correct answer.

34. **E** The first two lines of the passage contain the following: *Daddy was seeing an awful lot of his new friend. One of the rooms in his house was all of a sudden full of her stuff.* We don't know yet how the young girl is assessing the situation, so choice (E) is the only one of the choices with the appropriate amount of support in the passage. The other choices suggest that the girl is disapproving of her father's *new friend*, a claim that is not supported in the passage.

35. **E** The third line of the passage contains the following: *It had started with a few dinners and shopping trips, and now it seemed that their father's friend basically lived in the house, even shifting around some furniture that had been in place for as long as Sarah could remember.* The word *basically* suggests that Tess does not literally live in the house but that she spends as much time there as one who does live there, which is reflected in choice (E). The other choices contain some words from the passage, but the information in those choices is not supported in the passage.

36. **B** The third line of the passage contains the following: *It had started with a few dinners and shopping trips, and now it seemed that their father's friend basically lived in the house, even shifting around some furniture that had been in place for as long as Sarah could remember.* The idea of *shifting around some furniture* is offered as evidence that their father's friend *basically lived in the house.* It can be inferred, therefore, that *shifting around furniture* is something that is typically done by someone who lives in the house containing that furniture, as choice (B) suggests. Because the passage moves between ideas quickly, it doesn't say anything else about Sarah's perspective on this furniture moving, so none of the other answer choices are supported in the passage.

37. **D** In the first three sentences of the second paragraph, there are a number of words that imply a change: *then, became, now, eventually, introduced.* The quotation marks are evidence of that change, with the older people in the story now referring to themselves as part of Sarah's family, as choice (D) suggests. The words in quotes are not mean-spirited or slangy, eliminating choices (A) and (C), and nothing in the passage suggests that any of these terms are metaphorical, eliminating choice (E).

38. **B** The first two paragraphs of the passage explore Sarah's confusion over the more-frequent presence of her father's "new friend." Tess surprises Sarah after school one day to *take her shopping for a Junior Bridesmaid's dress.* Tess is surprised by the announcement, wondering *Bride?*, because she has not yet understood that Tess and her father are to be married. Choice (B) paraphrases this idea. Choices (A), (C), and (E) are too literal and are not supported in the passage. And although Sarah is not fully used to the idea of having Tess as a mother, she does not necessarily "resist" it, eliminating choice (D).

39. **B** The seventh paragraph states, *In the coming weeks, though, Sarah was not to be so involved again. She was usually asked to watch her brother as her daddy and Tess met with planners, caterers, and decorators.* A series of questions follows, outlining the kinds of questions they might be asking these *planners,*

caterers, and decorators, or naming the specific topics of their meetings with these wedding assistants, as choice (B) implies. The particular questions are not relevant to the larger idea of the story (a young girl coming to terms with her father's remarriage), so the other choices can be eliminated.

40. **D** The sentence listed in the question states the following: *Sarah had never seen him so calm—he was usually such an over-planner, barking orders at all within his sight.* There is a contrast here between her father's current *calm* and the fact that he is usually *barking orders*. Therefore, the answer must be the opposite of *calm*, as only choice (D) is.

41. **C** Sarah is asked to watch her brother as Tess and her father plan their wedding. She tries to eavesdrop subtly, but as her father's question implies, he is aware that she is listening to the conversation. Because the question immediately shifts back to Sarah's perception, we know little else about what the father thinks. Only choice (C) works, therefore, and the others can be eliminated.

42. **C** Toward the end of the passage, Sarah wishes more and more to be involved with her father's wedding: *She wanted to walk in there and take a seat at the table with them.* And later, *She wanted to be at the table, calling whatever shots she could.* There are hints of the other answer choices, but none has the textual support of choice (C).

43. **C** The first sentence says the following: *Online education hasn't freed itself of all the connotations, both positive and negative, that anything "online" could have.* In other words, online education has both *positive and negative* features, or *both good and bad aspects*, as choice (C) indicates. The other choices may be common ideas about online education, but they are not supported in the passage.

44. **C** The previous sentence states, *On the other hand, online education is, as much as any other product, a child of the market.* The sentence referred to in the question expands on this idea, as choice (C) indicates, stating the market benefits of online education. Although the sentence reflects the speech of administrators, it does not *mock* them, and it is not meant to sell the product to the reader, eliminating choices (A) and (D).

45. **E** Of face-to-face education, the author of Passage 1 states the following: *Perhaps the problem is deeper. Maybe "online" education is not such a new development: those students who are in face-to-face classes are not required to do their homework in Internet-free areas, and most students can browse the Internet freely in class. The Internet is already everywhere, and the undetected outcome may be lowered educational standards in general.* The author of Passage 2 states the following, *The "real thing," after all, had its own set of problems long before online education came along, and while students may be truant or distracted from online courses, they are just as likely to be so in face-to-face courses.* Both authors, therefore, suggest that face-to-face education is imperfect and susceptible to many of the same influences as online education, lending support to choice (E).

46. **E** Cross out the word in question, and fill in the blank with your own. The word appears in the following line: *And the belief that online education must be a _____ form of the "real thing" is simply misguided conservatism.* A term like *watered down* or a word like *lesser* would work here. While choices (B) and (C) may have meanings similar to *diluted*, only choice (E) works in this context.

47. **A** The author of Passage 1 outlines *the problem* as follows: *those students who are in face-to-face classes are not required to do their homework in Internet-free areas, and most students can browse the Internet freely in class. The Internet is already everywhere, and the undetected outcome may be lowered educational standards in general.* This agrees almost exactly with what the author of Passage 2 has to say, so the authors are essentially in agreement, as choice (A) suggests. While the author of Passage 1 might consider the lines in Passage 2 *respectful*, there is no reason to believe that she would consider them *exceedingly* so.

48. **B** The author of Passage 1 writes, *So how successful have these online courses been? According to a 2013 study, 77 percent of academic leaders rate the learning outcomes in online education as the same or superior to those in face-to-face classes.* The author of Passage 2 cites the same statistic, after stating, *Online education certainly has its benefits.* Both sentences reflect the benefits of online education as perceived by educators, lending support to choice (B). While online education may help these teachers to achieve their learning objectives, the authors do not bring up this statistic in order to discuss these learning objectives, but rather to show how effective teachers consider online learning, eliminating choice (E).

Section 4

21. **D** PITA! Start with choice (C), plugging in 4 for t. The first equation is then $4 < 6$, which is true, and the second is $16 < 16$, which is not true. Eliminate choices (C), (B), and (A) and go bigger. Try choice (D), plugging in 5 for t. The first equation is then $5 < 6$, which is true, and the second is $16 < 20$, which is also true. Since both equations are true, $t = 5$. The credited response is (D).

22. **A** Be safe: Plug In. Plug in 6 for the side of the square and label all of the sides 6. W, X, and Y are the midpoints, so label AW, WB, BX, XC, CY, and YD each as 3. Now $BC = 6$. Check all of the answer choices to find the one that does NOT equal 6. Choice (A) is $AD + AW = 6 + 3 = 9$. Choice (B) is $AW + XC = 3 + 3 = 6$. Choice (C) is $CD = 6$. Choice (D) is $DY + BW = 3 + 3 = 6$. Choice (E) is $AD = 6$. The credited response is (A).

23. **B** Solve for z. First subtract 6 from both sides of the equation to get $4z = 14$. Then divide both sides of the equation by 4 to get $z = \dfrac{14}{4}$. That is the only solution to the equation. The answer is (B).

24. **C** PITA! Start with (C), plugging in 5 for t. First, use the second equation to find $\sqrt{5} = s$. Use the calculator and find that s is approximately 2.24. Then plug in 2.24 for s in the second equation. Since $10 < 11.2 < 12$, t could equal 5. The credited response is (C).

25. **D** The total surface area of the solid is equal to the sum of the areas of all the individual faces. First, count the faces. There are 6 squares on the top, and therefore 6 on the bottom. There are 2 squares on the front, and therefore 2 on the back. There are 3 squares on the side, and therefore 3 on the other side. Thus, there are a total of $6 + 6 + 3 + 3 + 2 + 2 = 22$ squares. Since each square has an area of 3 square inches, the total surface area is $22 \times 3 = 66$ square inches. The credited response is (D).

26.   **E**   Variables in the answers: Plug In! Since $x > 0$, choose a positive number for x; in this case, $x = 2$. Since $\dfrac{y}{x}$ is negative, choose a negative number for y; in this case, $y = -8$. Check each answer choice to find which one is a negative number. (A) is $(2)^3 = 8$; eliminate it because it's positive. (B) is $(-8)^2 = 64$; eliminate it because it's positive. (C) is $-(-8) = 8$; eliminate it because it's positive. (D) is $2(2) = 4$; eliminate it because it's positive. (E) is -8; keep it because it's negative. The credited response is (E).

27.   **B**   Express the probability as a fraction: $\dfrac{want}{total} = \dfrac{red}{total} = \dfrac{1}{4}$. The total number of degrees in a circle is 360, so $\dfrac{red}{360} = \dfrac{1}{4}$. Solve to find that the red sectors have a total of 90°. There are two red sectors that each have a degree measure of r, so divide 90 by 2 to find that $r = 45°$. The credited response is (B).

28.   **C**   First, use the table to find $h(1)$. When the x column is 1 the $h(x)$ column is 3, so $h(1) = 3$. Since $g(x) = h(1)$, $g(x) = 3$. Now use the table to find the x value. When the $g(x)$ column is 3, the x column is 2, so $x = 2$. The credited response is (C).

29.   **6**   Plug in any of the (x, y) pairs from the table into the equation. The last (x, y) pair in the table is $(-2, -3)$, so $-2 = \dfrac{k}{-3}$. Multiply both sides of the equation by -3 to find that $k = 6$.

30.   **187**   Kevin makes 8 dollars for each chore, so divide 1,500 dollars by 8 to find the number of chores. $1{,}500 \div 8 = 187.5$, which is not an integer. Round up or round down? Try both to be safe. 188 chores times 8 dollars per chore equals 1,504 dollars, which is too big. 187 chores times 8 dollars per chore equals 1,496 dollars, which is less than 1,500.

31.   **50**   The lines are parallel, so all the big angles are equal and all the small angles are equal, and *big* + *small* = 180°. The small angle is 30°, so the big angle is 180° − 30° = 150°. The big angle is labeled $3x$, so $3x = 150°$. Divide both sides by 3 to find that $x = 50°$.

32.   **384**   If 36% of the juniors selected "Go to the beach" then the remaining 64% of the juniors selected a response other than "Go to the beach." 64% of the 600 total juniors is $\dfrac{64}{100} \times 600 = 384$.

33.   **22**   Write the area formula: $A = \pi r^2$. The area of circle P is 121π, so $121\pi = \pi r^2$ and $r = 11$. The diameter is twice the radius, so $d = 2r = 2 \times 11 = 22$.

34.   **36 or 72**

First find that $12 \times 9 = 108$. Is 108 a factor of z? To find z, first list the multiples of 12 and the multiples of 9 up to 120. The multiples that 12 and 9 have in common are possible values of z.

Multiples of 12: (12, 24, **36**, 48, 60, **72**, 84, 96, **108**)

Multiples of 9: (9, 18, 27, **36**, 45, 54, 63, **72**, 81, 90, 99, **108**, 117)

Therefore, the possible values of z are 36, 72, and 108. 108 is not a factor of 36; it is a possible answer because it proves the statement false. 108 is not a factor of 72; it is a possible answer because it proves the statement false. 108 is a factor of 108; it is not a possible answer because it proves the statement true.

35. 44 To find the shaded area, subtract the three small triangles from the large triangle. Write the area formula: $A = \frac{1}{2}bh$. The base of the large triangle is the sum of the bases of the small triangles. Use the formula to find the base of each small triangle. Each of the triangles is an isosceles right (45:45:90) triangle, so the base and the height are equal. Thus the formula can be written as $A = \frac{1}{2}b \times b$ or $A = \frac{1}{2}b^2$. Solve for the base of triangle A: $\frac{1}{2}b^2 = 18$ then $b^2 = 36$, so $b = 6$. Solve for the base of triangle B: $\frac{1}{2}b^2 = 8$ then $b^2 = 16$, so $b = 4$. Solve for the base of triangle C: $\frac{1}{2}b^2 = 2$ then $b^2 = 4$, so $b = 2$. The base of the large triangle is $6 + 4 + 2 = 12$ and so the area of the large triangle is $A = \frac{1}{2}12^2 = 72$. The sum of the areas of the small triangles is $18 + 8 + 2 = 28$. Subtract the unshaded area from the large area to get the shaded area: $72 - 28 = 44$.

36. $\frac{1}{12}$ or .083

Plug In! Plug in $a = 4$ and $b = 5$ to make the first equation true. Now plug in $a = 4$ the second equation to find c: $\frac{4}{c} = \frac{1}{15}$ so $c = 60$. Therefore, $\frac{b}{c} = \frac{5}{60} = \frac{1}{12}$. (Note: $\frac{5}{60}$ would also be counted as a correct answer.)

37. 252 Write out the pattern and then extrapolate. List the numbers from 100 to 199 that have at least one digit that is a four. {104, 114, 124, 134, 140, 141, 142, 143, 144, 145, 146, 147, 148, 149, 154, 164, 174, 184, 194}. There are 19 numbers in the one-hundreds that have at least one four. The same will be true of the two-hundreds, three-hundreds, five-hundreds, six-hundreds, seven-hundreds, eight-hundreds, and nine-hundreds. So far that's $19 \times 8 = 152$ numbers with at least one four. Then there are the four-hundreds: all 100 numbers from 400 to 499 have at least one four. So add that to the total to get $152 + 100 = 252$.

38. 60 This problem can be tackled as a rate problem using the formula or as an average problem using the average pie. Either way, set up an equation or a pie for both Ben and Carl. Since they both drove for the same amount of time, set your equation equal to time: $time = \frac{distance}{rate}$. If b represents the distance Ben drove, and he drove 15 miles further than Carl did, the distance Carl drove is $b - 15$.

Therefore, the equation for Ben is $t = \dfrac{b}{20}$ and the equation for Carl is $t = \dfrac{b-15}{15}$. The times are equal so set the two equations equal to each other: $\dfrac{b}{20} = \dfrac{b-15}{15}$. Cross multiply and solve for b:

$20b - 300 = 15b$, then $5b = 300$, so $b = 60$.

Section 5

1. **D**   The phrase, *The Great Wall of China, which was built to protect the Chinese Empire from invasion* is an incomplete thought. Since a comma combined with the word *and* can only be used to connect two complete thoughts, this sentence does not correctly connect the two ideas. Eliminate choice (A). Choice (B) makes both the first and the second thoughts complete, but connects the two with a comma. Therefore, choice (B) contains a comma splice error. In choice (C), the thought *The Great Wall of China, built to protect the Chinese Empire from invasion* is an incomplete thought. The phrase *therefore extending over more than 13,000 miles* is also incomplete. This choice contains two incomplete ideas that do not form a complete thought even when combined, so choice (C) is incorrect. In choice (E), the phrase *it was built to protect the Chinese Empire* is set off by commas, and should therefore contain unnecessary information. However, if you remove that part of the sentence, then the remaining thought is, *The Great Wall of China…extending over more than 13,000 miles*. This is an incomplete thought, so choice (E) does not contain a complete sentence, and is therefore incorrect. Choice (D) fixes the error in the original sentence and does not introduce any new errors, so choice (D) is the correct answer.

2. **B**   This sentence uses *ignoring*, rather than *ignore*, and therefore contains an incomplete thought. Choices (A), (C), and (E) all repeat the error in the original sentence and are therefore incorrect. Choice (D) adds the word *who*, which also makes the sentence incomplete. Therefore, the correct answer is choice (B), which fixes the original error and does not introduce any new errors.

3. **E**   The modifying phrase *Walking on the moon's surface for slightly more than two and a half hours* should describe Neil Armstrong and Buzz Aldrin, since those two men were the individuals who did the walking. However, as it is currently written, the phrase describes *numerous photos*, since that phrase appears immediately after the comma. Therefore, this sentence contains a misplaced modifier error. *Neil Armstrong and Buzz Aldrin* should appear immediately after the comma, so eliminate choices (A), (B), and (C). Choice (D) incorrectly places the prepositional phrase of *Little West Crater after took*, and is therefore incorrect. Choice (E) fixes the original error and does not introduce any new errors, so choice (E) is the correct answer.

4. **A** The way the sentence is currently written, the underlined verb phrase agrees with the non-underlined parts of the sentence in both number and tense, so choice (A) does not contain an error. Choice (B) adds a conjunction, *although,* to the beginning of the verb phrase and changes the form of the verb to *gaining.* This causes the entire sentence to become a fragment, so eliminate choice (B). Choice (E) repeats this same error, so eliminate choice (E) also. Choice (C) uses a comma and the word *but* to connect the two ideas in the sentence. However, only two complete ideas can be connected using a comma and the word *but.* Since *Chiropractic methods of treatment, once commonly criticized by many in the medical field,* is not a complete idea, it cannot be connected to the second half of the sentence using a comma and the word *but.* Eliminate choice (C). Choice (D) inappropriately changes the tense of the verbs by adding the future tense verb *will,* so choice (D) is also incorrect. Choice (A) is the correct answer.

5. **C** The verb *is* is singular, but the subject of the sentence is *rainforests,* which is plural. Therefore, this sentence contains a subject-verb agreement error. Eliminate choice (A). Choice (B) introduces the word *that,* which makes the sentence incomplete, so choice (B) is not the credited answer. Choices (D) and (E) incorrectly change the tense of the sentence, and are therefore not the credited answers. Choice (C) correctly changes the verb to the plural verb *are* and is the correct answer.

6. **D** This sentence contains two complete thoughts joined by a comma, which is a comma splice error. Choices (A), (B), and (C) repeat this error and are therefore incorrect. Choice (E) uses the singular verb *was,* but the subject of the verb is *mutated cells, ulcers, and cancer.* Since the verb is singular and the subject is plural, this choice contains a subject-verb agreement error. Choice (D) fixes the error in the original sentence and does not introduce any new errors. Therefore, choice (D) is the correct answer.

7. **B** This sentence contains the modifying phrase *Though most famous for her relationship with Beatles singer John Lennon.* This phrase should describe whatever appears after the comma. However, the phrase *the important contributions,* rather than *Yoko Ono,* appears after the comma. Therefore, this sentence contains a misplaced modifier. Both choices (A) and (D) repeat this error in the same way. In choice (C), the phrase *Yoko Ono's important contributions,* rather than *Yoko Ono,* appears right after the comma, so choice (C) also has a misplaced modifier error. In choice (E), the phrase *the works of Yoko Ono* appears after the comma, so choice (E) also has a misplaced modifier error. Only choice (B) fixes the error in the sentence.

8. **A** This sentence indicates that Genghis Khan did two things: he *united...tribes,* and *founded the Mongol Empire.* Since this sentence contains two verbs in a list, the verbs should be in the same form. As the sentence is currently written, the verbs are parallel, so keep choice (A). Choice (B) uses the word *who.* Since the word that appears immediately before the comma is *century,* this choice suggests that it is the century, not Genghis Khan, that founded the Mongol Empire. Thus, choice (B) is incorrect. Choice (C) uses the verb *found,* which is not parallel with *united,* so choice (C) creates a parallelism error. Choice (E) also creates a parallelism error by pairing *united* with

founding. Eliminate both choice (C) and choice (E). Choice (D) adds a subject to the second half of the sentence, thus turning that part of the sentence into a complete thought. Therefore, choice (D) contains two complete thoughts joined by a comma. Eliminate choice (D), since it has a comma splice error. Choice (A) is the correct answer.

9. E   As written, the verb *demonstrated* does not agree with the verb *prepares* in tense. Both verbs should be in present tense, so eliminate choice (A). Choices (B) and (C) use the singular pronoun *it* to refer to the plural noun classes, so both of these choices are incorrect. Choice (D) initially uses the plural pronoun *they*, but switches to the singular pronoun *it* later in the sentence. Thus choice (D) is incorrect. Choice (E) correctly uses plural pronouns to refer to *classes* and uses the correct verb tenses. Thus, choice (E) is the correct answer.

10. E   This sentence provides three verbs in a list: *chose, discovered,* and *was postponed*. However, items in a list should be parallel. In this case, the last verb in the list is not in the same form as the other two verbs. Therefore, this sentence contains a parallelism error. Choices (A), (C), and (D) all contain similar parallelism errors and are therefore incorrect. Choice (B) is also not parallel, because even though the verb is in the correct form, the choice also includes the subject *she*, unlike the second verb in the list. Choice (B) is also missing the conjunction *and*, which is needed before the last item in the list. Only choice (E) fixes the original error and does not introduce any new errors.

11. D   The words *simultaneously* and *as well* are redundant, so choice (A) is not the correct answer. Choice (C) repeats the error in the original sentence. Since the phrase *Ludovic built an enormous house of cards* is a complete thought, and *it was simultaneously very fragile* is also a complete thought, you cannot join the two thoughts with a comma. Therefore, choice (B) contains a comma splice error. Choice (E) changes the direction of the sentence by using *and* rather than *but*. Since the two ideas in the sentence—that the house was enormous and that the house was fragile—are opposite direction ideas, they should be joined with a conjunction that signals that they are opposites. Choice (D) fixes the redundancy error, so choice (D) is the correct answer.

12. B   The verb *wore* is in past tense, but the verb *start* is in present tense. Since nothing in the sentence indicates that a change of tense is required, this sentence contains a verb tense error. Eliminate choice (A). Choice (C) repeats the error in the original sentence and is therefore not the correct answer. Choice (D) uses the present perfect *had started dropping*. When a verb refers to something that began in the past and is still happening, the present perfect tense is appropriate, but this sentence refers to an event that occurred entirely in the past, so choice (D) is not the correct answer. Choice (E) uses *are beginning to drop*, which would also refer to an event happening in the present, rather than in the past, so choice (E) is incorrect. Choice (B) correctly uses the past tense, and does not introduce any new errors, so choice (B) is correct.

13. **C** In the original sentence, the phrase *originally a railroad bridge and part of the Poughkeepsie Bridge Route* is set off by commas, so the phrase should contain unnecessary information, and the sentence should make sense without it. Notice that if you eliminate the phrase, you are left with *Walkway Over the Hudson, now used by locals as a pedestrian walkway*. The main subject is *Walkway Over the Hudson*, but the subject is missing a verb, and the sentence is a fragment. Eliminate choice (A). Choice (B) uses the word *which*, and therefore changes the meaning of the sentence so that the phrase *is now used by locals as a pedestrian walkway* applies to *the Poughkeepsie Bridge Route* rather than to *Walkway Over the Hudson*. It also creates a fragment. Choice (C) adds the verb *is*, and therefore makes the sentence complete. Eliminate choice (D), since it contains the word being. Choice (E) connects the thoughts *Walkway Over the Hudson, originally a railroad bridge and used today by locals as a pedestrian walkway and it was once part of the Poughkeepsie Bridge Route* with a comma and the word *and*. However, in order to join two thoughts with a comma and the word *and*, both thoughts must be complete thoughts. Since the first thought is incomplete, this sentence does not correctly join the two thoughts. Eliminate choice (E). Choice (C) remains as the best answer.

14. **B** The original sentence compares *gecko's feet* to *other lizards*. Since the sentence should compare *lizard's feet* to *other lizard's feet* or *geckos* to *other lizards*, but not *feet* to *lizards*, there is a comparison error. Eliminate choice (A). Choices (D) and (E) contain similar comparison errors, and are therefore incorrect. Choice (C) correctly fixes the comparison error so that the sentence compares *gecko's feet* to *other lizard's feet*, but now the phrase *such as the iguana or the Komodo dragon* modifies *other lizard's feet*. Since the iguana and the Komodo dragon are examples of lizards, rather than of lizard's feet, this choice changes the meaning of the sentence, and is therefore not the correct answer. Since choice (B) correctly fixes the original error and does not introduce any new errors, it is the correct answer.

15. **D** The correct idiom is *similarities between one thing **and** another* rather than *similarities between one thing **with** another*. Therefore, this sentence contains an idiom error. Choices (A) and (B) repeat the original error and are therefore incorrect. The sentence should compare the results of the biologist's experiments to the results of Watson and Crick's experiments. However, choices (C) and (E) compare the results of the biologist's experiments to the experiments of Watson and Crick. Since these choices compare results to experiments rather than results to results, these choices contain comparison errors. Choice (D) fixes the original error in the sentence and does not introduce any new errors, so choice (D) is the correct answer.

16. **D** In the original sentence *By planning* is redundant with *why*, since both indicate a reason. Therefore, choice (A) is incorrect. In choice (B), the subject is *his planning* and the verb is *ended*. Since Carl, not the planning, is the one who actually did the action in the sentence, choice (B) puts the sentence into the passive voice, and is therefore incorrect. Choice (C) uses *plan of arriving*; however, the correct idiom is *plan to* rather than *plan of.* Thus, choice (C) contains an idiom error. Choice (E) incorrectly uses *He planned* as the subject of the verb *is*. However, the phrase *He planned*

already contains a subject and a verb, so it cannot be used as a subject. Choice (D) fixes the original error in the sentence and does not introduce any new errors, so choice (D) is the correct answer.

17.   C   The correct idiom is *not only...but also*. The original sentence uses *not only...but*, and omits the *also*. Therefore, this sentence contains an idiom error. Eliminate choice (A). Choice (B) makes a similar error by omitting *but* and is also incorrect. According to choice (D), the sentence lists two reasons that Tesla was remarkable: *because he made numerous contributions toward the fields of x-ray imaging and radio and because he patented also more than 300 inventions*. When you have items in a list, those items should be parallel. With the placement of *also* in the second part of the list, the items are not parallel, so choice (D) is incorrect. Choice (E) is similarly not parallel because the first item in the list uses *because*, whereas the second does not. Choice (C) fixes the error in the original sentence, and does not introduce any new errors, so choice (C) is the correct answer.

18.   A   The clause *Alzheimer's disease causes memory loss and confusion* is a complete thought. The clause *for instance, those affected frequently forget the names of close friends and relatives* is also a complete thought. These two thoughts are correctly joined by a semicolon, so choice (A) does not contain an error. Choices (B) and (E) change the intended meaning of the sentence by implying that Alzheimer's disease, rather than those affected by Alzheimer's disease, frequently forgets the names of close friends and relatives, so both choices are incorrect. Choice (C) uses a semicolon to connect the two thoughts in the sentence. However, a semicolon connects two complete thoughts, and *the phrase for instance, often forgetting the names of close friends and relatives* is not a complete thought. Choice (D) connects two complete thoughts with a comma, so choice (D) contains a comma splice error and is incorrect.

19.   E   The original sentence uses *finishing*, rather than *finished*, and thus does not contain a complete thought. In choice (B), the clause *In 1505, Michelangelo started building Pope Julius II's tomb* is a complete thought. The clause *however, it was never finished to his satisfaction, perhaps because he was constantly distracted by other tasks* is also a complete thought. Since this choice joins two complete thoughts with a comma, this choice contains a comma splice error. Choice (D) also contains two complete thoughts joined by a comma, and therefore repeats the error in choice (B). In choice (C), the modifying phrase *although distracted, perhaps, by other tasks* should describe whatever appears immediately after the comma. However, since *it*, rather than *he* appears immediately after the comma, this choice suggests that the Pope's tomb, rather than Michelangelo, was distracted. This choice contains a modifier error and is therefore incorrect. Choice (E) corrects the error in the original sentence and does not introduce any new errors, so choice (E) is the correct answer.

20.   B   The subject of the sentence is *claims*, which is plural, and the main verb is *has convinced*, which is singular. Therefore, this sentence contains a subject-verb agreement error. Choices (A) and (C) repeat this error, and are therefore incorrect. Choice (D) changes the intended meaning of the sentence by making it seem as though the claims of the witnesses, rather than the jury, returned a verdict of guilty. Choice (E) uses *they*, which is plural, to refer to *jury*, which is singular. Therefore choice (E) contains a pronoun agreement error. Choice (B) fixes the original error in the sentence, and does not introduce any new errors, so choice (B) is the correct answer.

21. **B** This sentence uses *having been outweighed*, rather than *have been outweighed*, and therefore does not contain a complete thought. Therefore, the correct answer is choice (B).

22. **C** The pronoun *her* is part of the plural subject *her* and *Tiffany*. However, *her* cannot be the subject of the sentence, because it is an object pronoun; *she* is the appropriate subject pronoun. Thus, choice (C) contains a pronoun error.

23. **B** This sentence uses the present perfect verb *have been received*, which suggests that the action in the sentence started in the past and is continuing in the present. However, the sentence begins with the phrase *when the impressionists began*, which indicates that the action occurred in the past. Therefore, choice (B) should not be in the present perfect tense, and contains a verb tense error.

24. **B** This sentence uses *which* to refer to Mao Zedong, who was a person. However, *who* refers to people, and *which* refers to things. Therefore, choice (B) contains an error and is the correct answer.

25. **B** This sentence lists two reasons that the grey squirrel has hidden nuts and seed: *to ensure its food source* and *preventing other competing species from consuming all of the available food*. The verbs *ensure* and *preventing* are not in the same form. Thus, choice (B) contains a parallelism error.

26. **A** This sentence couples the word *both* with the phrase *as well as*. However, the correct idiom is *both…and*. Therefore, choice (A) contains an idiom error, since the phrase *as well as* should be replaced by the word *and*.

27. **B** The correct idiom is *responded to*, rather than *responded at*. Therefore, choice (B) contains an idiom error.

28. **D** The subject of the sentence is *prevalence*, which is singular. However, the verb is *have increased*, which is plural. Therefore, choice (D) contains a subject-verb agreement error.

29. **B** This sentence uses *having* as the main verb in the sentence, which makes the thought in the sentence incomplete. Therefore, choice (B) contains a verb tense error, and is the correct answer.

30. **C** This sentence uses the adjective *quick* to describe the driver's action of changing lanes. However, you must use adverbs, rather than adjectives, to describe actions. Therefore, *quickly*, rather than *quick*, is the correct modifying word, and choice (C) is the credited answer.

31. **E** There is nothing in the sentence to indicate that there is more than one claim, so choice (A) is correct. Choice (B) is the correct verb form and tense. The singular verb is in choice (C) agrees with the singular subject *claim*, so choice (C) is correct. Choice (D) has a plural verb, *are*, but the subject for that verb is *objects*, so choice (D) is also correct. There are no errors, so the correct answer is (E).

32. **E** The possessive pronoun *whose* properly refers to *Amy*, who possesses volleyball skills. Therefore, choice (A) does not contain an error. Choice (B) is part of the present perfect verb *have respected*. Since the respect began in the past and continues in the present, the verb is in the correct tense. The subject of the verb is *I*, which agrees with the verb, so choice (B) does not contain a subject-

verb agreement error. Additionally, the verb is not in a list, so this choice does not contain any parallelism errors. Therefore, eliminate choice (B). Choice (C) uses the pronoun *I*. This sentence essentially says that *Amy…understands better than I do how to properly serve and spike the ball*, so the pronoun *I* is correct. The verb *do* is an understood verb that does not need to be directly written into the sentence. Since the pronoun in choice (C) is in the correct case, choice (C) does not contain a pronoun error. Finally, choice (D) uses the present tense verb *serve*. Since this verb agrees with the subject *I*, and is parallel with the verb *spike*, choice (D) does not contain an error. This sentence does not contain any grammatical errors, so the correct answer is choice (E).

33. **B** The correct idiom is *means to* rather than *means in*, and *protecting* should be *protect*. Therefore, choice (B) contains both an idiom and verb error, and is the correct answer.

34. **D** This sentence makes a comparison: *their reception would be less expensive than their friends.* However, since the expense of a wedding cannot be compared to people, this sentence contains a comparison error. In order to correctly compare the expense of Josh and Carla's wedding to the expense of their friends' weddings, the sentence would need to read *less expensive than their friends' weddings,* or *than those of their friends.*

35. **B** As it is currently written, sentence 3 does not contain a complete thought, and is therefore a fragment. Thus, choice (A) is not the credited answer. Choice (E) combines the sentences, but turns the resulting sentence into an incomplete thought and is therefore incorrect. Choices (B), (C), and (D) all fix the original problem by combining the two sentences. Of these three choices, (B) is the most concise, and it does not introduce any new errors, so the correct answer is choice (B).

36. **A** The first paragraph discusses the history of portrait painting and uses one particular portrait painter as an example, and the second paragraph begins by discussing the challenges of portrait paintings. Thus, a phrase that ties these two subjects together is needed to transition from one paragraph to the next. Choice (B) mentions the focus on photographic accuracy, which is not discussed in the first paragraph. Thus, choice (B) is not the correct answer. Choice (C) discusses the demand from subjects, which is not mentioned in either the first or the second paragraph, so choice (C) is incorrect. Since the paragraph does not contain any discussion of how attractive people are, choice (D) does not follow the flow of ideas in the paragraph and is therefore incorrect. Choice (E) references the time required to become a skilled painter, but this subject is not discussed in either the first or the second paragraph, so eliminate choice (E). Choice (A) refers back to the first paragraph by referencing the fact that portrait painters have been popular for centuries, and therefore creates a connection between the first paragraph and the second. Thus, choice (A) is the correct answer.

37. **E** As it is currently written, the sentence says that *this* is profitable. However, it is not clear whether *this* refers to the fact that Cézanne required so many sittings, or to the fact that he could spend hours painting a single feature. Therefore, the original sentence contains an error and choice (A) is not the correct answer. The paragraph does not discuss the fact that Cézanne painted Impressionist works, so choice (B) is incorrect. Choice (C) uses the incorrect past perfect verb *had* and is therefore not the credited answer. Choice (D) uses the present perfect verb *has*, which would imply

that the action is still ongoing. Since Cézanne is no longer painting, choice (D) is incorrect. Choice (E) correctly modifies the sentence to clarify that it was Cézanne's meticulousness that paid off, so choice (E) is the correct answer.

38. **D** The second paragraph ends by discussing the success of one of Cézanne's paintings, but the third paragraph begins by discussing paintings that have not been well received. Therefore, you need a sentence that connects these two ideas. Choice (A) relates back to paragraph 2, which discusses a famous artist, but it does not relate to paragraph 3. Therefore, choice (A) is not the correct answer. Since the third paragraph does not discuss the amount of time required to paint a portrait, choice (B) is incorrect. Choice (C) makes a statement of fact, but does not relate to the topics in either paragraph 2 or paragraph 3. Eliminate choice (C). Choice (E) implies that the third paragraph will prove something mentioned in the second paragraph to be true. However, since paragraph 3 does not prove anything from paragraph 2, choice (E) is incorrect. Choice (D) connects the two paragraphs by introducing the idea that not all portraits have been successful and, by using the phrase so *well received*, referring back to the portraits discussed in paragraph 2. Therefore, choice (D) is the correct answer.

39. **C** As it currently reads, the sentence indicates that *as a portrayal…John Trumbull's portrait…was rejected.* However, the painting was not rejected as a portrayal, but was simply rejected. Therefore, in the original sentence, the meaning is unclear. Choice (B) uses *following*, but since the sentence is not discussing one thing that comes after another, choice (B) is not the credited answer. Choice (D) changes the intended meaning by suggesting that perhaps it was the fact that the painting presented Washington at all that caused the painting to be rejected, so choice (D) is not the correct answer. Since the previous sentence discusses flattering portraits, rather than accurate portraits, choice (E) is incorrect. Choice (C) transitions from sentence 13, which discusses the fact that flattering paintings are sometimes rejected, to sentence 14, which gives an example of a portrait that was rejected. Since the fact that the painting of Washington was flattering relates the two sentences, choice (C) is the correct answer.

Chapter 9
Practice Test 3

PSAT

YOUR NAME: _____
(Print)   Last   First   M.I.

SIGNATURE: _____ DATE: ____ / ____ / ____

HOME ADDRESS: _____
(Print)   Number and Street

E-MAIL: _____

City   State   Zip

PHONE NO.: _____ SCHOOL: _____ CLASS OF: _____
(Print)

IMPORTANT: Please fill in these boxes exactly as shown on the back cover of your text book.

SCANTRON F-17982-PRP   P3 2803 628 5 4 3 2 1
© The Princeton Review, Inc.

5. YOUR NAME

First 4 letters of last name				FIRST INIT	MID INIT
Ⓐ	Ⓐ	Ⓐ	Ⓐ	Ⓐ	Ⓐ
Ⓑ	Ⓑ	Ⓑ	Ⓑ	Ⓑ	Ⓑ
Ⓒ	Ⓒ	Ⓒ	Ⓒ	Ⓒ	Ⓒ
Ⓓ	Ⓓ	Ⓓ	Ⓓ	Ⓓ	Ⓓ
Ⓔ	Ⓔ	Ⓔ	Ⓔ	Ⓔ	Ⓔ
Ⓕ	Ⓕ	Ⓕ	Ⓕ	Ⓕ	Ⓕ
Ⓖ	Ⓖ	Ⓖ	Ⓖ	Ⓖ	Ⓖ
Ⓗ	Ⓗ	Ⓗ	Ⓗ	Ⓗ	Ⓗ
Ⓘ	Ⓘ	Ⓘ	Ⓘ	Ⓘ	Ⓘ
Ⓙ	Ⓙ	Ⓙ	Ⓙ	Ⓙ	Ⓙ
Ⓚ	Ⓚ	Ⓚ	Ⓚ	Ⓚ	Ⓚ
Ⓛ	Ⓛ	Ⓛ	Ⓛ	Ⓛ	Ⓛ
Ⓜ	Ⓜ	Ⓜ	Ⓜ	Ⓜ	Ⓜ
Ⓝ	Ⓝ	Ⓝ	Ⓝ	Ⓝ	Ⓝ
Ⓞ	Ⓞ	Ⓞ	Ⓞ	Ⓞ	Ⓞ
Ⓟ	Ⓟ	Ⓟ	Ⓟ	Ⓟ	Ⓟ
Ⓠ	Ⓠ	Ⓠ	Ⓠ	Ⓠ	Ⓠ
Ⓡ	Ⓡ	Ⓡ	Ⓡ	Ⓡ	Ⓡ
Ⓢ	Ⓢ	Ⓢ	Ⓢ	Ⓢ	Ⓢ
Ⓣ	Ⓣ	Ⓣ	Ⓣ	Ⓣ	Ⓣ
Ⓤ	Ⓤ	Ⓤ	Ⓤ	Ⓤ	Ⓤ
Ⓥ	Ⓥ	Ⓥ	Ⓥ	Ⓥ	Ⓥ
Ⓦ	Ⓦ	Ⓦ	Ⓦ	Ⓦ	Ⓦ
Ⓧ	Ⓧ	Ⓧ	Ⓧ	Ⓧ	Ⓧ
Ⓨ	Ⓨ	Ⓨ	Ⓨ	Ⓨ	Ⓨ
Ⓩ	Ⓩ	Ⓩ	Ⓩ	Ⓩ	Ⓩ

1. TEST FORM

_____

6. DATE OF BIRTH

MONTH	DAY		YEAR	
○ JAN				
○ FEB				
○ MAR	Ⓞ	Ⓞ	Ⓞ	Ⓞ
○ APR	Ⓘ	Ⓘ	Ⓘ	Ⓘ
○ MAY	Ⓩ	Ⓩ	Ⓩ	Ⓩ
○ JUN	Ⓢ	Ⓢ	Ⓢ	Ⓢ
○ JUL		Ⓐ	Ⓐ	Ⓐ
○ AUG		Ⓢ	Ⓢ	Ⓢ
○ SEP		Ⓖ	Ⓖ	Ⓖ
○ OCT		Ⓣ	Ⓣ	Ⓣ
○ NOV		Ⓗ	Ⓗ	Ⓗ
○ DEC		Ⓞ	Ⓞ	Ⓞ

3. TEST CODE

⓪	⓪	⓪	⓪
①	①	①	①
②	②	②	②
③	③	③	③
④	④	④	④
⑤	⑤	⑤	⑤
⑥	⑥	⑥	⑥
⑦	⑦	⑦	⑦
⑧	⑧	⑧	⑧
⑨	⑨	⑨	⑨

4. PHONE NUMBER

(Bubbles ⓪ through ⑨ for each digit column)

7. SEX

○ MALE
○ FEMALE

8. OTHER

1 Ⓐ Ⓑ Ⓒ Ⓓ Ⓔ
2 Ⓐ Ⓑ Ⓒ Ⓓ Ⓔ
3 Ⓐ Ⓑ Ⓒ Ⓓ Ⓔ

1 READING

1 Ⓐ Ⓑ Ⓒ Ⓓ Ⓔ
2 Ⓐ Ⓑ Ⓒ Ⓓ Ⓔ
3 Ⓐ Ⓑ Ⓒ Ⓓ Ⓔ
4 Ⓐ Ⓑ Ⓒ Ⓓ Ⓔ
5 Ⓐ Ⓑ Ⓒ Ⓓ Ⓔ
6 Ⓐ Ⓑ Ⓒ Ⓓ Ⓔ
7 Ⓐ Ⓑ Ⓒ Ⓓ Ⓔ

8 Ⓐ Ⓑ Ⓒ Ⓓ Ⓔ
9 Ⓐ Ⓑ Ⓒ Ⓓ Ⓔ
10 Ⓐ Ⓑ Ⓒ Ⓓ Ⓔ
11 Ⓐ Ⓑ Ⓒ Ⓓ Ⓔ
12 Ⓐ Ⓑ Ⓒ Ⓓ Ⓔ
13 Ⓐ Ⓑ Ⓒ Ⓓ Ⓔ
14 Ⓐ Ⓑ Ⓒ Ⓓ Ⓔ

15 Ⓐ Ⓑ Ⓒ Ⓓ Ⓔ
16 Ⓐ Ⓑ Ⓒ Ⓓ Ⓔ
17 Ⓐ Ⓑ Ⓒ Ⓓ Ⓔ
18 Ⓐ Ⓑ Ⓒ Ⓓ Ⓔ
19 Ⓐ Ⓑ Ⓒ Ⓓ Ⓔ
20 Ⓐ Ⓑ Ⓒ Ⓓ Ⓔ
21 Ⓐ Ⓑ Ⓒ Ⓓ Ⓔ

22 Ⓐ Ⓑ Ⓒ Ⓓ Ⓔ
23 Ⓐ Ⓑ Ⓒ Ⓓ Ⓔ
24 Ⓐ Ⓑ Ⓒ Ⓓ Ⓔ

2 MATHEMATICS

1 Ⓐ Ⓑ Ⓒ Ⓓ Ⓔ
2 Ⓐ Ⓑ Ⓒ Ⓓ Ⓔ
3 Ⓐ Ⓑ Ⓒ Ⓓ Ⓔ
4 Ⓐ Ⓑ Ⓒ Ⓓ Ⓔ
5 Ⓐ Ⓑ Ⓒ Ⓓ Ⓔ
6 Ⓐ Ⓑ Ⓒ Ⓓ Ⓔ
7 Ⓐ Ⓑ Ⓒ Ⓓ Ⓔ

8 Ⓐ Ⓑ Ⓒ Ⓓ Ⓔ
9 Ⓐ Ⓑ Ⓒ Ⓓ Ⓔ
10 Ⓐ Ⓑ Ⓒ Ⓓ Ⓔ
11 Ⓐ Ⓑ Ⓒ Ⓓ Ⓔ
12 Ⓐ Ⓑ Ⓒ Ⓓ Ⓔ
13 Ⓐ Ⓑ Ⓒ Ⓓ Ⓔ
14 Ⓐ Ⓑ Ⓒ Ⓓ Ⓔ

15 Ⓐ Ⓑ Ⓒ Ⓓ Ⓔ
16 Ⓐ Ⓑ Ⓒ Ⓓ Ⓔ
17 Ⓐ Ⓑ Ⓒ Ⓓ Ⓔ
18 Ⓐ Ⓑ Ⓒ Ⓓ Ⓔ
19 Ⓐ Ⓑ Ⓒ Ⓓ Ⓔ
20 Ⓐ Ⓑ Ⓒ Ⓓ Ⓔ

3 READING

25 Ⓐ Ⓑ Ⓒ Ⓓ Ⓔ
26 Ⓐ Ⓑ Ⓒ Ⓓ Ⓔ
27 Ⓐ Ⓑ Ⓒ Ⓓ Ⓔ
28 Ⓐ Ⓑ Ⓒ Ⓓ Ⓔ
29 Ⓐ Ⓑ Ⓒ Ⓓ Ⓔ
30 Ⓐ Ⓑ Ⓒ Ⓓ Ⓔ
31 Ⓐ Ⓑ Ⓒ Ⓓ Ⓔ
32 Ⓐ Ⓑ Ⓒ Ⓓ Ⓔ

33 Ⓐ Ⓑ Ⓒ Ⓓ Ⓔ
34 Ⓐ Ⓑ Ⓒ Ⓓ Ⓔ
35 Ⓐ Ⓑ Ⓒ Ⓓ Ⓔ
36 Ⓐ Ⓑ Ⓒ Ⓓ Ⓔ
37 Ⓐ Ⓑ Ⓒ Ⓓ Ⓔ
38 Ⓐ Ⓑ Ⓒ Ⓓ Ⓔ
39 Ⓐ Ⓑ Ⓒ Ⓓ Ⓔ
40 Ⓐ Ⓑ Ⓒ Ⓓ Ⓔ

41 Ⓐ Ⓑ Ⓒ Ⓓ Ⓔ
42 Ⓐ Ⓑ Ⓒ Ⓓ Ⓔ
43 Ⓐ Ⓑ Ⓒ Ⓓ Ⓔ
44 Ⓐ Ⓑ Ⓒ Ⓓ Ⓔ
45 Ⓐ Ⓑ Ⓒ Ⓓ Ⓔ
46 Ⓐ Ⓑ Ⓒ Ⓓ Ⓔ
47 Ⓐ Ⓑ Ⓒ Ⓓ Ⓔ
48 Ⓐ Ⓑ Ⓒ Ⓓ Ⓔ

The Princeton Review
PSAT

4

MATHEMATICS

21 (A) (B) (C) (D) (E)
22 (A) (B) (C) (D) (E)
23 (A) (B) (C) (D) (E)
24 (A) (B) (C) (D) (E)

25 (A) (B) (C) (D) (E)
26 (A) (B) (C) (D) (E)
27 (A) (B) (C) (D) (E)
28 (A) (B) (C) (D) (E)

ONLY ANSWERS ENTERED IN THE OVALS IN EACH GRID AREA WILL BE SCORED.
YOU WILL NOT RECEIVE CREDIT FOR ANYTHING WRITTEN IN THE BOXES ABOVE THE OVALS.

29 30 31 32 33

34 35 36 37 38

5

WRITING SKILLS

1 (A) (B) (C) (D) (E)
2 (A) (B) (C) (D) (E)
3 (A) (B) (C) (D) (E)
4 (A) (B) (C) (D) (E)
5 (A) (B) (C) (D) (E)
6 (A) (B) (C) (D) (E)
7 (A) (B) (C) (D) (E)
8 (A) (B) (C) (D) (E)
9 (A) (B) (C) (D) (E)
10 (A) (B) (C) (D) (E)
11 (A) (B) (C) (D) (E)
12 (A) (B) (C) (D) (E)
13 (A) (B) (C) (D) (E)

14 (A) (B) (C) (D) (E)
15 (A) (B) (C) (D) (E)
16 (A) (B) (C) (D) (E)
17 (A) (B) (C) (D) (E)
18 (A) (B) (C) (D) (E)
19 (A) (B) (C) (D) (E)
20 (A) (B) (C) (D) (E)
21 (A) (B) (C) (D) (E)
22 (A) (B) (C) (D) (E)
23 (A) (B) (C) (D) (E)
24 (A) (B) (C) (D) (E)
25 (A) (B) (C) (D) (E)
26 (A) (B) (C) (D) (E)

27 (A) (B) (C) (D) (E)
28 (A) (B) (C) (D) (E)
29 (A) (B) (C) (D) (E)
30 (A) (B) (C) (D) (E)
31 (A) (B) (C) (D) (E)
32 (A) (B) (C) (D) (E)
33 (A) (B) (C) (D) (E)
34 (A) (B) (C) (D) (E)
35 (A) (B) (C) (D) (E)
36 (A) (B) (C) (D) (E)
37 (A) (B) (C) (D) (E)
38 (A) (B) (C) (D) (E)
39 (A) (B) (C) (D) (E)

SECTION 1
Time — 25 minutes
24 Questions
(1–24)

Directions: For each question in this section, select the best answer from among the choices given and fill in the corresponding circle on the answer sheet.

Each sentence below has one or two blanks, each blank indicating that something has been omitted. Beneath the sentence are five words or sets of words labeled A through E. Choose the word or set of words that, when inserted in the sentence, <u>best</u> fits the meaning of the sentence as a whole.

Example:

Desiring to ------- his taunting friends, Mitch gave them taffy in hopes it would keep their mouths shut.

(A) eliminate   (B) satisfy   (C) overcome
    (D) ridicule   (E) silence

---

1. The gourmet restaurant was primarily known for its ------- cuisine, but the dining room was rarely crowded due to the ------- demeanor of the wait staff.

    (A) delectable . . exuberant
    (B) unremarkable . . downbeat
    (C) exciting . . dreary
    (D) original . . primitive
    (E) affordable . . inviting

2. Since the ------- of the honeybee population is currently underway, food production may be altered since these insects are ------- to this industry in the United States.

    (A) surging . . irrelevant
    (B) flattening . . inconsequential
    (C) renouncing . . robust
    (D) declining . . vital
    (E) pollinating . . anathemas

3. The Leaning Tower of Pisa, although regarded as one of the most remarkable buildings in the world, is actually a ------- architectural effort since it unintentionally tilts to one side.

    (A) shoddy   (B) superior   (C) towering
        (D) repugnant   (E) tumultuous

4. The early years of professional sports were -------- the basic concept of safety; players hit and ran into each other with such careless abandon that it seemed no one was interested in ------- play.

    (A) cognizant of . . structured
    (B) oblivious to . . cautious
    (C) unaware of . . reckless
    (D) presupposed to . . honest
    (E) acclimated to . . considerate

5. Unlike an artist who works in the Photorealistic style, ------- to recreate every single detail of the painting's subject, an artist working in the Expressionist style uses color to create an emotional impact.

    (A) endeavoring   (B) disdaining   (C) loath
        (D) collaborating   (E) surrendering

6. In order to ------- a victory during the state science fair, the teacher only ------- the work from her honors physics class.

    (A) ensure . . capitulated
    (B) cinch . . showcased
    (C) sabotage . . presented
    (D) snare . . assimilated
    (E) transpire . . invited

7. The recent exploits of the daring adventurer did nothing to dampen the public's enthusiasm for his penchant for -------, but also confirmed that he had no intention of worrying about his own safety.

    (A) cleverness   (B) orthodoxy   (C) synergy
        (D) profundity   (E) imperilment

8. The actions of the criminal could only be described as -------; even after he was convicted of his crime, he mean-spiritedly mocked and taunted his victims in the courtroom

    (A) impetuous   (B) indifferent   (C) extraneous
        (D) pernicious   (E) sanctimonious

GO ON TO THE NEXT PAGE

The passages below are followed by questions based on their content; questions following a pair of related passages may also be based on the relationship between the paired passages. Answer the questions on the basis of what is <u>stated</u> or <u>implied</u> in the passage and in any introductory material that may be provided.

Questions 9-10 are based on the following passage.

A natural result of the Romantic and Surrealist literary movements, which often attributed idealistic, even supernatural, elements to their stories and characters, was the
Line Naturalist literary movement, a logical response to wishful
5 thinking that illustrated more realistic scenarios. Specifically, Naturalism derived from the idea that one's environment played a much more pivotal role in determining one's destiny than choice and action. This is particularly exemplified in Stephen Crane's 1893 novel *Maggie, A Girl of the Streets,* in
10 which the author's titular heroine watches the dissolution of her own family and descends into homelessness, which ultimately leads to her suicide. While certainly tragic, Crane's protagonist was ultimately doomed not because of herself, but because of the environment into which she was born.

9. The author suggests that the "Naturalist literary movement" (line 4) was

   (A) the most realistic literary period
   (B) depressing for most readers
   (C) a seemingly inevitable response to Romanticism
   (D) pioneered by Stephen Crane's *Maggie, A Girl of the Streets*
   (E) primarily focused on the environment

10. In lines 8-12, the author mentions Maggie's eventual suicide in order to

    (A) illustrate her unsatisfying family life
    (B) suggest that her story would likely not appear in a Surrealist literary novel
    (C) indicate that many naturalist stories had tragic endings
    (D) highlight how the Romantic movement was a more satisfactory literary genre
    (E) show how her environment played a greater role in her life than her decisions

Questions 11-12 are based on the following passage.

The advent of social media sites such as Facebook and Twitter has had a dichotomous effect on the cultural landscape over the past decade. Many of the effects of
Line these tools are considered problematic, such as their
5 near-elimination of privacy and their role in increasing users' narcissism. But these seemingly frivolous forms of technology have also played a great role in societal change over the past decade, in both subtle and blatant ways. Facebook and Twitter have played small roles in local and
10 national elections by informing younger voters of the issues attached to certain politicians. In addition to initiating minor alterations to government, Twitter has also been responsible for a complete overhaul in government as it was the primary tool used to inform the world of the regime changes that
15 occurred in Iran in 2009. This event has since, not ironically, been coined "The Twitter Revolution."

11. Lines 1-3 ("The advent . . . past decade") primarily serve to

    (A) bemoan the spike in social media during the past several years
    (B) introduce the differing consequences of these particular forms of communication
    (C) criticize those who use Twitter for selfish reasons
    (D) celebrate technology and its effect on our environment
    (E) consider the roles of social media and the Internet in our daily lives

12. The author uses the term "not ironically" in line 15 in order to

    (A) suggest that regime change was impossible without social media
    (B) highlight the flippant attitude towards the revolution in Iran
    (C) underscore that social media was integral to societal change
    (D) show how narcissistic uses of social media pale in comparison with those that have real consequences
    (E) cast doubt on those who view the revolution in Iran as a result of Twitter's popularity

GO ON TO THE NEXT PAGE →

Questions 13-24 are based on the following passages.

Passage 1

Music in Peril confirms most of our worst suspicions. The 2011 survey gives an interesting but ultimately saddening assessment of the state of music in schools. In a span of
5 only thirty years, the number of children who play musical instruments has been cut in half. If you've ever enjoyed a symphony or film score, or if you simply care about the quality of the cultural life in this country, you are probably as worried now as many of the rest of us are.

Music in Peril is not the collection of urban legends that
10 most of its critics will accuse it of being. It is a set of data collected from elementary and middle schools all over the country. With schools represented from each of the 50 states, it accounts for all the great diversity in this country—not merely race and gender diversity, but class and regional
15 diversity as well. Given the broad reach of the survey, and the fact that it has collected its data in at least the five most populous towns in each state, *Music in Peril* is a statistically sound document. Although the survey covers a wide range of topics relating to music education, the basic results go
20 something like this: music education and instrument-playing have decreased dramatically among all children aged 6-18, regardless of race, gender, or region, and this decrease is occurring at a higher rate than in the past. Anyone who comes to this report looking for good news about the art of music in
25 the United States is looking in the wrong place.

Even if the data in the report are potentially disturbing, these data are hardly unexpected, unless we did not realize just how widespread music education was in the past. *Music in Peril* has simply put what everyone knows—that state and
30 federal governments have cut music out of public schools at an alarming rate—into the language of statistics. The ability to play a musical instrument and to appreciate music is not in-born, even if some people seem to have "natural" talents. True musical proficiency is the result of many years of encouraging
35 musical education, and not only for those who eventually become musicians. Ours is a dire world indeed when not only have our musicians lost the ability to play but also the broader populace has lost the discernment and ability to hear them.

Passage 2

Music in Peril is hardly surprising in our era of
40 apocalyptic surveys, yet more evidence that all the bad things we suspect are worse than we even knew. These surveys are the bread and butter of cultural critics, who are always looking for social-scientific support for their own suspicions. These critics were already speaking of "decline" and "death,"
45 and now these surveys just give more fodder to their calls for "reinvention" and "change." Now, for the first time in history, the story goes, fewer children are learning instruments than ever before.

Nevertheless, *Music in Peril* misses the important fact that
50 music is as interesting as it has ever been, even if the average teen doesn't know a Beethoven symphony from a Chopin

etude. In the age of the iPod, people are listening to music all the time, even if they're not doing it in quite the ways or the places that musical conservatives want them to.

55 It would be naïve, however, to say that *Music in Peril*'s findings are completely wrongheaded. Music programs have been slashed at many public schools, and less than half as many children today are learning instruments than were the generations of forty or fifty years earlier. And this statistical
60 certainty is not limited to the less fortunate areas of the country: "Indeed," write the statisticians, "the 50 percent reduction is only the median. While some schools have seen more modest declines, many schools have cut out their music education and appreciation programs almost entirely."

65 So what is the lesson of the survey? The musical landscape is changing, yes, but not in the distressing way that *Music in Peril* wants to suggest. The survey can't capture the fact that classical music is not the only place to find interesting, complex music anymore, except by the
70 most conservative, crustiest definitions. China and Germany still produce more young violinists than we do, but how meaningful is this statistical fact when we consider that high-art music is no longer so dependent on the traditional orchestral instruments? Listen to any of the new experimental
75 music in genres like post-rock, math rock, and tech-noire, and you'll see that classical music no longer has an exclusive hold on musical virtuosity. You'll see that, in surveys like *Music in Peril*, the only real decline is in musical categories that don't apply anymore. All that is happening is that the institutions of
80 old are trying to hold on for dear life and actually belong in the same irrelevant pile as studies on the decline of cursive or telephone conversations.

---

13. Lines 3-5 ("In a … half") suggest that the situation described should be considered

(A) rapid
(B) suspicious
(C) inevitable
(D) essential
(E) promising

14. The author of Passage 1 suggests that a "set of data" (line 10) should ideally be

(A) taken from the same set as previous surveys
(B) diverse enough to reflect the group it represents
(C) randomly selected from a computer database
(D) made up of elementary-school-aged children
(E) comprised of equal numbers from each race

GO ON TO THE NEXT PAGE ➡

15. The author of Passage 2 would most likely argue that the "reach" (Passage 1, line 15) is

(A) less representative of racial diversity than the author of Passage 1 promises
(B) more biased toward a particular gender than the author of Passage 1 hopes
(C) less relevant to the study than the author of Passage 1 believes
(D) drawn from a group that does not represent the diversity that the author of Passage 1 assumes
(E) more similar to the reach of previous studies than the author of Passage 1 knows

16. The final paragraph of Passage 1 (lines 26-38) serves primarily to

(A) discount the survey's findings by showing that they are already well-known
(B) argue for a new approach that the survey's results show is inevitable
(C) take issue with the statisticians who collected the data for the survey
(D) suggest the cultural implications of the trend it is describing
(E) offer an alternative conclusion based on the same set of data

17. The author of Passage 2 would most likely consider the final two sentences of Passage 1 (lines 33-38) to be

(A) overstated
(B) ironic
(C) shrewd
(D) revolutionary
(E) dishonest

18. Which of the following would the author of Passage 2 most likely consider another "apocalyptic" idea (line 40)?

(A) An editorial that argues that the trend toward text messaging has led to a decline in the number of E-mails sent per year
(B) An article that shows that reading among teenagers has increased since the popularization of e-readers
(C) A slideshow that details the 20 most environmentally conscious cities in the United States
(D) A sociologist who argues that the use of smartphones among teenagers will lead to a significant increase in driver fatalities
(E) A historical document that predicted that health care legislation would be passed in the United States by the 1970s

19. Lines 55-64 ("It would … entirely'") focus on which aspect of the "statistical certainty"?

(A) Its obviousness
(B) Its ridiculousness
(C) Its range
(D) Its conservatism
(E) Its bias

20. The author of Passage 2 indicates that the "landscape" referred to in line 66 is

(A) characterized by a lack of expertise
(B) based on regional preferences and racial identity
(C) filled with more appreciation of old favorites than anyone realizes
(D) shifting and thus not possible to describe
(E) no longer defined by its traditional parameters

21. In line 70, "crustiest" most nearly means

(A) most ineffective
(B) cruelest
(C) warmest
(D) most inflexible
(E) filthiest

22. The author of Passage 1 would most likely respond to the last statement in Passage 2 (lines 79-82) by asserting that

(A) a survey of musical-education programs has broader cultural importance
(B) classical music is as essential to well-rounded citizens as cursive
(C) *Music in Peril* is one of the first studies of school-aged children
(D) surveys like the one in *Music in Peril* are run by respected statisticians
(E) the average reader will be able to spot faulty data in any survey

GO ON TO THE NEXT PAGE

23. Which best describes the tone of the first paragraph of Passage 1 and the tone of the first paragraph of Passage 2, respectively?

(A) Morose *vs.* elated
(B) Alarmist *vs.* ignorant
(C) Sensitive *vs.* offensive
(D) Conservative *vs.* dismissive
(E) Concerned *vs.* skeptical

24. Which best conveys the primary relationship between the two passages?

(A) Passage 2 discusses some of the findings that undermine the survey described in Passage 1.
(B) Passage 2 takes issue with some of the premises that shape the argument made in Passage 1.
(C) Passage 2 offers the cultural context that adds support to the conclusions drawn by the author of Passage 1.
(D) Passage 2 uses the predictions offered in Passage 1 as a way to argue for a revolutionary change.
(E) Passage 2 provides new data that disproves the conclusions from the survey discussed in Passage 1.

STOP
If you finish before time is called, you may check your work on this section only.
Do not turn to any other section in the test.

SECTION 2
Time — 25 minutes
20 Questions
(1–20)

Directions: For this section, solve each problem and decide which is the best of the choices given. Fill in the corresponding circle on the answer sheet. You may use any available space for scratchwork.

Notes

1. The use of a calculator is permitted.

2. All numbers used are real numbers.

3. Figures that accompany problems in this test are intended to provide information useful in solving the problems. They are drawn as accurately as possible EXCEPT when it is stated in a specific problem that the figure is not drawn to scale. All figures lie in a plane unless other wise indicated.

4. Unless otherwise specified, the domain of any function f is assumed to be the set of all real numbers x for which $f(x)$ is a real number.

Reference Information

    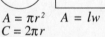

$A = \pi r^2$ $A = lw$ $A = \frac{1}{2}bh$ $V = lwh$ $V = \pi r^2 h$ $c^2 = a^2 + b^2$ Special Right Triangles

$C = 2\pi r$

The number of degrees of arc in a circle is 360.

The sum of the measures in degrees of the angles of a triangle is 180.

---

1. If $2rst = 60$ and $st = 6$, then $r =$

(A) 2

(B) $\dfrac{10}{3}$

(C) 5

(D) 6

(E) 45

2. What is the positive difference between $(x + 5)^2$ and $\sqrt{x+5}$ when $x = 4$?

(A) 36

(B) 56

(C) 78

(D) 81

(E) 84

GO ON TO THE NEXT PAGE

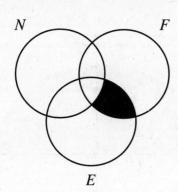

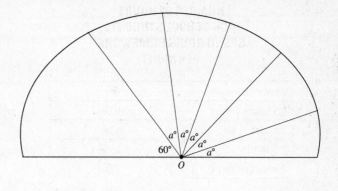

3. In the diagram above, circle N represents the set of all negative integers, circle F represents the set of all multiples of 5, and circle E represents the set of all even integers. Which of the following numbers would be in the shaded region?

(A) −15
(B) −8
(C) 7
(D) 25
(E) 30

5. In the figure above, O is the center of the semicircular region. What is the value of a ?

(A) 12
(B) 24
(C) 30
(D) 36
(E) 42

4. Which of the following equations is satisfied by both $n = 4$ and $n = 5$?

I. $3n = 12$
II. $n^2 - 9n + 20 = 0$
III. $(n - 4)(n - 5) = 0$

(A) I only
(B) III only
(C) I and II only
(D) II and III only
(E) I, II, and III

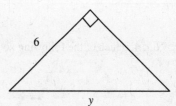

6. One leg of the isosceles right triangle above is 6. What is the value of y ?

(A) 6
(B) $6\sqrt{2}$
(C) $6\sqrt{3}$
(D) 12
(E) $12\sqrt{2}$

GO ON TO THE NEXT PAGE

**NUMBER OF HOURS
HIGH SCHOOL STUDENTS
SPEND DOING HOMEWORK
PER NIGHT**

1 hour or less	5%
1.5 hours	10%
2 hours	63%
2.5 hours	15%
3 hours or more	p%

7. The students at High School X were asked how many hours per weeknight they typically spend doing homework, and the results are shown in the chart above. Of the 800 students at this school, how many typically spend 3 hours or more on homework per night?

(A) 56
(B) 64
(C) 160
(D) 200
(E) 296

8. If $2 < 2x - 6 < 4$, which of the following could be the value of x ?

(A) –6

(B) –3

(C) 4

(D) $\dfrac{9}{2}$

(E) 5

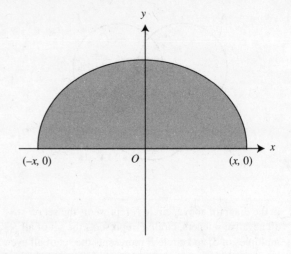

9. In the xy-plane above, the shaded semicircular region has an area of 18π. What is the value of x ?

(A) 3
(B) 6
(C) 9
(D) 12
(E) 18

10. Jar L contains 196 pennies, jar M contains 184 pennies, and jar N contains 175 pennies. Pennies are to be transferred only from jar L to jar N. What is the least number of pennies that must be transferred so that jar N will contain more pennies than each of the other two jars?

(A) 11
(B) 12
(C) 13
(D) 14
(E) 15

GO ON TO THE NEXT PAGE

0	12
7	16
14	20
21	24
...	...

11. In the left column of the table above, the first term of the sequence is 0 and each term after the first is 7 more than the preceding term. In the right column, the first term in the sequence is 12, and each term after the first is 4 more than the preceding term. If these sequences continue indefinitely, in how many of the rows of the table will the terms for both sequences be equal?

(A) More than three
(B) Three
(C) Two
(D) One
(E) None

12. A woman is taking a cab ride to the airport. The fare consists of a one-time charge of $2.50 for the ride and a $3 charge for each mile traveled. If m represents the number of miles travelled, which of the following represents the total fare, in dollars, per mile?

(A) $m + 2.50$

(B) $2.50 + 3m$

(C) $2.50m + 3m$

(D) $\dfrac{2.50 + 3m}{m}$

(E) $\dfrac{2.50m + 3}{m}$

GO ON TO THE NEXT PAGE

13. Function *g* is defined such that there is exactly one value of *x* for which *g*(*x*) = 0. Which of the following could be the graph of function *g* ?

(A)

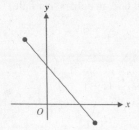

(B)

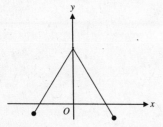

(C)

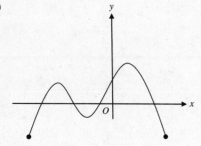

(D)

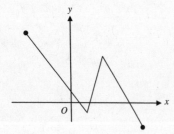

(E)

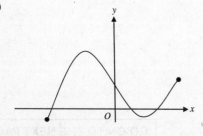

14. If one face of a rectangular solid is known to be a square, what is the greatest number of faces of the solid that could be rectangles that are <u>not</u> square?

(A) Zero
(B) One
(C) Two
(D) Three
(E) Four

x	1	2	3	4	5
p(x)	4	3	5	7	2

15. The table above shows the values for the function *p*. What is the value of 3*p*(4) + *p*(2) ?

(A) 6
(B) 8
(C) 12
(D) 18
(E) 24

GO ON TO THE NEXT PAGE

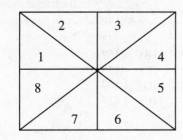

Note: Figure not drawn to scale.

16. A game is played by dropping two pebbles, one onto each of the game boards in the figure above. The score is the sum of the numbers in the regions where the two pebbles land. The pebbles must land inside one of the numbered regions, and it is equally likely that the pebbles will land in any one of the numbered regions. What is the probability that the score will be at least 10 ?

(A) $\dfrac{1}{12}$

(B) $\dfrac{1}{8}$

(C) $\dfrac{3}{16}$

(D) $\dfrac{1}{4}$

(E) $\dfrac{3}{8}$

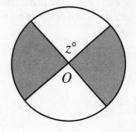

17. In the circle above with center O, the average (arithmetic mean) of the areas of the unshaded regions is equal to the sum of the areas of the shaded regions. What is the value of z ?

(A) 45
(B) 60
(C) 90
(D) 120
(E) 135

18. Three points lie on a number line with coordinates f, g, and h such that $f < g < h$. If f, g, and h are each integers, and fgh is a negative even integer, which of the following must be true?

    I. $f < 0$
   II. $gh > 0$
  III. f, g, and h are each even integers

(A) I only
(B) II only
(C) I and II only
(D) II and III only
(E) I, II, and III

GO ON TO THE NEXT PAGE

19. Points M and N lie in the same plane. How many points in the same plane as M and N could be 6 units from M and 2 units from N ?

   (A) More than three
   (B) Three
   (C) Two
   (D) One
   (E) None

20. How many positive integers less than 1,500 do not have a 5 as any digit?

   (A) 1,133
   (B) 1,152
   (C) 1,176
   (D) 1,189
   (E) 1,227

STOP

If you finish before time is called, you may check your work on this section only.
Do not turn to any other section in the test.

NO TEST MATERIAL ON THIS PAGE.

GO ON TO THE NEXT PAGE

SECTION 3
Time — 25 minutes
24 Questions
(25–48)

Directions: For each question in this section, select the best answer from among the choices given and fill in the corresponding circle on the answer sheet.

Each sentence below has one or two blanks, each blank indicating that something has been omitted. Beneath the sentence are five words or sets of words labeled A through E. Choose the word or set of words that, when inserted in the sentence, best fits the meaning of the sentence as a whole.

Example:

Hoping to ------- the dispute, negotiators proposed a compromise that they felt would be ------- to both labor and management.

   (A) enforce . . useful
   (B) end . . divisive
   (C) overcome . . unattractive
   (D) extend . . satisfactory
   (E) resolve . . acceptable

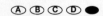

25. Even though it claimed to always place the needs of the customer above all else, the popular chain store lately has forgotten customer service in favor of making money: it consistently ------- patrons while primarily focusing on -------.

   (A) hordes . . losses
   (B) shuns . . profits
   (C) celebrates . . earnings
   (D) upends . . savings
   (E) neglects . . philanthropy

26. Basset hounds are always classified as -------, though not -------: they are slow to get up from rest, but are always aware of their surroundings.

   (A) energetic . . perceptive
   (B) idle . . oblivious
   (C) agreeable . . lazy
   (D) shiftless . . conscious
   (E) devout . . active

27. Always one to ------- excessively about his accomplishments, David was known for his braggadocio and arrogance.

   (A) boast (B) belittle (C) verbalize
   (D) minimize (E) dwindle

28. 1970s cinema is often lauded for its -------: depicting undoubtedly realistic situations, these films were a welcome respite from fantastical elements from earlier eras.

   (A) verisimilitude (B) austerity (C) implausibility
   (D) chicanery (E) euphemism

29. Portraying the common field cricket's movements as -------, the entomologist's research belied hundreds of years of assumptions that the field cricket was a ------- creature.

   (A) tense . . hackneyed
   (B) excitable . . vague
   (C) ebullient . . vivacious
   (D) spasmodic . . fitful
   (E) kinetic . . placid

GO ON TO THE NEXT PAGE

The passages below are followed by questions based on their content; questions following a pair of related passages may also be based on the relationship between the paired passages. Answer the questions on the basis of what is <u>stated</u> or <u>implied</u> in the passage and in any introductory material that may be provided.

Questions 30-33 are based on the following passages.

Passage 1 (2003)

When it comes to generating solar electricity from panels, the idea behind the technology is fantastic, but the practice is less efficient than it could be. Natural light has many different wavelengths, including visible, infrared, and ultraviolet. The solar panels that are available today use cells made of silicon to absorb light for conversion to electricity. But because the silicon can only absorb a narrow band of the solar spectrum, a majority of the solar energy is lost as heat. Typically, a solar panel will convert less than 20 percent of the solar energy into electricity. The best sunlight-conversion rate from an available panel is 21.5 percent. Solar electricity is a renewable resource that has a lot of potential, but is also limited by the technology currently available.

Passage 2 (2013)

A group of physicists led by Harry Atwater is working on a device that would generate two times the solar power generated by existing panels available today. The possibility arose with the advances in manipulating light on a much smaller scale. Current devices with silicon semiconductors can only absorb a small band of light from the sun, but Atwater's device would split the sunlight (as a prism does) into separate bands of light. Each band would then be directed to a semiconductor made to absorb that particular band of light. The device would have an efficiency of at least 50 percent, much higher than the current models. "Within a few years," Atwater says, "there won't be any point to working on technology that has efficiency that's less than 20 percent."

30. This pair of passages considers which of the following?

(A) The inefficiency of current solar panels in absorbing bands of light

(B) The tendency of some brands of solar panels to overheat

(C) The faulty conductivity of silicon semiconductors

(D) The development of a solar panel that is more effective than current models.

(E) The need for funding research to develop renewable energy

31. Atwater would most likely consider the last sentence in Passage 1 (lines 11-13) to be

(A) an accurate claim

(B) a controversial statement

(C) a logical fallacy

(D) an exciting revelation

(E) a disputable finding

32. The tone of lines 24-27 ("Within...percent") is best described as

(A) argumentative

(B) optimistic

(C) sarcastic

(D) nostalgic

(E) technical

33. Both passages mention the silicon in semiconductors to

(A) cite an example of a material that performs more efficiently than expected

(B) present a type of device that physicists are still developing

(C) reference a material that is useful but limited

(D) identify the main fault with solar panels

(E) clarify a mistaken statement about infrared and ultraviolet light

GO ON TO THE NEXT PAGE

Questions 34-42 are based on the following passage.

This passage, adapted from a 1995 short story set in Mexico, is about a girl named Catalina who has left her small town and gone to university in Mexico City, the capital city of Mexico.

The girls in her room, after a few weeks of getting used to some of her atypical habits and learning her way of showing friendship, began to take her in as one of their own. The
Line oldest girl, Araceli, really started to warm up to Catalina, and
5 she was the first to invite Catalina into her room for help with homework, to watch a video clip on the computer, or just to chat about the day. Araceli could not resist Catalina's look of awe and enjoyment, and she took to the younger girl quickly. Catalina wondered if Araceli, too, had come to the big city
10 from a small town like hers and thought of it when she was sad or lonely. Araceli could be stern, and sometimes a little mean, but Catalina knew now how hard the adjustment from small town to big city was, and she forgave her older friend a bit of overadjustment.

15 But it was a girl who lived on the floor above, Clara, who was really the one to shape how the next years of Catalina's life were to go. It was toward the end of the semester, and the weather outside was oppressively hot—not even the gorditas and horchata from the girls' favorite stand could offset it.
20 As Catalina sat reading beneath a tree, Clara, with her face painted and her hands full of signs, approached her.

"You coming?" she asked, "Ever been to a protest? We're going to the Federal District right now—we want to get as many people as we can. See?" she asked, showing her protest
25 sign, *Farm Reform, No Sharecroppers,* to an oddly moved Catalina, who felt that the sign was a key that had unlocked something inside of her. Clara explained some of the working conditions of Mexican farmers, especially in small towns. "Terrible, right? You want to come protest with me? Yeah, let's
30 go—I'll let you hold one of these signs—and if you want, we can paint your face for the next one. Do you not have class now? Good, because this is usually the time that we go to the District. It can be pretty frustrating sometimes, but if you're like me, you just can't stand to see these injustices keep going
35 and keep going. I want to go into politics when I'm done with school. Have you decided what you want to do yet?"

Catalina was shocked that Clara really wanted her to come along, that she really thought Catalina had some kind of special insight into a political topic. Clara's questions were
40 so casual, but they hit Catalina hard: maybe she would go into politics, too. She had seen the small farmer protests at home, and she knew how her own father had struggled to make a life for their family. She felt for the first time that she might be able to make a difference for people like her father.

45 So she went to the protest, and went to every other protest she could until school ended, some without Clara, and became as well-informed on the issues as she could. Maybe she was always meant to do something like this, but what a random chain of events had to happen before she could get
50 to it.

34. The primary purpose of the passage is to describe
   (A) Catalina's unhappiness at her new school
   (B) a formative encounter with a new friend
   (C) an uncomfortable meeting between two students
   (D) Catalina's homesickness after leaving her small town
   (E) Catalina's relationship with Araceli at school

35. The first sentence of the passage (lines 1-3) suggests that the "girls in her room" initially regarded Catalina as
   (A) prudish
   (B) ridiculous
   (C) unattractive
   (D) unhygienic
   (E) alien

36. The action described in lines 5-6 ("she ... homework") exemplifies Araceli's
   (A) intelligence
   (B) beauty
   (C) hospitality
   (D) condescension
   (E) anger

37. Which of the following LEAST accurately characterizes Araceli as she is represented in lines 3-14?
   (A) Familiar
   (B) Nurturing
   (C) Stern
   (D) Sympathetic
   (E) Local

38. The primary purpose of Clara's various questions in lines 22-36 is to
   (A) encourage Catalina to join her at the protest
   (B) interrogate Catalina about her childhood
   (C) spark a political dialogue with Catalina
   (D) force Catalina to change her political views
   (E) test whether Catalina is able to protest

GO ON TO THE NEXT PAGE

39. The author uses the image of the "key" (line 26) to convey the impression of

    (A) a visual representation of protest
    (B) opening things that had been hidden away
    (C) an important political point
    (D) a locked government building
    (E) a protest song

40. The repetition of the word "really" in lines 37-39 serves to emphasize Catalina's

    (A) consternation
    (B) astonishment
    (C) misanthropy
    (D) befuddlement
    (E) dishonesty

41. The fourth paragraph (lines 37-44) represents Catalina as

    (A) hopeful
    (B) suspicious
    (C) deceptive
    (D) apathetic
    (E) thoughtful

42. The last paragraph (lines 45-50) suggests that, until she met Clara, Catalina

    (A) believed that she would return to her village after graduation
    (B) had no sympathy for the sufferings of local farmers
    (C) did not have an intense interest in politics
    (D) felt that the government represented her interests
    (E) had decided not to go to political protests any more

GO ON TO THE NEXT PAGE ➡

Questions 43-48 are based on the following passage.

The following passage is from a 2011 article on the state of wild orchids throughout the world.

Many horticulturalists who study orchid populations do so in a broad way and on a global scale, and their findings can give us pause. But for those who study orchid populations
Line on a local level, the results are far more alarming. The
5 Euro-American craze for these exotic flowers began in the 1800s, and it has grown ever since. But as the global trade has grown, and as orchids have become more easily accessible in grocery stores and other mass-purchasing sites, the effects on local communities can be devastating. These effects mirror
10 those of the trade in aloe throughout the world, which had been harvested at truly overwhelming rates for its medicinal qualities and now faces extinction in certain regions.

In Tanzania, local farmers have made a business of harvesting their local orchids, and they argue that the
15 plant continues to thrive. They're more concerned with the illegal trade in Zambia and a decline in prices than with the extinction of these flowers that grow like weeds but that Westerners can't seem to get enough of. Some farmers have had to move to more remote locations or to employ
20 environmentally questionable methods, but this, they argue, is not an outgrowth of shortage. A Tanzanian farmer considers the allegations of extinction ridiculous, pointing to the fact that many of his colleagues got into the business in 1983 and are still thriving.
25 These farmers are certainly closer to the orchid crops than any more broadly-focused scientist could be. In addition, their need to earn a living for themselves does not allow them to be concerned with results thirty or forty years down the line. And the orchid is so essential to this part of Tanzania, the
30 "Serengeti of Flowers," that life is in some ways inconceivable without it. Here, the orchid is just as prized for its nutritional value as for its aesthetic value. The tubers of the orchids taste of liver when boiled in a certain way, and what remains is mixed with wood ash into a fine flour and used to prepare
35 "kinaka," an orchidean sausage and prized Tanzanian delicacy. Moreover, to meet the demand for orchids, many farms have been devoted exclusively to growing orchids, ensuring that the orchids can be harvested in a productive but controlled way, thus promoting the continued survival of many orchid
40 species that could not have thrived in this way in the wild. Unfortunately, these data cannot overtake the obvious fact that the international orchid population is dwindling, and even for those Tanzanian farmers, it can take three days to fill a bucket of orchids, where it used to take one.

45 In the face of the scientific evidence, some Asian and African governments have promised measures to protect orchids and the orchid industry at the same time. The governments of Tanzania and Nepal, for example, understand that extinction of these flowers could lead to
50 serious economic collapse, all the while having an intimate knowledge of the local significance of the orchid. The Tanzanian government, for example, has plans to make the Kitulo Plateau (host to a "staggering" array of flowers) into a national park, following the lead of the Singapore National
55 Parks Board, which created its National Orchid Garden in 1995.

43. The author refers to "aloe" (line 10) primarily to illustrate

(A) how Tanzania's record of farming orchids has a historical precedent
(B) why farmers consider the models of scientists untrustworthy
(C) why some horticulturalists consider the trends in orchid farming troubling
(D) why Tanzanian farmers are concerned about the state of orchids in their region
(E) what Tanzanian farmers have done to increase their production of orchids

44. In line 21, "outgrowth" most nearly means

(A) onset
(B) effect
(C) overharvest
(D) dearth
(E) parasite

45. The author supports the claim in lines 25-26 ("These … be") by asserting that farmers

(A) have avoided orchid extinction since 1983
(B) have favored the creation of national parks protecting orchids
(C) are occasionally required to move to find more orchid crops
(D) use orchid crops for things other than international flower sales
(E) have their own set of scientific data about global orchid crops

GO ON TO THE NEXT PAGE →

46. The author uses the statement in lines 29-31 ("And … it")
to emphasize that

(A) the main purchasers of orchids come from orchid-
farming regions

(B) the extinction of aloe plants is not likely to be
mirrored in orchid crops

(C) horticulturalists understand the cultural role of
orchids better than farmers do

(D) in certain areas, orchids have more than just an
aesthetic value

(E) scientists who study orchids refuse to see the local
importance of the flowers

47. The passage suggests that all of the following are true of
orchids EXCEPT

(A) they can be eaten and used in other food products

(B) they have been popular on international markets
since the 1800s

(C) they grow in many of the same places as aloe
crops

(D) there are legal restrictions on how they can be farmed
and sold

(E) the health of the species is often assessed on an
international level

48. The author indicates that "some Asian and African
governments" (lines 45-46) do which of the following?

(A) Encourage aggressive farming techniques

(B) Restrict how much orchid material local populations
can eat

(C) Employ orchid farmers to curate national parks

(D) Plan to take measures to protect orchid crops

(E) Boycott countries whose farmers harvest orchids
illegally

STOP

If you finish before time is called, you may check your work on this section only.
Do not turn to any other section in the test.

SECTION 4
Time — 25 minutes
18 Questions
(21–38)

Directions: For this section, solve each problem and decide which is the best of the choices given. Fill in the corresponding circle on the answer sheet. You may use any available space for scratchwork.

Notes

1. The use of a calculator is permitted.

2. All numbers used are real numbers.

3. Figures that accompany problems in this test are intended to provide information useful in solving the problems. They are drawn as accurately as possible EXCEPT when it is stated in a specific problem that the figure is not drawn to scale. All figures lie in a plane unless other wise indicated.

4. Unless otherwise specified, the domain of any function f is assumed to be the set of all real numbers x for which $f(x)$ is a real number.

Reference Information

 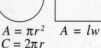   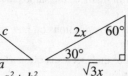

$A = \pi r^2$ $A = lw$ $A = \frac{1}{2}bh$ $V = lwh$ $V = \pi r^2 h$ $c^2 = a^2 + b^2$ Special Right Triangles

The number of degrees of arc in a circle is 360.

The sum of the measures in degrees of the angles of a triangle is 180.

21. If $c^2 = 9$, then $c^4 =$

   (A) 18
   (B) 36
   (C) 72
   (D) 81
   (E) 6,561

22. What is the average (arithmetic mean) of the first seven positive even integers?

   (A) 6
   (B) 6.5
   (C) 7
   (D) 8
   (E) 8.5

GO ON TO THE NEXT PAGE

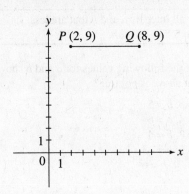

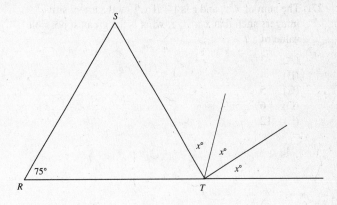

23. In the *xy*-coordinate system above, $\overline{PQ}$ is one side of an isosceles right triangle. Which of the following coordinates could be a vertex of this triangle?

(A) $(-4, 9)$
(B) $(2, 6)$
(C) $(6, 14)$
(D) $(8, 5)$
(E) $(8, 15)$

25. In $\triangle RST$ above, $RT = ST$. What is the value of x ?

(A) 30
(B) 35
(C) 50
(D) 75
(E) 105

24. What is the largest integer whose square root is less than 4 ?

(A) 9
(B) 12
(C) 15
(D) 16
(E) 25

26. If there are s seconds in m minutes, what is s in terms of m ?

(A) $\dfrac{m}{30}$

(B) $\dfrac{60}{m}$

(C) $60 - 2m$

(D) $m + 60$

(E) $60m$

GO ON TO THE NEXT PAGE

27. The sum of x, y, and z is 14. If x, y, and z are positive integers such that $x \geq y \geq z$, what is the greatest possible value of z ?

 (A) 3
 (B) 4
 (C) 5
 (D) 6
 (E) 12

For all integers a and b that are less than 5, $5a - b > ab$.

28. Which of the following values for a and b show that the statement above is <u>not</u> true?

 (A) $a = 5, b = 5$
 (B) $a = 4, b = 6$
 (C) $a = 3, b = 4$
 (D) $a = 2, b = -3$
 (E) $a = -4, b = 6$

GO ON TO THE NEXT PAGE

Directions for Student-Produced Response Questions

Each of the remaining 10 questions requires you to solve the problem and enter your answer by marking the ovals in the special grid, as shown in the examples below. You may use any available space for scratch work.

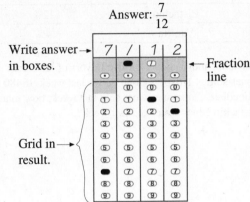

Answer: $\frac{7}{12}$

Write answer → in boxes.

← Fraction line

Grid in → result.

Answer: 2.5

← Decimal point

Note: You may start your answers in any column, space permitting. Columns not needed should be left blank.

- Mark no more than one circle in any column.

- Because the answer sheet will be machine-scored, **you will receive credit only if the circles are filled in correctly.**

- Although not required, it is suggested that you write your answer in the boxes at the top of the columns to help you fill in the circles accurately.

- Some problems may have more than one correct answer. In such cases, grid only one answer.

- No question has a negative answer.

- **Mixed numbers** such as $3\frac{1}{2}$ must be gridded as

  3.5 or 7/2. (If ┌3│1│/│2┐ is gridded, it will be

  interpreted as $\frac{31}{2}$, not $3\frac{1}{2}$.)

- **Decimal Answers:** If you obtain a decimal answer with more digits than the grid can accommodate, it may be either rounded or truncated, but it must fill the entire grid. For example, if you obtain an answer such as 0.6666..., you should record your result as .666 or .667. **A less accurate value such as .66 or .67 will be scored as incorrect.**

Acceptable ways to grid $\frac{2}{3}$ are:

---

29. 200 people attended a concert for band Q. Band Q earned $15 for each person who attended the concert and an additional $10 for each T-shirt sold. If 132 people bought one T-shirt each, how much, in dollars, did band Q earn from the concert? (Disregard the $ sign when gridding your answer.)

30. If $.5943 = (59.43)10^{-t}$ what is the value of t?

GO ON TO THE NEXT PAGE ⟩

31. If $\frac{1}{6}$ of m is 200 and $\frac{1}{5}$ of n is 500, what is the value of $n - m$?

ICE CREAM SALES AT KRISPY'S CONE PARLOR	
Ice Cream Cone Flavor	Percent Sold
Strawberry	3%
Mint Chocolate Chip	60%
Rocky Road	21%
Pistachio	12%
Vanilla	4%

33. The table above shows the five flavors of ice cream cones sold at Krispy's Cone Parlor last week. If 480 Mint Chocolate Chip cones were sold last week, how many Pistachio cones were sold last week?

32. In the figure above, *ABCD* and *WXYZ* are squares with areas 4 and 49, respectively. *DCXQ* is a rectangle with area 16. What is the area of rectangle *PDQW* ?

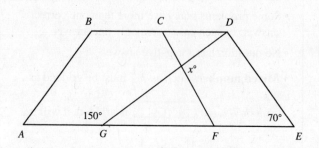

34. In the figure above, $\overline{AE} \parallel \overline{BD}$ and $\overline{CF} \parallel \overline{DE}$. What is the value of x ?

GO ON TO THE NEXT PAGE

35. For a certain magic trick, Jen is asked to choose a number between 1 and 500. If Jen chooses an even number that is divisible by both 3 and 23, what is one possible number that Jen could have chosen?

36. If $-2 \leq a \leq 3$ and $-4 \leq b \leq 2$, what is the maximum value

of $\dfrac{|a - b|}{8}$?

37. The total cost of 9 roses and 5 tulips is the same as the total cost of 6 roses and 9 tulips. The cost of each tulip is p times the cost of each rose. What is the value of p ?

38. In the xy-plane, the line $cx - dy = 2$, where c and d are constants, intersects the y-axis where $y = -8$. What is the value of d ?

STOP
If you finish before time is called, you may check your work on this section only.
Do not turn to any other section in the test.

SECTION 5
Time — 30 minutes
39 Questions
(1–39)

Directions: For each question in this section, select the best answer from among the choices given and fill in the corresponding circle on the answer sheet.

The following sentences test correctness and effectiveness of expression. Part of each sentence or the entire sentence is underlined; beneath each sentence are five ways of phrasing the underlined material. Choice A repeats the original phrasing; the other four choices are different. If you think the original phrasing produces a better sentence than any of the alternatives, select choice A; if not, select one of the other choices.

In making your selection, follow the requirements of standard written English; that is, pay attention to grammar, choice of words, sentence construction, and punctuation. Your selection should result in the most effective sentence—clear and precise, without awkwardness or ambiguity.

EXAMPLE:

Bobby Flay baked his first cake <u>and he was thirteen years old then</u>.
(A) and he was thirteen years old then
(B) when he was thirteen
(C) at age thirteen years old
(D) upon the reaching of thirteen years
(E) at the time when he was thirteen

Ⓐ ● Ⓒ Ⓓ Ⓔ

---

1. In 1900, Wilbur Wright and his brother, *West Side News* publisher Orville Wright, journeyed to Kitty Hawk, North Carolina, <u>they began their first experiments with manned air gliders there</u>.

   (A) they began their first experiments with manned air gliders there
   (B) it was where they began their first experiments with manned air gliders
   (C) that was where they began their first experiments with manned air gliders
   (D) when the first experiments with manned air gliders were begun by them
   (E) where they began their first experiments with manned air gliders

2. When Beethoven was thirteen years old, he <u>has already begun</u> composing and publicly performing music; however, not until seventeen years later would he write his first symphony.

   (A) has already begun
   (B) was already beginning
   (C) is already to begin
   (D) will already begin
   (E) had already begun

3. The lead guitarist and the drummer fought constantly, <u>and this caused the guitarist starting</u> his own new band.

   (A) and this caused the guitarist starting
   (B) so the guitarist started
   (C) the guitarist was starting
   (D) so as the guitarist was starting
   (E) effecting in that the guitarist started

4. James Dean, having died shortly after the filming of *Rebel Without a Cause*, <u>and he was only able to receive</u> an Academy Award for Best Actor posthumously.

   (A) and he was only able to receive
   (B) then he was only able to be receiving
   (C) was only able to receive
   (D) he was only able to receive
   (E) therefore he was only able to receive

5. The school <u>board, in enacting new anti-truancy laws that would discourage students from</u> cutting class and encourage regular school attendance.

   (A) board, in enacting new anti-truancy laws that would discourage students from
   (B) board is enacting new anti-truancy laws, they will discourage students
   (C) board enacted new anti-truancy laws that would discourage students from
   (D) board, which enacted new anti-truancy laws will discourage students from
   (E) board, who enacted new anti- truancy laws that will discourage students

GO ON TO THE NEXT PAGE →

6. Eugene Fama, <u>a Nobel prize winner and one of the world's most distinguished American economists, is extolled by many</u> as an authority on portfolio theory and asset pricing.

(A) a Nobel prize winner and one of the world's most distinguished American economists, is extolled by many

(B) a Nobel prize winner and one of the world's most distinguished economists, and extolled by many

(C) being a Nobel prize winner and one of the world's most distinguished economists, and by many to be extolled

(D) he is a Nobel prize winner and one of the world's most distinguished economists, many extolling him

(E) as a Nobel prize winner and one of the world's most distinguished economists, and by many to be extolled as

7. The Willis (formerly Sears) Tower, with its 108 stories and 1,451 feet, <u>are easily considered</u> Chicago's most famous landmark.

(A) are easily considered

(B) easily considered

(C) which are easily considered

(D) given easy consideration as

(E) is easily considered

8. Pollsters canvassing public opinion are discovering that most voters want improved economic conditions, better health care, and <u>have more social services programs for the elderly</u>.

(A) have more social services programs for the elderly

(B) with more social services programs for the elderly

(C) to have more social services programs for the elderly

(D) more social services programs for the elderly

(E) having more social services programs for the elderly

9. The strategy board game Chinese <u>checkers, an easy game to learn,</u> it allows players only single-step moves or moves in which pieces jump over other pieces, and the basic goal is simply to reach the other side of the board before any opponents do the same.

(A) checkers, an easy game to learn,

(B) checkers is an easy game to learn,

(C) checkers is an easy game to learn because

(D) checkers, an easy game to learn because

(E) checkers, an easy game to learn in that

10. The teacher explained that copying <u>or by otherwise using</u> another student's work to solve the problem was considered cheating.

(A) or by otherwise using

(B) or otherwise using

(C) or otherwise used

(D) or to otherwise use

(E) or if otherwise used

11. NASA astronauts, before going into space, are required <u>to accumulate a number of flight hours in military jets in order to become a pilot</u> certified to fly the space shuttle.

(A) to accumulate a number of flight hours in military jets in order to become a pilot

(B) to accumulate a number of flight hours in military jets, they thus become pilots

(C) they will accumulate a number of flight hours in military jets, thus becoming a pilot

(D) that they accumulate a number of flight hours in military jets in order to become a pilot

(E) to accumulate a number of flight hours in military jets in order to become pilots

12. The critic claimed that the paintings from Picasso's Blue Period were more representative of early twentieth-century modern art than <u>other artists who painted during his time</u>.

(A) other artists who painted during his time

(B) those artists from the same time in art history

(C) artists of his time

(D) those of any other artists of his time

(E) the same time in modern art

GO ON TO THE NEXT PAGE

13. While learning to ride the new bicycle, a pink one with green tassels and a banana seat, a dog ran in front of Rebekah and caused her to swerve into a fire hydrant.

    (A) While learning to ride the new bicycle, a pink one with green tassels and a banana seat, a dog ran in front of Rebekah and caused her to swerve into a fire hydrant.

    (B) A dog ran in front and caused Rebekah's swerve into a fire hydrant while learning to ride the new bicycle, a pink one with green tassels and a banana seat.

    (C) A dog ran out while learning to ride the new bicycle, a pink one with green tassels and a banana seat, and it caused Rebekah to swerve into a fire hydrant.

    (D) While learning to ride the new bicycle, a pink one with green tassels and a banana seat, a fire hydrant was run into by Rebekah when she swerved to avoid a dog.

    (E) While Rebekah was learning to ride the new bicycle, a pink one with green tassels and a banana seat, a dog ran in front of her and caused her to swerve into a fire hydrant.

14. Daily exercise involving cardiovascular activities <u>are proven to reduce</u> the risk of conditions such as diabetes and high blood pressure.

    (A) are proven to reduce
    (B) have been proven to reduce
    (C) has been proven as reducing
    (D) has been proven to reduce
    (E) prove that they reduce

15. <u>It possessed the most advanced safety features available in its time, and it</u> was generally considered unsinkable, the *RMS Titanic* sank along with 1,500 of its passengers on April 15, 1912.

    (A) It possessed the most advanced safety features available in its time, and

    (B) During its time, it possessed the most advanced safety features available, and

    (C) Although it possessed the most advanced safety features available in its time and

    (D) Despite it possessing the most advanced safety features available during its time,

    (E) It possessed the most advanced safety features available in its time, although

16. Each year hundreds of bicyclists from around the world pack up their belongings, travel <u>to France to participate in the Tour de France bicycle race</u>.

    (A) to France to participate in the Tour de France bicycle race

    (B) and in France they participate in the Tour de France bicycle race

    (C) to France, participating in the Tour de France bicycle race

    (D) to France, and the Tour de France bicycle race is participated in

    (E) to France, and participate in the Tour de France bicycle race

GO ON TO THE NEXT PAGE →

17. If more travelers <u>were to check their bags rather than bring carry-ons</u>, the lines through airport security would be much shorter than they currently are.

   (A) were to check their bags rather than bring carry-ons

   (B) were to check their bags rather than instead take carry-ons

   (C) will check their bags rather than instead taking carry-ons

   (D) check their bags rather than bring carry-ons

   (E) check their bags but rather instead bring carry-ons

18. Jana must move her belongings to the new apartment today regardless <u>of whether she will be able to unpack them promptly when she arrives</u>.

   (A) of whether she will be able to unpack them promptly when she arrives

   (B) of if she can unpack it promptly upon arrival

   (C) of whether or not she will be able to unpack it promptly upon arriving

   (D) of if she could unpack them immediately upon arrival

   (E) of whether she can unpack it promptly when she arrives

19. Famous for founding the world's first private detective agency, <u>another fact about Eugène Vidocq is that before he became a detective, he was a criminal and an army deserter</u>.

   (A) another fact about Eugène Vidocq is that before he became a detective, he was a criminal and an army deserter

   (B) before becoming a detective he was a criminal and an army deserter is another fact about Eugène Vidocq

   (C) Eugène Vidocq's career before he became a detective was that of a criminal and an army deserter

   (D) another fact about Eugène Vidocq is that before he became a detective, he was a criminal and an army deserter

   (E) Eugène Vidocq was a criminal and an army deserter before he became a detective

20. The reigns of Atilla the <u>Hun, like many other early rulers of the Hun tribes, were</u> marked by bloody conquests and ceaseless wars.

   (A) Hun, like many other early rulers of the Hun tribes, were

   (B) Hun and many other early rulers of the Hun tribes were

   (C) Hun, like those of many other early rulers of the Hun tribes, was

   (D) Hun and many other early rulers of the Hun tribes was

   (E) Hun, like those of many other early rulers of the Hun tribes, had been

GO ON TO THE NEXT PAGE

The following sentences test your ability to recognize grammar and usage errors. Each sentence contains either a single error or no error at all. No sentence contains more than one error. The error, if there is one, is underlined and lettered. If the sentence contains an error, select the one underlined part that must be changed to make the sentence correct. If the sentence is correct, select choice E. In choosing answers, follow the requirements of standard written English.

EXAMPLE:

The other players and her significantly improved
   A   B   C

the game plan created by the coaches. No error
           D   E

21. Traveling to Rome, skiing in the Alps, and to swim with
        A   B

dolphins are among the activities that I want to do this
         C   D

year. No error
     E

22. Between the ages of 9 and 11, Janis made at least three
                             A

visits to the hospital emergency room per year, the
                      B

majority of it due to minor mishaps she had while playing
       C   D

soccer. No error
      E

23. Unlike those of many authors, Kurt Vonnegut's stories
             A

cannot be described as belonging to a single genre, since
      B   C   D

they equally blend satire, dark humor, and science fiction.

No error
  E

24. The annual running of the bulls in Pamplona and other
                 A

Spanish towns attracts thousands of tourists, who
          B

gather to participate in a tradition that originated from the
     C   D

fourteenth century. No error
          E

25. In the 1960s, master potter Shoji Hamad influenced
                            A

significant the way that Japanese potters created
      B

traditional ceramics, encouraging new emphasis on
              C   D

mingei and other utilitarian styles of pottery. No error
                                 E

26. Most professors maintain that one who studies hard is
            A   B

likely to succeed, especially when they attends class
   C   D

regularly. No error
        E

27. The Montreal Biodome being composed of four zones,
         A   B

each of which replicates a different ecosystem and allows
          C

visitors to experience a different climate without leaving
       D

the building. No error
       E

GO ON TO THE NEXT PAGE

28. His unreasonably strict rules for submitting homework
   <u>   A</u>

have made the professor so unpopular that he has little
<u> B</u>   <u>C</u>

chance of having anyone sign up for his <u>next course.</u>
                                           D

<u>No error</u>
  E

29. Different <u>types</u> of stars have a <u>different temperature;</u> blue
           A   B

stars, for instance, <u>are</u> typically above 33,000 Kelvin,
                 C

white stars are <u>about</u> 8,000 Kelvin, and brown stars are
               D

anywhere from 500 to 1,300 Kelvin. <u>No error</u>
                                E

30. We <u>would be</u> sad to leave Dublin had the weather <u>been</u>
       A   B

<u>pleasant enough during our stay</u> to allow us to <u>engage in</u>
                  C   D

outdoor activities. <u>No error</u>
                  E

31. Economists <u>have predicted</u> that the Brazilian economy
               A

will continue to <u>decline</u> throughout 2013; <u>it has</u> prompted
           B   C

them to express concern that the country's credit rating

may soon begin to suffer. <u>No error</u>
           D   E

32. <u>Along</u> <u>the western bank</u> of Lake Nasser sits the
    A   B   <u>C</u>

Great Temple of Ramses II and the Small Temple of

Nefertiti, each of which <u>was originally carved</u> out of a
                             D

mountainside. <u>No error</u>
               E

33. After Frank insisted <u>to present</u> his paper <u>at the conference,</u>
                 A   B

he also <u>tried</u> to convince his coworkers <u>to give him</u>
          C   D

transportation to the event. <u>No error</u>
                      E

34. That the state of Maine has <u>less than</u> 42 residents per
          A   B

square mile sometimes <u>comes</u> as a <u>shock to</u> those who
                   C   D

move there from more densely populated areas. <u>No error</u>
                                         E

GO ON TO THE NEXT PAGE

Directions: The following passage is an early draft of an essay. Some parts of the passage need to be rewritten.

Read the passage and select the best answers for the questions that follow. Some questions are about particular sentences or parts of sentences and ask you to improve sentence structure or word choice. Other questions ask you to consider organization and development. In choosing answers, follow the requirements of standard written English.

Questions 35-39 are based on the following passage.

(1) Many think that spending hours studying vocabulary flashcards and books on grammar are the best way to learn a foreign language. (2) Most linguists, however, would also suggest interacting with native speakers. (3) Doing so helps one improve one's accent and forces one to practice speaking as well as listening. (4) When individuals practice speaking in foreign language, they strengthen muscles that they do not use when speaking in their own tongue and therefore become better speakers in the new language.

(5) Dedicating regular time to study is also essential to learning a new language, according to many experts. (6) The fact of being irregular in your studies, they find, is the worst action you can take if you want to become fluent in a new language. (7) In other words, when you study regularly, whether you study for two hours per day or for thirty minutes per day, you are exercising your new skills and preventing yourself from forgetting what you have learned. (8) Practice is essential for improving other skills, such as playing an instrument, too.

(9) Learning a new language sometimes requires you to make a fool of yourself. (10) For a language learning process to be effective, you must practice new skills in settings that include others. (11) When individuals practice their language skills by interacting with native speakers, they are literally going back to being two year-olds, and are likely to make mistakes. (12) And during a conversation, when speech is impromptu, they are more likely to occur than during planned presentations or in essays.

35. Which of the following is the best revision of the underlined part of sentence 1 (reproduced below)?

Many think that spending hours studying vocabulary flashcards and books on grammar are the best way to learn a foreign language.

(A) (as it is now)
(B) spending hours studying vocabulary flashcards and books on grammar is
(C) the hours they spent studying vocabulary flashcards and books on grammar were
(D) if you spend hours studying vocabulary flashcards and books on grammar, that is
(E) after spending hours studying vocabulary flashcards and books on grammar one will have discovered

36. In context, which of the following is the best version of the underlined part of sentence 6 (reproduced below)?

The fact of being irregular in your studies, they find, is the worst action you can take if you want to become fluent in a new language.

(A) (as it is now)
(B) Such irregularity
(C) Being irregular like that
(D) Studying irregularly
(E) To be so irregular

37. In context, which of the following is the best revision of the underlined part of sentence 11 (reproduced below)?

When individuals practice their language skills by interacting with native speakers, they are literally going back to being two year-olds, and are likely to make mistakes.

(A) (as it is now)
(B) are despite this
(C) are, in contrast,
(D) are, for example,
(E) are, as it were,

GO ON TO THE NEXT PAGE ⇨

38. In context, the pronoun "they" in sentence 12 refers to which of the following?

(A) Individuals who study foreign languages

(B) Conversations between those who study a foreign language and native speakers of that language

(C) New skills gained by practicing conversation in a foreign language

(D) Conversational mistakes made by foreign language students

(E) Settings that include both native and non-native speakers of a language

39. Which of the following is unnecessary and should be deleted from the passage?

(A) Sentence 3

(B) Sentence 4

(C) Sentence 7

(D) Sentence 8

(E) Sentence 11

STOP

If you finish before time is called, you may check your work on this section only.
Do not turn to any other section in the test.

PRACTICE TEST 3 ANSWERS

Section 1	Section 2	Section 3	Section 4	Section 5	
1. C	1. C	25. B	21. D	1. E	31. C
2. D	2. C	26. B	22. D	2. E	32. C
3. A	3. E	27. A	23. E	3. B	33. A
4. B	4. D	28. A	24. C	4. C	34. B
5. A	5. B	29. E	25. C	5. C	35. B
6. B	6. B	30. A	26. E	6. A	36. D
7. E	7. A	31. A	27. B	7. E	37. E
8. D	8. D	32. B	28. C	8. D	38. D
9. C	9. B	33. C	29. 4,320	9. C	39. D
10. E	10. A	34. B	30. 2	10. B	
11. B	11. D	35. E	31. 1,300	11. E	
12. C	12. D	36. C	32. 40	12. D	
13. A	13. A	37. E	33. 96	13. E	
14. B	14. E	38. A	34. 100	14. D	
15. C	15. E	39. B	35. 138,	15. C	
16. D	16. C	40. B	276,	16. E	
17. A	17. D	41. A	or	17. A	
18. D	18. C	42. C	414	18. A	
19. C	19. C	43. C	36. .875	19. E	
20. E	20. A	44. B	or $\frac{7}{8}$	20. B	
21. D		45. D		21. B	
22. A		46. D	37. $\frac{3}{4}$	22. C	
23. E		47. C	or .75	23. E	
24. B		48. D		24. D	
			38. $\frac{1}{4}$	25. B	
			or .25	26. D	
				27. B	
				28. E	
				29. B	
				30. A	

You will find a detailed explanation for each question beginning on page 253.

SCORING YOUR PRACTICE PSAT

Critical Reading

After you have checked your answers against the answer key, you can calculate your score. For the two Critical Reading sections (Sections 1 and 3), add up the number of correct answers and the number of incorrect answers. Enter these numbers on the worksheet on the next page. Multiply the number of incorrect answers by .25 and subtract this result from the number of correct answers. Then round this to the nearest whole number. This is your Critical Reading "raw score." Next, use the conversion table to convert your raw score to a scaled score.

Math

Calculating your Math score is a bit trickier, because some of the questions have five answer choices (for these, the incorrect answer deduction is .25), and some are Grid-Ins (which have no deduction for wrong answers).

First, check your answers to all of the problem-solving questions on Sections 2 and 4. For Section 2 and questions 21–28 of Section 4, enter the number of correct answers and the number of incorrect answers into the worksheet on the next page. Multiply the number of incorrect answers by .25 and subtract this result from the number of correct answers. For questions 29–38 of Section 4, the Grid-In questions, simply enter the number of correct answers. Now, add up the totals for both types of math questions to give you your total Math raw score. Then you can use the conversion table to find your scaled score.

Writing Skills

The Writing Skills section should be scored just like the Critical Reading sections. Add up the number of correct answers and the number of incorrect answers from Section 5, and enter these numbers on the worksheet on the next page. Multiply the number of incorrect answers by .25 and subtract this result from the number of correct answers. Then round this to the nearest whole number. This is your Writing Skills raw score. Next, use the conversion table to convert your raw scores to scaled scores.

WORKSHEET FOR CALCULATING YOUR SCORE

Critical Reading

	Correct	**Incorrect**	

A. Sections 1 and 3 _____ – (.25 × _____) =

A

B. Total rounded Critical Reading raw score

B

Math

	Correct	**Incorrect**

C. Sections 2 and 4—Problem Solving _____ – (.25 × _____) =

C

D. Section 4—Grid-Ins _____ =

D

E. Total unrounded Math raw score (C + D)

E

F. Total rounded Math raw score

F

Writing Skills

Correct   **Incorrect**

Section 5 _____ – (.25 × _____) =

Total rounded Writing Skills raw score

SCORE CONVERSION TABLE

Math Raw Score	Math Scaled Score	Critical Reading Raw Score	Critical Reading Scaled Score	Writing Skills Raw Score	Writing Skills Scaled Score
38	80	48	80	39	80
37	77	47	80	38	80
36	74	46	78	37	78
35	72	45	76	36	77
34	70	44	74	35	76
33	68	43	72	34	74
32	66	42	71	33	73
31	65	41	69	32	71
30	64	40	68	31	69
29	62	39	67	30	68
28	61	38	66	29	66
27	60	37	64	28	65
26	59	36	63	27	63
25	58	35	62	26	62
24	57	34	62	25	60
23	55	33	61	24	59
22	54	32	60	23	57
21	53	31	59	22	56
20	52	30	58	21	55
19	51	29	57	20	54
18	50	28	56	19	52
17	48	27	55	18	51
16	47	26	54	17	50
15	46	25	54	16	49
14	45	24	53	15	48
13	44	23	52	14	46
12	43	22	51	13	45
11	42	21	50	12	44
10	41	20	49	11	43
9	40	19	48	10	41
8	39	18	47	9	40
7	38	17	46	8	39
6	36	16	45	7	37
5	35	15	44	6	36
4	34	14	43	5	35
3	32	13	42	4	33
2	30	12	41	3	32
1	29	11	40	2	31
0	26	10	39	1	30
		9	38	0	29
		8	37		
		7	36		
		6	34		
		5	33		
		4	32		
		3	30		
		2	29		
		1	27		
		0	25		

Chapter 10
Practice Test 3:
Answers and
Explanations

Section 1

1. **C** Start with the second blank. Since the restaurant was *rarely crowded* due to the *wait staff*, replace the blank with a negative word such as "rude" or "disrespectful." Eliminate everything except choices (B) and (C). Now move to the first blank and notice the trigger word *but*, which indicates that even though the wait staff was negative, the cuisine must be positive. Eliminate choice (B) since *unremarkable* is not a positive word. Choice (C) is the correct answer.

2. **D** Start with the second blank. Since the sentence states that *food production will be altered* due to what's happening to the honeybee, the honeybee must be important to food production, so replace the second blank with "important." Eliminate choices (A), (B), and (E). Since the honeybees have an effect on food production, replace the first blank with a word that indicates a change in the population, such as "increase" or "decrease." Eliminate choice (C) since *renouncing* doesn't fit either of those words. Choice (D) is the correct answer.

3. **A** The sentence states that the *Leaning Tower of Pisa… is regarded as one of the most remarkable buildings in the world*, but this statement is preceded by the trigger word *although*. Therefore the blank should be replaced with something that means "unremarkable" or "inferior." Eliminate choices (B) and (C) since they are the opposite of the clue, and also choice (E) because it isn't a negative. Choice (D) is too strong since repugnant means "very ugly or distasteful." Choice (A) is the correct answer.

4. **B** Start with the second blank. The second part of this sentence mentions that players hit each other with *careless abandon* and that *no one was interested* in a particular type of play. Therefore, the second blank should be the opposite of *careless*, so choose a word that means "careful." Eliminate choices (C) and (D). Because of the semicolon, which is a same-direction trigger, the first part of the sentence must agree with the second. Fill in the first blank with something such as "not caring" or "not knowing." Eliminate choices (A) and (E). Choice (B) is the correct answer.

5. **A** The sentence contrasts the *Photorealistic style* and the *Expressionist style*. In contrast to the Expressionist painter, who *uses color to create an emotional impact*, the Photorealistic painter would "try" to copy every detail. The missing word must mean "try." *Endeavor* means "attempt," making choice (A) the correct answer.

6. **B** Start with the second blank. The sentence states that the physics instructor wanted a *victory* and did something with the work of her *honors physics class*. Since a *victory* was needed, replace the second blank with "display" or "used." Eliminate everything but choices (B) and (C). If the teacher only used the best work, she must have wanted to "guarantee" a victory. Use that word for the first blank and eliminate choice (C) since it's the opposite of "guarantee." Choice (B) is the correct answer.

7. **E** The sentence states that the explorer's *recent exploits...confirmed that he had no intention of worrying about his own safety*, so the trigger word *but* should indicate that the *exploits* were the opposite of safe, so replace the blank with "danger." Choice (E) is the correct answer.

8. **D** The blank in this question must match the clues, which are *mean-spiritedly mocked* and *taunted*, so recycle a word from the sentence and replace the blank with "mean-spirited." Choice (D) is the only choice that has a negative meaning, and it means "causing harm" or "evil/wicked," so choice (D) is the correct answer.

9. **C** The correct answer to this question must be stated directly in the passage, so go to the answer choices and eliminate anything that cannot be proven. Choice (A) is too extreme, so eliminate it. Choice (B) doesn't work since nothing is said about *most readers*. Choice (C) could work since the first line states that the Naturalist movement was the "natural result of Romanticism and Surrealism." Choice (D) seems okay at first, but the passage only states that Crane's is as example of Naturalism, not that it was the first Naturalist novel. Choice (E) uses the wrong meaning of the word *environment*. Choice (C) is the correct answer.

10. **E** The author uses Maggie's suicide as an example of something found in a Naturalist novel. Choice (A) doesn't work because the passage never explicitly states that Maggie's home life was unsatisfying. There is no evidence that Maggie's story wouldn't be told in a Surrealist novel, so eliminate choice (B). Eliminate choice (C) since this is only one example of a Naturalist novel. Choice (D) is wrong since the passage is not focused on the Romantic movement. Choice (E) fits since the passage states that, in the Naturalist movement, *one's environment played a much more pivotal role in determining one's destiny than choice and action*, so it is the correct answer.

11. **B** The first sentence states that *The advent of social media sites such as Facebook and Twitter has had a dichotomous effect on the landscape*, so look for an answer that says something about having conflicting or different effects on the world. Eliminate choices (A) and (C) since this passage is neutral, and there is no evidence to support *bemoan* or *criticize*. Choice (D) is also out since *celebrate* is positive. Choice (B) fits since it says *differing* consequences. Eliminate choice (E) since our *daily lives* is irrelevant. Choice (B) is the correct answer.

12. **C** Since this passage states that *Twitter has also been responsible for a complete overhaul in government in Iran*, the use of *not ironically* indicates that stating Twitter played this role is serious and not meant as a joke. Eliminate (A) since *impossible* is too extreme. Eliminate choice (B) because there is no mention of anyone having a *flippant attitude*. Choice (C) could work since it states Twitter's role was *integral*, which matches complete *overhaul*. Eliminate choice (D) because the passage does not make such a comparison. Eliminate choice (E) since the author isn't trying to cast doubt on anyone. Choice (C) is the correct answer.

13. **A** The full lines read as follows: *In a span of only thirty years, the number of children who play musical instruments has been cut in half.* The word *only* indicates the quickness with which this transformation has occurred, lending support to choice (A). The author goes on to list the troubling aspects of this trend, so none of the other choices work in this context.

14. **B** The author of Passage 1 discusses the survey in the first part of the second paragraph: *Music in Peril is not the collection of urban legends that most of its critics will accuse it of being. It is a set of data collected from elementary and middle schools all over the country. With schools represented from each of the 50 states, it accounts for all the great diversity in this country.* From this statement, it can be inferred that the author disapproves of *urban legends* and approves of data collected from *all over the country that accounts for all the great diversity in this country.* The author is most concerned with span and diversity, as choice (B) suggests. While choice (D) does partially describe *Music in Peril's* data, it does not account for all the data, so it can be eliminated. Choice (E) addresses the issue of race, but not the other types of diversity described in the passage.

15. **C** The author of Passage 2 does not dispute the methods employed by the statisticians described in Passage 1. She instead thinks the criteria should be changed. As she writes in the last paragraph, *The survey can't capture the fact that classical music is not the only place to find interesting, complex music anymore, except by the most conservative, crustiest definitions.* In this sense, the author of Passage 2 would likely consider the diversity of the groups surveyed irrelevant because the survey is based on faulty premises, as suggested in choice (C). The author of Passage 2 does not take issue with Passage 1's data but more with its premises and conclusions.

16. **D** The main point of the final paragraph of Passage 1 comes through in the last two sentences: *True musical proficiency is the result of many years of encouraging musical education, and not only for those who eventually become musicians. Ours is a dire world indeed when not only have our musicians lost the ability to play but also the broader populace has lost the discernment and ability to hear them.* In other words, musical education does not only affect schoolchildren but affects society as a whole, as choice (D) paraphrases. While choice (B) may be implied in the passage, it is never directly stated, so this answer choice has to be eliminated.

17. **A** The author of Passage 2 refers to Passage 1's conclusions as *apocalyptic* and *evidence that all the bad things we suspect are worse than we even knew.* Passage 2's sarcastic, dismissive language suggests that the author thinks Passage 1's conclusions are a bit dramatic, or overstated, as choice (A) suggests. Although she disagrees with these conclusions, she does not refer to the author of Passage 1 as *dishonest*, merely misguided, eliminating choice (E).

18. **D** The author of Passage 2 refers to these *apocalyptic surveys as providing evidence that all the bad things we suspect are worse than we even knew.* The survey in the answer choices must therefore describe a negative trend, eliminating choices (B), (C), and (E). Choice (A) describes a trend, but it is one that is simply true. It does not contain within it the value judgment that choice (D) does. Only choice (D) remains, as exactly the kind of *apocalyptic survey* she considers commonplace.

19.   C   The third paragraph of Passage 2 states the following: *Music programs have been slashed at many public schools, and less than half as many children today are learning instruments than were the generations of forty or fifty years earlier. And this statistical certainty is not limited to the less fortunate areas of the country.* Words like *many* and *limited* refer to the *range* of the problem, as choice (C) suggests. The author of Passage 2 does accuse *Music in Peril* of both *conservatism* and *bias*, but in these lines, she is conceding that the study describes a wide-ranging trend, eliminating choices (D) and (E).

20.   E   The word *landscape* is used in the beginning of the fourth paragraph: *The musical landscape is changing, yes, but not in the distressing way that* Music in Peril *wants to suggest. The survey can't capture the fact that classical music is not the only place to find interesting, complex music anymore.* In other words, the typical definition suggests that *classical music* is the only *interesting, complex* type of music—a claim that the author disputes, lending support to choice (E). Choice (D) is correct to say *shifting*, but the trend is not *impossible to describe*, as the author tries to describe it.

21.   D   Throughout the fourth paragraph, the author uses terms like *most conservative, traditional, musical categories that don't apply anymore, institutions of old,* and *irrelevant*. In other words, the categories are still being used even though they have not changed to reflect current realities and are therefore *inflexible*, as choice (D) suggests. Other terms may provide alternate meanings for the slangy word *crusty*, but they do not apply here.

22.   A   The last sentence of Passage 2 says the following: *All that is really happening is that the institutions of old are trying to hold on for dear life and actually belong in the same irrelevant pile as studies on the decline of cursive or telephone conversations.* The key word here is *irrelevant*, and the author of Passage 1 would likely respond by noting the larger relevance of the project, as choice (A) does. There is no support in Passage 1 for choices (B), (C), and (E). Choice (D) may be true, but it would not respond to Passage 2's criticism.

23.   E   Compare the first sentences of both passages. Passage 1 states, Music in Peril *confirms most of our worst suspicions,* suggesting a concerned or saddened tone. Passage 2 states, Music in Peril *is hardly surprising in our era of apocalyptic surveys, yet more evidence that all the bad things we suspect are worse than we even knew,* which is far more sarcastic and dismissive. Choice (A) is correct only for Passage 1, and choice (D) is correct only for Passage 2. The only choice that correctly identifies the tone in each of the passages is choice (E).

24.   B   Passage 2 is primarily a critique of the ideas in Passage 1, which eliminates choices (C) and (D). Passage 2 does not, however, provide new findings or new data, which eliminates choices (A) and (E). Only choice (B) remains, and it correctly identifies Passage 2's issue with the premises of Passage 1's argument, namely that classical music is the main outlet for interesting, important music.

Section 2

1. **C** Start by writing out the equation and plugging in the given information. Since $st = 6$, the equation becomes $2r(6) = 60$. Multiply the 2 and the 6 on the left side to get $12r = 60$. It is possible to Plug In The Answers (PITA) at this point, but it is quicker to simply divide each side of the equation by 12. Therefore, $r = 5$ and (C) is the credited response.

2. **C** This is a Plugging In question for which the number to plug in is provided. Start by plugging $x = 4$ into the two expressions. $(x + 5)^2$ becomes $(4 + 5)^2$, which is $(9)^2$ or 81. $\sqrt{x+5}$ becomes $\sqrt{4+5}$, which is $\sqrt{9}$ or 3. "Difference" means subtraction, so subtract 3 from 81 to get 78. Choice (C) is the credited response.

3. **E** The question only asks about a number in the overlap between sets E and F, so the correct answer cannot be in set N. Therefore, (A) and (B) can be eliminated, as those are negative numbers. Check each remaining answer choice to determine if it is in set E and set F. The numbers in (C) and (D) are not even, so those can be eliminated. The number in (E) is even, and it is a multiple of 5, so (E) is the credited response.

4. **D** This is a Plugging In question in which the values for the variable are provided. Start with case I and plug in $n = 4$. This yields $3(4) = 12$, which is true. Now plug in $n = 5$. $3(5)$ is 15, which is not equal to 12. Since the equation is not satisfied by both values of n, case I is false. Therefore, (A), (C), and (E) can be eliminated. Choices (B) and (D) both contain case III, so it must be true and does not need to be tested. Only case II needs to be evaluated to determine whether (B) or (D) is the credited response. Plug $n = 4$ into case II, which yields $(4)^2 - 9(4) + 20 = 0$. This becomes $16 - 36 + 20 = 0$, or $-20 + 20 = 0$. This is true, so test $n = 5$. The equation becomes $(5)^2 - 9(5) + 20 = 0$, which equals $25 - 45 + 20 = 0$ or $-20 + 20 = 0$. This is also true, so both cases II and III are true, and (D) is the credited response.

5. **B** If the shape in the figure is a semicircle, then the line across the bottom is the diameter and a straight line. There are 180° in a straight line, so $60 + a + a + a + a + a = 180$. This simplifies to $60 + 5a = 180$. From here, the equation can be solved for a. PITA will work as well, since the question asks for a specific amount. If $a = 30$, the value in (C), the equation is $60 + 5(30) = 180$. This becomes $60 + 150 = 180$, or $210 = 180$. This is not true, so (C) can be eliminated. That value for a was too large, so (D) and (E) can be eliminated as well. Try the value in (B), $a = 24$, and the equation is $60 + 5(24) = 180$, or $60 + 120 = 180$. This is true, so (B) is the credited response.

6. **B** Isosceles right triangles have two equal legs. The angles of isosceles right triangles are 45°, 45°, and 90°. It is one of the special right triangles, so the sides have a predictable relationship of $x:x: x\sqrt{2}$. If the leg is x, then the hypotenuse is $x\sqrt{2}$. In this triangle, the leg is 6, so the hypotenuse, which is y, is $6\sqrt{2}$. Therefore, (B) is the credited response. Knowing the special right triangles saves time on the test, but it is not necessary to solve this problem. If both legs are equal to 6, the Pythagorean Theorem states that $6^2 + 6^2 = y^2$. This can also be used to solve for y.

7. **A** First, determine what percent of the students typically spent 3 hours or more doing homework each night. The percents must add up to 100, so $5 + 10 + 63 + 15 + p = 100$. This simplifies to $93 + p = 100$, so $p = 7\%$. Now find 7% of the total number of students. Translating the English to math, 7% means 7 out of 100, "of" means to multiply, and the total number of students equals 800. The number of students who spent 3 hours or more equals $\frac{7}{100} \times 800 = 56$, so (A) is the credited response.

8. **D** When asked for a specific value and given numbers in the answer choices, PITA. Start with (C) and plug in 4 for x. The inequality becomes $2 < 2(4) - 6 < 4$, or $2 < 8 - 6 < 4$. This becomes $2 < 2 < 4$, which is not true, so (C) can be eliminated. A larger value is needed for x to make the inequality true, so (A) and (B) can also be eliminated. Only choices (D) and (E) remain, and the value in (E) is easier to plug in. If $x = 5$, the inequality becomes $2 < 2(5) - 6 < 4$. This simplifies to $2 < 10 - 6 < 4$, or $2 < 4 < 4$. This is also not true, so (E) can be eliminated, and (D) is the credited response.

9. **B** When asked for a specific value and given numbers in the answer choices, PITA. Start with the value in (C), which is 9. If $x = 9$, the radius of the semicircle is 9. The area of the semicircle is $\frac{1}{2}\pi r^2$ or $\frac{1}{2}\pi(9)^2$. This equals $\frac{1}{2}\pi(81)$, which is 40.5π. The question states that the area of the semicircle is 18π, so (C) can be eliminated. This value is too large, so (D) and (E) can be eliminated as well. For (B), if $x = 6$, the radius is 6 and the area is $\frac{1}{2}\pi(6)^2$ or $\frac{1}{2}\pi(36)$. This equals 18π, so (B) is the credited response.

10. **A** When asked for a specific value and given numbers in the answer choices, PITA. This question asks for the *least* value that will work, so start with the value in (A). If 11 pennies are transferred from jar L to jar N, jar L will have 185 pennies in it and jar N will have 186 pennies in it. Since jar M has only 184 pennies in it, jar N has more pennies than each of the other two jars. Therefore, (A) is the credited response.

11. **D** This is a pattern question, and the fact that the sequences "continue indefinitely" makes it sound like it will be a lot of work. The best approach is to simply start writing the sequences out until a pattern emerges, which it is likely to do fairly quickly. The sequence in the left column will be: 0, 7, 14, 21, 28, 35, 42, 49, 56, 63, etc. The sequence in the right column will be 12, 16, 20, 24, 28, 32, 36, 40, 44, 48, etc. At this point, both sequences contain the number 28 as the 5th term, so there is at least one row in which the terms are equal. Therefore, (E) can be eliminated. From the 6th term on, the number in the sequence in the left column is larger than the corresponding number in the right column. The sequence on the left will continue to increase faster than the one on the right, so the two sequences will never have equal numbers in any row again. There was only one match, so (D) is the credited response.

12. **D** With variables in the answer choices, Plug In. If the woman's ride to the airport is 10 miles, $m = 10$. Her total fare would be $2.50 for the one-time charge and $3 for each of the 10 miles travelled, or $2.50 + 3(10)$, which is $32.50. Now, to find the cost "per mile," divide the fare of $32.50 by the number of miles, which equals 10. This results in $3.25, which is the target answer. Now plug $m = 10$ into the answer choices to see which one equals $3.25. Choice (A) becomes $10 + 2.50$, which equals 12.50. This is not the target answer, so (A) can be eliminated. Choice (B) becomes $2.50 + 3(10)$, which equals 32.50. This is the total fare, not the fare per mile, so (B) is a trap answer and can be eliminated. Choice (C) becomes $2.50(10) + 3(10)$, which is much too large and can be eliminated without even calculating. Choice (D) becomes $\frac{2.50 + 3(10)}{10}$, which equals $\frac{32.50}{10}$ or $3.25. This is the target answer, but all 5 answer choices must be checked when Plugging In, in case more than one results in the target answer. Choice (E) becomes $\frac{2.50(10) + 3}{10}$, which equals $\frac{28}{10}$ or $2.80. This is not the target answer, so (D) is the credited response.

13. **A** When dealing with graphs of functions, $f(x)$ or $g(x)$ is the y value for any given x. The question asks which graph has exactly one value of x that makes $g(x) = 0$, so draw a line on each graph in the answer choices at $y = 0$. This is also the x-axis of the xy-coordinate plane in each graph. The number of points of intersection between the graph of $g(x)$ and the line drawn will be the number of values for which x makes $g(x) = 0$. For (A), the graph will look like the following:

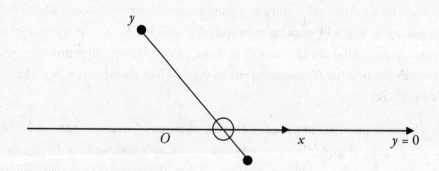

There is only one point of intersection between the graph and the line $y = 0$, at the circled point. If the same steps are followed with (B), there are two points of intersection. For (C), there are four, and (D) and (E) each have three points of intersection. Therefore, (A) is the credited response.

14.   **E**   For geometry questions that do not have a figure, draw one. If one side of the rectangular solid is a square, the opposite side must also be a square. Draw the other 4 sides as rectangles that are <u>not</u> square, if possible. This will determine what the greatest number of "not square" sides can be. The rectangular solid could look something like the following:

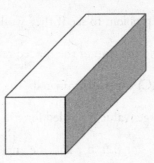

The front and back are squares, but the other four sides are <u>not</u> square. Therefore, (E) is the credited response.

15.   **E**   When dealing with functions, the value in parentheses is the *x* value, and *f(x)* or *p(x)* is the value that comes out of the function when that *x* value is put in. To find the value of *p*(4), look up where *x* = 4 on the chart and find the corresponding *p(x)* value. According to the chart, *p*(4) = 7. Now find where *x* = 2 to determine that *p*(2) = 3. Plug these values into the equation 3*p*(4) + *p*(2) to get 3(7) + 3 = 21 + 3 = 24. Therefore, (E) is the credited response.

16.   **C**   Probability is defined as the number of outcomes that fulfill the requirements divided by the total number of possible outcomes. The total number of possible outcomes consists of the 4 options from the board on the left multiplied by the 8 options from the board on the right. This yields 32 total possible outcomes. Now, to determine how many scores are at least 10, the best method is to start listing them out. Be systematic so that none get overlooked. If the number on the board on the left is 4, the numbers from the board on the right that will result in a score of at least 10 are 8, 7, and 6. If the number of the left is 3, the numbers on the right that will result in a score of at least 10 are 8 and 7. If the number on the left is 2, the number on the right must be 8. There are no other combinations that will have a sum of 10 or more, so there are 6 outcomes that fulfill the requirements. Therefore, the probability is $\frac{6}{32}$, which reduces to $\frac{3}{16}$. Choice (C) is the credited response.

17. **D** When asked for a specific value and given numbers in the answer choices, PITA. Start with the middle choice, (C) and assume that $z = 90°$. If it does, the angle opposite z will also be 90°. This leaves 180° out of the total 360° in the circle for the shaded regions. This 180° is divided equally between the two shaded regions, so each of those is 90° as well. Now check these values with the information given in the problem to see if they work. The average of the unshaded regions is $\frac{90+90}{2}$, which equals 90, and the sum of the shaded regions is 90 + 90, which equals 180. These two values are not equal, so (C) can be eliminated. The sum of the shaded regions was too large, so to make those smaller, a larger value is needed for z in the unshaded regions. Therefore, (A) and (B) can be eliminated as well. For (D), if z and the angle opposite z each equal 120°, they add to 240°. There are 120° left for the shaded regions, so each of those equals 60°. Now the average of the unshaded regions is $\frac{120+120}{2}$, which equals 120, and the sum of the shaded regions is 60 + 60, which equals 120. These two results are equal, so (D) is the credited response.

18. **C** For questions with unknown variables, Plug In for those variables, following any restrictions set forth in the question. In this case, when the three numbers are multiplied together, the result is a negative number. This means that either one of the numbers is negative and two are positive, or all three are negative. Start with the first situation and pick a negative integer for f, since it is less than the other two numbers, and positive integers for g and h. If $f = -2$, $g = 3$, and $h = 4$, $fgh = -24$. This fits the requirements, so these numbers work. For these values, cases I and II are true, but case III is false. Therefore, (D) and (E) can be eliminated, as those contain case III. Now try other values for the variables, making all three of them negative. If $f = -5$, $g = -3$, and $h = -1$, $fgh = -15$. These values still fit the requirements and cases I and II are still true. Try a few more combinations of numbers, just to be certain that cases I and II are always true. Since they are, (C) is the credited response.

19. **C** When given a geometry question with no figure, draw one. Start with points M and N.

M ●   ● N

Now draw a point that could be 6 units from M and 2 units from N. It could look like the following:

●

M ●   ● N

Another point could be below line $\overline{MN}$ in the same position, like this

There are no other points that can be drawn that are 6 units away from M and 2 units away from N, so (C) is the credited response.

20. **A** The numbers in these answer choices are very large. Rather than count the number of integers that do <u>not</u> have 5 as any digit, count the number that <u>do</u> and subtract them from the total number of integers less than 1,500. This will still be a lot of integers, so start by listing out those with a 5 in them until a pattern emerges. Between 1 and 99, the integers that contain a 5 as any digit are 5, 15, 25, 35, 45, 50, 51, 52, 53, 54, 55, 56, 57, 58, 59, 65, 75, 85, and 95, for a total of 19 integers. For the numbers 100-199, there will again be 19 integers with a 5 as a digit. The same is true for 200-299, 300-399 and 400-499. For the numbers between 500 and 599, every one of them will contain at least one 5 as a digit, so that adds 100 more to the list. There will be 19 more integers added to the list from each of the following sets of 100: 600-699, 700-799, 800-899, 900-999, 1,000-1,099, 1,100-1,199, 1,200-1,299, 1,300-1,399, and 1,400-1,499. In total, the number of integers with a 5 as any digit will include the 100 from 500 to 599 and the 19 from each of the other 14 sets of 100 listed above. Therefore, Total = 100 + 19(14) = 100 + 266 = 366. Now subtract 366 from the total number of integers <u>less than</u> 1,500, which is 1,499, to get 1,499 − 366 = 1,133. Choice (A) is the credited response.

Section 3

25. **B** Start with the second blank. The sentence states that the *popular chain store lately has forgotten customer service in favor of making money*, so replace the second blank with "money." Eliminate everything except choices (B) and (C). Since the first part of the clue states that the *chain store has forgotten customer service*, replace the first blank with "forgets." Eliminate choice (C). Choice (B) is the correct answer.

26. **B** Start with the first blank. The sentence says that basset hounds are *slow to get up from rest, but are always aware of their surroundings*. Replace the first blank with "slow" and eliminate everything except choices (B) and (D). Replace the second blank with "unaware." Eliminate choice (D). Choice (B) is the correct answer.

27. **A** David is described in this sentence as being *known for his braggadocio and arrogance*, so replace the first blank with "brag." Choice (A) is a good fit. Choice (C) might work, but *verbalize* only means to talk, so there is no hint of *braggadocio and arrogance*. Choice (A) is the correct answer.

28.   **A**   The sentence states that 1970s cinema is celebrated for *depicting undoubtedly realistic situations*, in contrast to the *fantastical elements from earlier eras*, so replace the blank with "honest." Choice (A) is a good fit. Choice (B) means "serious," which doesn't match "honest" as well as choice (A) does. Eliminate choices (C) and (D) since both are the opposite of "honest" and choice (E) since it doesn't match "honest." Choice (A) is the correct answer.

29.   **E**   The sentence doesn't have any clues about the *common field cricket* other than *the research that belied a common assumption*. Therefore, the blanks will stand in contrast of each other, so look for answers that contain words that are opposites. Eliminate choices (C) and (D) since they contain words that are similar to each other. Eliminate choices (A) and (B) since neither contains words that are opposites of one another. Choice (E) is a good fit since *kinetic* means "movement" while *placid* means "not moving much." Choice (E) is the correct answer.

30.   **A**   Both passages discuss the low sunlight-conversation rate of current solar panels. Passage 1 explains that *because the silicon can only absorb a narrow band of the solar spectrum, a majority of the solar energy is lost as heat* while Passage 2 also references the fact that *current devices with silicon semiconductors can only absorb a small band of light from the sun*. Choice (A) fits what both passages say. Passage 1 does say that a majority of the sun's energy is lost as heat, but it doesn't say anything about the panels overheating, so choice (B) can be eliminated. Choice (C) can also be eliminated because, although the silicon isn't particularly efficient, it isn't actually faulty. Choice (D) might initially look good, but it only addresses Passage 2. Choice (E) isn't mentioned in either passage. Choice (A) is the correct response.

31.   **A**   The final sentence of Passage 1 describes why Atwater is working on the new device, so he would agree with the statement. That eliminates choices (B), (C), and (E). He already knows the information—it isn't anything *exciting*—so choice (D) can also be eliminated. Choice (A) is the correct answer.

32.   **B**   Atwater is *working on the device*; it isn't available yet. His statement shows that he feels the research and development is very promising. Choice (B) is the correct answer.

33.   **C**   Passage 1 states that *silicon can only absorb a narrow band of the solar spectrum*, while Passage 2 agrees that *silicon semiconductors can only absorb a small band of light from the sun*. Choice (A) is the opposite of what the both passages state, so it can be eliminated. Physicists are developing a new solar panel, but the silicon semiconductors are not a part of that, and the new device is also mentioned only in Passage 2, so eliminate choice (B). Choice (C) agrees with both passages. Choice (D) may initially look attractive, but the silicon is not actually mentioned as a fault, just as a limitation. There are no mistaken statements, so choice (E) can be eliminated. The best answer is choice (C).

34. **B** The initial paragraphs set the scene for the passage's central event: Catalina's meeting with Clara and her growing interest in politics. Choice (B) best captures this central event. Choice (A) does not take any of Catalina's friendships into account, nor does choice (D), and neither answer is supported in the passage. And choice (E) addresses one of Catalina's friendships, but not the most important one.

35. **E** The first sentence of the passage reads as follows: *The girls in her room, after a few weeks of getting used to some of her atypical habits and learning her way of showing friendship, began to take her in as one of their own.* In other words, these girls had to get used to some of Catalina's habits, so they initially considered her *foreign* or *alien*, as choice (E) suggests. The other choices are too harsh and have no support in the passage.

36. **C** The full sentence reads as follows: *The oldest girl, Araceli, really started to warm up to Catalina, and she was the first to invite Catalina into her room for help with homework, to watch a video clip on the computer, or just to chat about the day.* The three things that Araceli does are evidence of how *she took* to Catalina and made her feel at home, as choice (C) best captures. These are kind gestures, which eliminates choices (D) and (E). And while Araceli may be beautiful or intelligent, there is nothing specific in the passage to support either.

37. **E** Araceli is the first of the girls to *warm up to Catalina*, showing that she is *familiar, nurturing,* and *sympathetic,* eliminating choices (A), (B), and (D) because this question asks for the answer that LEAST describes Araceli. She is also described as *stern* in the final sentence of the paragraph, eliminating choice (C). Araceli does not seem *local* to Catalina, however, she wonders whether Araceli *had come to the big city from a small town like hers,* making choice (E) the LEAST descriptive of Araceli and therefore the correct answer.

38. **A** Clara is on her way to a protest when she finds Catalina reading outside. Clara wants Catalina to join her, as evidenced by her questions, *You coming?* And *You want to come to the protest with me?* Choice (A) reflects Clara's intention. Because Catalina is apparently not responding, except by joining Clara at the protest, there is no support for any of the other answer choices, which all suggest that Clara asks Catalina questions to gain information.

39. **B** The line containing this simile describes *an oddly moved Catalina, who felt that the sign was a key that had unlocked something inside of her.* In other words, Catalina believes she has had these feelings and that that they were locked away inside of her, or *hidden,* as choice (B) suggests. Choice (A) describes the sign, not the *key.* Choices (C), (D), and (E) provide alternate meanings of the word *key,* but they do not work in this context.

40. **B** Catalina is charmed and flattered that Clara wants her to come to the protest and that Clara is interested in her political views. She is not upset by Clara's questions, eliminating choices (A), (C), and (E). And while she is surprised by Clara, there is no evidence that she is confused, or *befuddled,* as choice (D) suggests. Only choice (B), *astonishment,* correctly captures Catalina's reaction, which the passage describes as *shocked.*

41.   A   Read the last sentence of the paragraph carefully: *She felt for the first time that she might be able to make a difference for people like her father.* In other words, she is *hopeful* that she can make a difference, as choice (A) suggests. Her feelings are mainly positive, which eliminates all the other answer choices, which are either negative or neutral.

42.   C   Catalina's meeting with Clara was the beginning of a new phase in her life, one in which she *went to every other protest she could* and *became as well-informed on the issues as she could.* In other words, by the end of the passage, Catalina has taken a more intense interest in politics than she had before, as choice (C) suggests. Choice (B) is too extreme, and choice (E) assumes that Catalina had gone to political protests before, which the passage suggests that she had not.

43.   C   The author says the effects of orchid farming *mirror those of aloe throughout the world*, effects which have produced near-extinction for the medicinal plant. Scientists fear that orchids could come to a similar fate, lending support to choice (C). The passage only states that the effects of farming orchids and those of farming aloe mirror one another, but there are no other links listed in the passage, which eliminates all other answer choices.

44.   B   The word *outgrowth* appears in this sentence: *Some farmers have had to move to more remote locations or to employ environmentally questionable methods, but this, they argue, is not an outgrowth of shortage.* In other words, farmers claim that they are not resorting to these methods *because* of shortage or *as a response to* shortage. Choice (B), *effect*, best captures this relationship. Choices (C) and (D) represent common themes of the passage (*overharvest* is one of the practices that is damaging orchid populations, and *dearth* is the lack that is created when orchids no longer grow in a particular place), but they do not apply in this particular sentence.

45.   D   The author states that the farmers are *closer* to the orchids than scientists are. The author offers as evidence that *the orchid is...essential to life in Tanzania.... Here, the orchid is just as prized for its nutritional value as for its aesthetic value.* In other words, farmers in this region use the orchid for more things in their daily lives, and thus have a more complex, or closer, relationship with it. Choice (D) states this idea in a very general way. Choices (A) and (C) may be true, but they do not support the claim given in the question.

46.   D   The full statement reads as follows: *And the orchid is so essential to this part of Tanzania, the "Serengeti of Flowers," that life is in some ways inconceivable without it.* The author goes on to add that, in this region, *the orchid is just as prized for its nutritional value as for its aesthetic value*, as choice (D) suggests. The other choices use words from the passage, but the statements in those answer choices are not supported by textual evidence.

47.   C   The passage states that the trends in orchid farming *mirror* those of aloe farming, but it does not state that the two crops grow in the same regions, thus making choice (C) the correct answer. Choice (A) is supported throughout the third paragraph. Choice (B) is stated in the first paragraph. Choice (D) is implied in the discussion of Zambia in the second paragraph. Choice (E) is stated in the first line of the passage.

48. **D** The first sentence of the last paragraph states, *In the face of the scientific evidence, some Asian and African governments have promised measures to protect orchids and the orchid industry at the same time.* Choice (D) gives a very simple paraphrase of this sentence and of the ideas that follow in the paragraph. The other choices are not supported in this paragraph and can therefore be eliminated.

Section 4

21. **D** First, take the square root of both sides of the first equation to find that $c = 3$. Then use your calculator for find $3^4 = 81$. The credited response is (D).

22. **D** First, list the first seven positive even integers: 2, 4, 6, 8, 10, 12, 14. Then use the average pie to calculate the average. The sum of the integers is 56; put that at the top of the pie. The number of things is 7; put that in the lower left of the pie. Divide 56 by 7 to find that the average is 8. The credited response is (D).

23. **E** PITA! Plot the coordinates in the answer to see which makes the isosceles right triangle. Use the two given points, (2, 9) and (8, 9), to find that one side of the triangle is 6. Choices (A) and (C) do not make right triangles. Choices (B) and (D) make right triangles, but the sides are 3 and 5, respectively, not 6. Choice (E) makes a right triangle with a side of 6. The credited response is (E).

24. **C** PITA! Since the question asks for the "largest integer," start with choice (E). The square root of 25 is 5, which is not less than 4, so eliminate it and move to (D). The square root of 16 is 4, which is not less than 4, so eliminate it and move to (C). The square root of 15 is approximately 3.87 (use your calculator), which is less than 4, so it's the answer. The credited response is (C).

25. **C** Label what you know. Since $RT = ST$, angle R must equal angle S. Label both angles 75°. There are 180 degrees in a triangle, so $75 + 75 + \angle RTS = 180$. Solve to find that $\angle RTS = 30$. Now look at the straight line. Straight lines have 180 degrees, so $30 + x + x + x = 180$. Solve for x to find that $3x = 150$, so $x = 50$. The credited response is (C).

26. **E** Plug In! In 2 minutes there are 120 seconds, so plug in $s = 120$ and $m = 2$. Then plug 2 in for m in each of the answer choices to find which one equals 120. Choice (E) is $60 \times 2 = 120$. Remember to check all the answer choices. The credited response is (E).

27. **B** PITA! Since the question asks for the "largest integer," start with choice (E). Plug in 12 for z. The smallest x and y could each be is 12. The sum ($12 + 12 + 12 = 36$) is larger than 14, so eliminate (E). For (D), plug in 6 for z. The smallest x and y could each be is 6. The sum ($6 + 6 + 6 = 18$) is larger than 14, so eliminate (D). For (C), plug in 5 for z. The smallest x and y could each be is 5. The sum ($5 + 5 + 5 = 15$) is larger than 14, so eliminate (C). For (B), plug in 4 for z. The smallest x and y could each be is 4, but they could be bigger. If $x = 5$ and $y = 5$, then the sum ($5 + 5 + 4 = 14$) could equal 14. The credited response is (B).

28. **C** PITA! Read carefully and plug the values from the answer choices into the given equation. Since *a* and *b* are integers less than 5, eliminate choices (A), (B), and (E); they each contain numbers that are 5 or greater. Plug in choice (C): $5(3) - 4 > (3)(4)$ becomes $11 > 12$. Since this is <u>not</u> true, the credited response is (C).

29. **4,320** Take it in bite-sized pieces. First, the band earned $15 for each person, so $15 × 200 = $3,000. Next, the band earned $10 for each T-shirt, so $10 × 32 = $1,320. Therefore the total amount earned is $3,000 + $1,320 = $4,320.

30. **2** To get from 59.43 to 0.5943, the decimal moves two places to the left. That means that 59.43 is divided by 100. Multiplying by 10^{-2} is the same as dividing by 100, so $t = 2$. Use your calculator to verify.

31. **1,300** Take it in bite-sized pieces. First, translate the first phrase into math: $\frac{1}{6}$ of *m* is 200 translates to $\frac{1}{6} \times m = 200$. Multiply both sides by 6 to find that $m = 1,200$. Next, translate the second phrase into math: $\frac{1}{5}$ of *n* is 500 translates to $\frac{1}{5} \times n = 500$. Multiply both sides by 5 to find that $n = 2,500$. Finally, subtract to find that $n - m = 2,500 - 1,200 = 1,300$.

32. **40** Write your formulas and label everything. The area of *ABCD* is 4, so write the formula and find the side: $A = s^2 = 4$, so $s = 2$. Label each side of *ABCD* as 2. The area of *WXYZ* is 49, so write the formula and find the side: $A = s^2 = 49$, so $s = 7$. Label each side of *WXYZ* as 7. The area of *DCXQ* is 4, so write the formula and find the missing sides: $A = b \times h = 16$, $b \times 2 = 16$, so $b = 8$. Label sides *CX* and *DQ* as 8. Finally, to find the area of *PDQW*, find the side and then use the formula. Since $XW = 7$ and $XQ = 2$, subtract to find that $QW = 5$. Now write the area formula: $A = b \times h = 8 \times 5 = 40$.

33. **96** One approach is to set up the proportion: $\dfrac{Pistachio}{Mint\ Chocolate\ Chip} = \dfrac{12}{60}$. There are 480 Mint Chocolate Chip, so $\dfrac{Pistachio}{480} = \dfrac{12}{60}$. Multiply both sides by 480 to find that Pistachio = 96.

34. **100** Extend out the parallel lines and find the angles that are equal. First extend the parallel lines $\overline{CF}$ and $\overline{DE}$. Rotate the page if needed. Notice that line $\overline{AE}$ cuts those parallel lines therefore all the small angles are the same. $\angle DEF = 70$, so $\angle CFG = 70$. $\overline{AE}$ is a straight line, so if $\angle AGD = 150$, $\angle DGF = 30$. Next look at the center triangle with a base of $\overline{GF}$. All triangles have 180 degrees, so the third angle at the top (next to *x*) will be $180 - 30 - 70 = 80$. Lastly, $\overline{GD}$ is a straight line, $x = 180 - 80 = 100$.

35. **138, 276, or 414**

   Since the number Jen chose was divisible by 2 (even), 3 and 23, it must be divisible by their product: $2 \times 3 \times 23 = 138$. Therefore Jen chose a number less than 500 that is a multiple of 138: 138, 276, or 414.

36.   .875 or $\dfrac{7}{8}$

To make the fraction as large as possible, the numerator must be as large as possible. Since $a - b$ is in an absolute value, its value must be as large as possible <u>or</u> as small as possible. To make $a - b$ large, start with the largest value for a and subtract the smallest value of b: $a - b = 3 - (-4) = 7$. To make $a - b$ small, start with the smallest value for a and subtract the largest value of b: $a - b = (-2) - 2 = -4$. Since the absolute value of 7 is 7 and the absolute value of -4 is 4, the maximum value of $|a - b|$ is 7. Therefore, the maximum value of $\dfrac{|a - b|}{8}$ is $\dfrac{7}{8}$ or .875.

37. $\dfrac{3}{4}$ or .75

Translate the English into math. The first sentence translates to $9r + 5t = 6r + 9t$. Combine like terms to get $3r = 4t$. Then translate the second sentence to $t = pr$. Substitute rp for t in the first equation to get $3r = 4pr$. Divide both sides by $4r$ to find that $p = \dfrac{3}{4}$ or .75.

38. $\dfrac{1}{4}$ or .25

The question provides the y-intercept, so rewrite the equation in the $y = mx + b$ format: $y = \dfrac{cx}{d} + \dfrac{2}{-d}$. In this form, the y-intercept is represented by $\dfrac{2}{-d}$. Since the y-intercept is -8, write $\dfrac{2}{-d} - 8$. Solve for d and find that $d = \dfrac{1}{4}$ or .25.

Section 5

1.   E   The first part of the sentence, *In 1900, Wilbur Wright and his brother,* West Side News *publisher Orville Wright, journeyed to Kitty Hawk, North Carolina,* is a complete thought. The underlined portion of the sentence also contains a complete thought. Since you cannot join two complete thoughts with a comma, this sentence contains a comma splice error. Eliminate choice (A). Choices (B) and (C) repeat the original error and are also incorrect. Choice (D) begins the underlined phrase with *when*. However, since the word *when* modifies *Kitty Hawk, North Carolina*, which is a place, rather than a time, you cannot use *when* here. Additionally, the phrase *experiments…were begun by them* is passive. Choice (D) is therefore not the correct answer. Choice (E) fixes the error in the original sentence and does not introduce any new errors, so choice (E) is the correct answer.

2.   E   The non-underlined portion of the sentence uses the past tense verb *was*. Since the sentence is discussing a past event, rather than an event that is currently occurring, the present perfect verb *has begun*, which refers to an event that began in the past but is still occurring in the present, is incorrect. Therefore, this sentence contains a verb tense error. Eliminate choice (A). Choice (C) is

also in the present tense, and is therefore incorrect. Choice (B) uses *was beginning*. However, *was beginning composing and publicly performing* is incorrect; you would need *was beginning to compose and publicly perform*. Thus, choice (B) also contains a verb form error. Choice (D) switches to the future tense by using *will begin*, and is thus not the credited answer. Choice (E) fixes the original error and does not introduce any new errors, so choice (E) is correct.

3. **B** The two halves of the sentence are joined by a comma and the word *and*. However, in order to join two thoughts in this way, you must have two complete thoughts. Since the second half of the sentence uses *starting*, rather than *to start*, the second half of the sentence is incomplete. Therefore, the original sentence contains an error, and choice (A) is incorrect. Choice (D) contains a similar error, and uses *so as*, which is idiomatically incorrect, so choice (D) is not the correct answer. Choice (C) contains a comma splice error and is incorrect. Finally, choice (E) uses *effecting in that*, which is idiomatically incorrect, so you can eliminate choice (E). Choice (B) fixes the error and does not introduce any new errors, so choice (B) is the correct answer.

4. **C** If you join two thoughts with a comma and the word *and*, you should be joining two complete thoughts. However, since the first part of the sentence, *James Dean, having died shortly after the filming of* Rebel Without a Cause does not contain a complete thought, choice (A) contains an error. Choice (B) does not contain a complete thought, and is therefore not the credited answer. Choices (D) and (E) both use *he*, so that the sentence reads, *James Dean…he was only able to receive*. The word *he* is unnecessary, and since using *he* changes the sentence so that the subject *James Dean* does not have a verb associated with it, both choices (D) and (E) are incorrect. Choice (C) fixes the error in the original sentence and does not introduce any new errors, so choice (C) is the correct answer.

5. **C** As it is currently written, this sentence does not contain a complete thought. Therefore, eliminate choice (A). Choices (D) and (E) similarly do not contain complete thoughts, and are also therefore incorrect. In choice (B), the clause *The school board is enacting new anti-truancy laws* is a complete thought. The clause *they will discourage students cutting class and encourage regular school attendance* is also a complete thought, although idiomatically the word *from* should appear before the word *cutting*. Since choice (B) contains two complete thoughts joined by a comma, choice (B) contains a comma splice error. Choice (C) fixes the problem in the original sentence and does not introduce any new errors, so the correct answer is choice (C).

6. **A** As written, the underlined portion of the sentence contains a modifier that correctly modifies the subject of the sentence, *Eugene Fama*. It also contains a singular verb, *is*, which agrees with the subject. Choices (B), (C), and (E) eliminate the main verb of the sentence. This makes the sentences fragments, so you can eliminate choices (B), (C), and (E). Choice (D) incorrectly uses *he*, so that the clause *he is a Nobel prize winner and one of the world's most distinguished economists* becomes a complete thought, but the main part of the sentence—*Eugene Farma…many extolling him as an authority on portfolio theory and asset pricing*—does not contain a complete thought. Thus, choice (D) is not the credited answer. Choice (A) is the correct answer.

7. **E** The subject of the sentence is *Tower*, which is singular, but the verb is *are*, which is plural. Therefore, this sentence contains a subject-verb agreement error, so eliminate choice (A). Choice (C) repeats the original error and is also incorrect. Choice (B) removes the main verb from the sentence and thus does not contain a complete thought. Choice (D) changes the meaning of the sentence, and is therefore not the correct answer. Choice (E) fixes the error in the original sentence and does not introduce any new errors, so the correct answer is choice (E).

8. **D** This sentence gives three items in a list: *improved economic conditions, better health care, and have more social services programs.* Items in a list should be parallel, but the first two items are nouns and the last item is a verb. Therefore, the original sentence contains a parallelism error, so eliminate choice (A). Choices (C) and (E) repeat the original error. Choice (B) uses *with*, therefore making the last item in the list not parallel with the first two, so choice (B) is incorrect. Choice (D) fixes the error in the original sentence and does not introduce any new errors, so choice (D) is the correct answer.

9. **C** In the original sentence, the first half is missing a verb, and therefore does not contain a complete thought. Thus, you can eliminate choice (A). In choice (B), the first half of the sentence contains a complete thought, and the second half of the sentence also contains a complete thought. Since these two parts of the sentence are joined by a comma, this choice contains a comma splice error. Eliminate choice (B). Choice (C) fixes the error in the original sentence and does not introduce any new errors, so choice (C) is the credited answer. Choices (D) and (E) illustrate the same error as in choice (A), so they are eliminated.

10. **B** This sentence contains a list of two things that are considered cheating: *copying* and *by otherwise using another student's work.* However, the two items are not in the same form, and are therefore not parallel. Eliminate choice (A). Choices (C) and (E) both contain the past tense verb *used*, which is not parallel with *copying*, so both choices are incorrect. Choice (D) contains the verb *to use*, which is also not parallel with *copying*, so you can eliminate choice (D). Choice (B) fixes the original error and does not introduce any new errors, so choice (B) is the correct answer.

11. **E** The original sentence refers to *NASA astronauts* as *a pilot.* Since *astronauts* is plural, but *pilot* is singular, this sentence contains a noun agreement error. Eliminate choice (A). Choices (C) and (D) repeat the original error and are therefore incorrect. Choice (B) contains two complete thoughts joined by a comma, so choice (B) contains a comma splice error. Choice (E) fixes the original error and does not introduce any new errors, and is therefore the correct answer.

12. **D** As it is currently written, this sentence compares two things: *paintings from Picasso's Blue Period* and *other artists.* Since you must compare paintings to paintings and artists to artists, rather than paintings to artists, this sentence contains a comparison error. Eliminate choice (A). Choices (B) and (C) make similar comparison errors, and are therefore incorrect. Choice (E) compares *paintings* to *the same time*, and is also incorrect. Choice (D) fixes the comparison error by comparing *paintings* to *those of*, or paintings of, *other artists.* Thus, choice (D) is the correct answer.

13. **E**   This sentence contains the modifying phrase *While learning to ride the new bicycle*. The phrase *a pink one with green tassels and a banana seat* contains extra information that simply modifies *bicycle*. If you eliminate this phrase, you are left with *While learning to ride the new bicycle...a dog*. As it is currently written, the sentence suggests that a dog, rather than Rebekah, was learning to ride the bicycle. Therefore, this sentence contains a misplaced modifier. Eliminate choice (A). Choices (B) and (C) similarly suggest that the dog, rather than Rebekah, was learning to ride the bicycle, so both choices are incorrect. Choice (D) seems to suggest that the fire hydrant, rather than Rebekah, was learning to ride the bicycle, and is also not the credited answer. Choice (E) correctly changes the sentence so that Rebekah is the person learning to ride the bike. Therefore, choice (E) is correct.

14. **D**   The subject of the sentence is *exercise*, which is singular, but the verb is *are proven*, which is plural. Therefore, this sentence contains a subject-verb agreement error. Eliminate choice (A). Choices (B) and (E) also use plural verbs and are therefore incorrect. Choice (C) uses *proven as reducing*, rather than *proven to reduce*, and therefore contains an idiom error. Choice (D) correctly uses the singular verb *has been proven*, and does not introduce any new errors. Thus, choice (D) is the correct answer.

15. **C**   The clause *It possessed the most advanced safety features available in its time, and it was generally considered unsinkable* is a complete thought. The clause *the RMS Titanic sank along with 1,500 of its passengers on April 15, 1912* is also a complete thought. This sentence joins two complete thoughts with a comma, and therefore contains a comma splice error. Eliminate choice (A). Choices (B) and (E) repeat the original error and are therefore incorrect. Choice (D) uses the word *despite*, which should indicate a contrast. However, the phrase *possessing the most advanced safety features available during its time* is in the same direction, rather than the opposite direction, as *considered unthinkable*. Thus, choice (D) is incorrect. Choice (C) fixes the error in the original sentence and does not introduce any new errors, so it is the correct answer.

16. **E**   As it is currently written, the sentence does not contain a complete thought. Therefore, choice (A) is incorrect. Choice (C) repeats this error and is also incorrect. Choice (B) lists three things that the bicyclists do: *pack, travel,* and *they participate*. Since the three actions should be in parallel form, choice (B) contains a parallelism error. Choice (D) is similarly not parallel, as well as passive. Choice (E) fixes the error in the original sentence while also keeping the three items in the list parallel, so choice (E) is the credited answer.

17. **A**   This sentence correctly uses the subjunctive voice by using the *if...were* construction. Choice (B) uses the word *instead*, which is redundant since the sentence already uses *rather than*, so choice (B) is incorrect. Choice (C) uses the future tense verb *will*, which you cannot use with the word *if*, so choice (C) is not the credited answer. Using the subjunctive voice and the word *if* requires *were* plus the infinitive form of the verb, rather than the present tense, so choices (D) and (E) are incorrect. Since the original sentence does not contain any errors, choice (A) is the correct answer.

18. **A** The correct idiom is *regardless of whether*, not *regardless of if*. Therefore, eliminate choices (B) and (D). The phrase *whether or not* in choice (C) is redundant, and the singular pronoun *it* doesn't agree with the plural noun *belongings*, so eliminate choice (C). Choice (E) also uses the singular pronoun *it*, so eliminate that choice as well. The correct answer is choice (A).

19. **E** The modifying phrase *Famous for founding the world's first private detective agency* should modify whatever appears immediately after the comma. However, as it is currently written, this phrase modifies *another fact*. Since it is Eugène Vidocq, not a fact, who founded the detective agency, Eugène Vidocq should appear immediately after the comma. Therefore, eliminate choices (A), (B), and (D). Note that in choice (C) *Eugène Vidocq's career*, rather than *Eugène Vidocq*, appears right after the comma. Since the man, rather than his career, founded the detective agency, eliminate choice (D). Choice (E) fixes the error in the original sentence and does not introduce any new errors, so choice (E) is the correct answer.

20. **B** As it is currently written, this sentence compares *The reigns of Atilla the Hun to many other early rulers*. Since you need to compare *reigns* to *reigns*, rather than *reigns* to *rulers*, this sentence contains a comparison error. Eliminate choice (A). The subject of the sentence in choice (A) is *reigns*, which is plural, but the verb is *was*, which is singular. Choice (C) therefore contains a subject-verb agreement error and is incorrect. Choice (D) repeats this error and is also incorrect. Choice (E) uses the past perfect verb *had been*. Since this sentence does not contain two past events, one of which occurred before the other, the past perfect tense is incorrect for this sentence. Eliminate choice (E). Choice (B) removes the incorrect comparison and does not introduce any new errors, so choice (B) is the correct answer.

21. **B** This sentence lists three things that the author wants to do: *traveling, skiing,* and *to swim*. Items in a list should be in parallel form, so choice (B) contains a parallelism error, since *to swim* should be *swimming*. Choice (B) is therefore the correct answer.

22. **C** As the sentence is currently written, the singular pronoun *it* refers to the plural pronoun *visits*. Therefore, choice (C) contains a pronoun agreement error and is the correct answer.

23. **E** Choice (A) correctly compares the stories of other authors to those of Vonnegut. Choice (B) is the correct verb, choice (C) is the correct adverb, and choice (D) is the correction conjunction. Therefore, there are no errors, and choice (E) is the correct answer.

24. **D** The correct idiom is *originate in*, not *originate from*. Choice (D) is the correct answer.

25. **B** The word *significant* is an adjective, but it modifies *influenced*, which is a verb. Since adverbs, not adjectives, modify verbs, choice (C) contains an error; the correct modifier is *significantly*.

26. **D** The pronoun early in the sentence is *one*, which is singular. The plural *they* in choice (D) does not agree with *one*. Therefore, choice (D) is the correct answer.

27. **B** The main clause in the sentence, *The Montreal Biodome being composed of four zones*, does not contain a complete thought, since the verb is *being composed*. In order to make the thought complete, the verb must be changed to *is composed*.

28. **E** Choice (A) correctly uses an adverb to describe an adjective, so there is no error there. The plural verb *have made* in choice (B) agrees with the plural subject *rules*. The singular verb *has* in choice (C) agrees with the singular subject *he*, and choice (D) does not contain an error. This sentence is correct as written, so choice (E) is the correct answer.

29. **B** The sentence is discussing *different types of stars*, and is therefore discussing plural items. However, *a temperature* is singular and does not agree with *types of stars*. Correctly written, choice (B) should read *different temperatures*. Thus, choice (B) contains a noun agreement error, and is the correct answer.

30. **A** Because the verb in the non-underlined part is past tense, the future tense in choice (A) creates an error in tense. Choice (A) is the correct answer.

31. **C** The pronoun *it* does not clearly refer to any one noun; it seems to replace *predicted*, but since you cannot use a pronoun to replace a verb, the pronoun *it* cannot replace *predicted*. Therefore, choice (C) contains an error.

32. **C** The verb *sits* is singular, but the subject of the sentence is *the Great Temple of Ramses II and the Small Temple of Nefertiti*. Two singular nouns joined by the conjunction *and* make a plural subject, so the subject of this sentence is plural. Therefore, this sentence contains a subject-verb agreement error, and the correct answer is choice (C).

33. **A** The correct idiom is *insisted that*, rather than *insisted to*. In order to read correctly, the sentence would need to read *Frank insisted that he be allowed to present his paper at the conference*, or something similar. Therefore, choice (A) contains an error and is the correct answer.

34. **B** Use *less* for items that are not countable, and *fewer* for items that are countable. Since *residents* are countable, choice (B) contains an error.

35. **B** The subject of the sentence is *spending*, which is singular, but the verb is *are*, which is plural. Thus, this sentence contains a subject-verb agreement error. Eliminate choice (A). Choice (C) also has a plural verb and is therefore incorrect. In choice (D), the word *that* does not clearly refer to any single noun, so choice (D) is incorrect. Choice (E) fixes the subject-verb agreement error but is unnecessarily wordy. Choice (B) fixes the error by using the singular verb *is* and is more concise than choice (E), so choice (B) is the correct answer.

36. **D** As it is currently written, the sentence seems to suggest that *the fact*, rather than *studying irregularly*, is the worst action you can take. Therefore, as it is currently written, the sentence contains an error. Choice (B) uses the word *such*, which would imply that irregularity was discussed in the previous sentence. However, since that is not the case, choice (B) is not the correct answer. Choice (E)

uses the word *so*, and thus contains a similar error. Choice (C) is unnecessarily wordy and uses the word *being*, which is often used incorrectly in PSAT grammar questions. Therefore, choice (C) is not the credited answer. Choice (D) fixes the error in the original sentence, and does not introduce any new errors, so choice (D) is the correct answer.

37. E Since those who practice speaking in a foreign language do not literally become children again, since their ages do not change, the word *literally* is not used correctly in this sentence. Eliminate choice (A). The sentence does not discuss a contrast, so both choices (B) and (C) are incorrect. The sentence does not contain an example, so choice (D) is not the credited answer. The sentence is attempting to explain that those who practice speaking in a foreign language often speak as if they were two year-olds, so choice (E) correctly captures the intended meaning of the sentence, and is the correct choice.

38. D The end of sentence 11 mentions that individuals practicing a foreign language *are likely to make mistakes.* Since sentence 12 shortly thereafter mentions that *they are likely to occur, they* most probably refers to *mistakes.* Thus, the correct answer is choice (D).

39. D The passage as a whole discusses the process of learning a new language. With the exception of sentence 8, each of the sentences in the answer choices discusses some factor related to studying a foreign language. However, sentence 8 introduces the idea of learning to play an instrument, which is unrelated to the topic discussed in the rest of the passage. Hence, the correct answer is choice (D).

NOTES

NOTES

NOTES

Score Your Best on Both of the Tests

Get proven prep for the SAT and ACT at **PrincetonReviewBooks.com**

More SAT Guides

Essential SAT Vocabulary (Flashcards)
978-0-375-42964-4
$16.99/$21.99 Can.

11 Practice Tests for the SAT and PSAT, 2015 Edition
978-0-8041-2509-3
$24.99/$28.99 Can. *(June 2014!)*

Are You Ready for the SAT & ACT?
978-0-8041-2521-5
$14.99/$17.99 Can.
eBook: 978-0-8041-2522-2

Cracking the SAT with 5 Practice Tests, 2015 Edition
978-0-8041-2465-2
$21.99/$25.99 Can.
eBook: 978-0-8041-2466-9

Cracking the SAT Premium Edition with 8 Practice Tests, 2015
978-0-8041-2467-6
$34.99/$41.99 Can.

Crash Course for the SAT, 4th Edition
978-0-375-42831-9
$9.99/$10.99 Can.

Math Workout for the SAT, 3rd Edition
978-0-375-42833-3
$17.99/$20.99 Can.

Reading and Writing Workout for the SAT, 2nd Edition
978-0-375-42832-6
$16.99/$18.99 Can.

Crack the ACT, Too!

Cracking the ACT with 3 Practice Tests, 2014 Edition
978-0-8041-2438-6
$19.99/$22.95 Can.
eBook: 978-0-8041-2439-3

Cracking the ACT with 4 Practice Tests & DVD, 2014 Edition
978-0-8041-2440-9
$31.99/$36.95 Can.

Crash Course for the ACT, 4th Edition
978-0-375-42762-6
$9.99/$11.99 Can.

Essential ACT (Flashcards)
978-0-375-42806-7
$17.99/$19.99 Can.

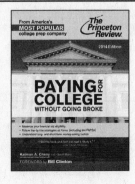

Admissions Advice from the Experts

The Best 379 Colleges, 2015 Edition
978-0-8041-2479-9
$23.99/$27.99 Can. *(August 2014!)*

Paying for College Without Going Broke, 2014 Edition
978-0-8041-2436-2
$20.00/$23.00 Can.
eBook: 978-0-8041-2437-9

The Best Value Colleges, 2014 Edition
978-0-8041-2447-8
$21.99/$24.95 Can.

The Complete Book of Colleges, 2015 Edition
978-0-8041-2520-8
$26.99/$32.00 Can. *(August 2014!)*

The Princeton Review.

Find tools for boosting your scores on AP tests, SAT Subject Tests, and more at PrincetonReviewBooks.com